AFRICAN AMERICANS IN THE
FURNITURE CITY

RANDAL MAURICE JELKS

African Americans in the Furniture City

THE STRUGGLE FOR CIVIL RIGHTS IN GRAND RAPIDS

UNIVERSITY OF ILLINOIS PRESS

URBANA AND CHICAGO

⊗ This book is printed on acid-free paper.

Library of Congress Cataloging-in-Publication Data
Jelks, Randal Maurice, 1956–
African Americans in the Furniture City : the struggle for
civil rights in Grand Rapids / Randal Maurice Jelks.
p.   cm.
Includes bibliographical references and index.
ISBN-10: 0-252-03040-0 (cloth : alk. paper)
ISBN-13: 978-0-252-03040-6 (cloth : alk. paper)
ISBN-10: 0-252-07347-9 (paper : alk. paper)
ISBN-13: 978-0-252-07347-2 (paper : alk. paper)
1. African Americans—Civil rights—Michigan—Grand
Rapids—History. 2. Civil rights movements—Michigan—
Grand Rapids—History. 3. African Americans—
Michigan—Grand Rapids—Social conditions. 4. Grand
Rapids (Mich.)—Race relations. 5. Grand Rapids (Mich.)—
Social conditions. I. Title.
F574.G7J45   2006
305.8'96073'077455—dc22   2006022113

In memory of my mother,
Marjorie Louise Baptiste Nelson
(September 9, 1934–March 5, 1996)

She left New Orleans, but it never left her—
her gumbo was fiery, creative, and passionate.

And in memory of my grandmother,
Priscilla Edith Carter
(August 9, 1906–May 23, 1999)

A woman of unbending pride, pugnacious
temperament, and a prayerful heart

Contents

Acknowledgments

The great challenge in writing the history of any community is locating documentation and constructing a readable narrative. Locating documentation both oral and written requires a great deal of collaboration with libraries, important community institutions, individuals, and fellow historians. This book owes profound debts of gratitude to Darlene Clark Hine, a mentor and friend; all scholars whose ideas and insights helped shape this book, especially David Katzman, Dennis Dickerson, Michelle Loyd-Paige, Felix Armfield, Jacqueline McLeod, James Bratt, and Dale Van Kley, who read all or parts of this manuscript; retired Grand Rapids city historian Gordon Olson, whose constant support and haranguing prompted me to complete this project; Richard Harms, formerly the assistant city historian of Grand Rapids, who consistently found articles and archival sources that added depth to this study; Carl Bajema of Grand Valley State University, a biologist and an able natural historian who graciously opened his personal files of nineteenth- and early-twentieth-century Grand Rapids newspaper clippings to me; and Mary Edmonds and the women of Alpha Kappa Alpha sorority for building the African American collections at the Grand Rapids Public Library: without these sources, I would have been lost. Thank you for your efforts to preserve the history of the Grand Rapids African American community.

Without the use of great archives, libraries, and librarians, this book would be awash. My love and thanks go out to the staff to the Grand Rapids Public Library's local history department, especially Martha Bloem, Betty Gibout, M. Christine Byron, and Rebecca Mayne, for dealing with my demands with graciousness and professional courtesy. I would also like to acknowledge the wonderful assistance I received from the Bentley Historical Library at the University of Michigan; the Michigan Regional Archives in Kalamazoo; the Library of Congress; the Michigan Historical Library; the National Archives; the Calvin College library staff and Heritage Room; the Ithaca Public Library; Cornell University Special Collections; Kalamazoo College Special Collections; University of Minnesota YMCA Archives; David Mook of the Sioux City Public Library; and Michael Maxson of the Flat River Community Library. For opening their records to me for this research, I also owe thanks to the Fountain Street Church, Park Congregational Church, St. Philip's Episcopal Church, True Light Baptist Church, and the First Community African Methodist Episcopal Church.

Special recognition is due all my colleagues at Calvin College. I would especially like to thank the history department for high intellectual conversation, camaraderie, and great laughter. I owe an unpayable debt to the administrative assistants in the history department, especially Jane Haney, who is now retired, and the late Lori Menninga, whose untimely death prevented her from seeing this book in final form. They endured my silly word-processing queries and corrected my grammatical lapses with graciousness beyond anything I deserve. I would also like to thank Shelly LeMahieu Dunn, whose keen editorial scrutiny assisted me in making this book much better than it would have been otherwise.

Finally, I thank my family. I belong to a tribe too numerous to chronicle here. I thank my wife Mari Beth Johnson-Jelks for her enduring love and support. I also thank my children for asking me basic questions about why I was writing this book. They reminded me that the scholarly world is about simple curiosity toward the most basic of life's questions. Thanks, Johannah and Jonathan, for keeping me on task. Finally, I would like to offer this book as homage to my deceased mother, Marjorie Louise Baptiste Nelson. Mother, thank you for taking me to the Philip Street Library in New Orleans at age four: it finally paid off.

Preface

The city of Grand Rapids was chartered in 1850. Running through the middle of the city and snaking its way from Lake Michigan is a rapidly flowing river the original inhabitants of the region called the *Owashtanong*, "the faraway waters." The river's name was first translated into French and then into English as "the Grand."[1] The river was the city's artery; the dense hardwood forest that shadowed the city was its exploitable natural resource. For a person traveling west along the river by steamboat, Grand Rapids was one or two hours from Lake Michigan, where lumber products were shipped west to Chicago and north to Canada. Once the rail lines fully connected the country from east to west and north to south, lumber products from the area were shipped all over the nation. Shortly after the Civil War, the second wave of the Industrial Revolution made the city a bustling district teeming with local manufacturers, the most adroit of which became wealthy as result of their ability to exploit the area's natural resources along with a pool of low-priced labor. The city became the home to numerous companies that crafted exquisitely designed home furniture.[2] During the 1880s, the Furniture Manufacturer's Association colluded to stamp all furniture produced in the city with the label "made in Grand Rapids," regardless of who the local manufacturer was. From then until the late 1920s, Grand Rapids was known throughout the United States as "the Furniture City."[3]

Grand Rapids was a part of the large industrial manufacturing corridor strung around the Great Lakes from Buffalo to Chicago to Menominee. The city therefore shared a regional history that reflects industrialization, the pull and push of Southern migrants and European immigrants, the formation of ghettos, labor discord, and racial/ethnic antagonisms. As a result, the history of African Americans in Grand Rapids shares many features of the regional history of black community formation in the Great Lakes industrial corridor.[4] The particular pattern the African American community in Grand Rapids followed is one found in smaller cities of the region, having egalitarian traditions based in politics and religious heritage.[5] This history, then, is not about black working-class activism, the making of ghettos, black proletarianization, or the creation of culturally important institutions—although these themes are certainly to be found as a part of it. Rather, the central theme for African Americans living in Grand Rapids was the quest for middle-class status based on religious notions about equality and self-accountability before God, both of which played a defining and mediating role in community-building.

A Protestant religious ethos fashioned much of the local culture.[6] Retired Episcopal Bishop of Massachusetts John Melville Burgess, a native of Grand Rapids, wrote in 1969 that "[l]ittle has been written by students of society about the Negro in the ordinary town or small city of the North. It has been more popular and attractive to uncover the dismal facts of the great urban ghettos, to trace there the causes and incidents of crime and delinquency, to mark the decline of family life, to describe the crushed and maimed victims of outright prejudice and exploitation." Burgess's comments were intended to emphasize that not all black people were from large urban centers. He described his hometown, Grand Rapids, as a city "under 100,000 citizens and a Negro community of a few hundred."[7] More important, Bishop Burgess recognized the cultural ethos of his youth:

> Since my maternal grandparents had arrived [in Grand Rapids] in the early 1870s, we considered ourselves, along with several other Negro families, among the old settlers. As a young person, I was not particularly aware of racial discrimination or even of racial identity. The town was so dominated by a Dutch majority that all other racial or ethnic groups underwent certain disabilities as "Gentiles." The two Reformed denominations in no way reflected their South African counterparts, but maintained an aloofness from the Negro as from the Italian, from the Methodist as from the Roman Catholic. Negroes seemed no better or worse than their white neighbors. Grand Rapids, living under strict Calvinism, was a clean, law-abiding Republican city. Solid citizens owned their homes and went to church; and Negroes reflected much of this atmosphere.[8]

Studying a small African American community in a city where Protestant Christianity is a vital component leads in a direction that urban historians have not fully explored. Religion and religious ethos may help to explain the actions and reactions of African Americans as they developed a black, urban, middle-class culture. To be certain, the middle-class cultural attitudes and the anti-middle-class sentiments that formed in the city were shaped in part by religious institutions and beliefs systems.[9]

Research into the African American community of Grand Rapids in particular points to religious institutions as the starting place for understanding local race relations, politics, and the ways in which African Americans struggled with one another to define themselves as middle-class. This quest for middle-class respectability was politically dynamic, interjecting itself into labor and class stratification, denominations and religious communities, and regional identity. It was also the instrument used to reject racial oppression and assert a constructive communal identity. The pressure, and perhaps necessity, of adopting middle-class mores was not only a phenomenon in America; it also spread throughout industrializing European urban centers of the nineteenth century. However, very few studies of African American urban history have reflected on the notion of the Protestant work ethic as it informed black urban life. Max Weber's *The Protestant Ethic and the Spirit of Capitalism* has some relevancy here because underlying African Americans' struggle to achieve respectability was the force of Protestant Christianity.[10]

In this study, "respectability" deriving from a Protestant ethos has a politically multidimensional definition. First, respectability is defined as the larger process of embracing the urban, middle-class culture that existed in nearly every urban community in the Western world throughout the nineteenth century. Urbanization moved people from an agrarian existence toward membership in the working classes and beyond by transitioning them from extended families to nuclear ones, pushing them to be concerned about the formal education of their children (to better their economic and class status) and about achieving the power to purchase material goods that satisfied both actual needs and new, consumer-driven desires. Additionally, as author Eric Hobsbawm recognized, this quest for respectability served in the West as a part of the working-class acceptance of and resistance to the structural forces of capitalism. He points out that respectability "expressed simultaneously the penetration of middle-class values and standards, and also the attitudes without which working-class self-respect would have been difficult to achieve, and a movement of collective struggle impossible to build: sobriety, sacrifice, the postponement of gratification."[11] As Hobsbawm further explains, the adjustment of the working class to the culture of respectability was also an effort to win demands for fair wages and social progress. As a working-class and laboring people, African Americans joined in this wider effort and used the ideas of respectability as one of their armors in the fight against racial and economic segregation. As historian Elizabeth Brooks Higginbotham has shown, respectability became one of the important internal struggles for African Americans as they sought to define what it meant to be middle-class Americans.[12] In this regard, African Americans placed heavy emphasis on the behavioral norms of black people as one means to successfully integrate into American life.

Respectability possessed yet another dimension in the vocabulary of individual self-respect.[13] To African American Southerners migrating to the region, self-respect meant controlling their own spheres of family life, churches, and civic associations. They, too, wanted access to the larger society—but on terms that would not make them feel inferior or injured. Historians James Grossman and Kimberly Phillips have shown that African Americans migrating to Chicago and Cleveland arrived with their own notions of respectability rooted in black southern culture, which was largely protestant. Their sense of community was formed in states like Mississippi—states that provided models of respectability derived from slave community and agrarian living.[14] Key to this Southern experience was a sense of blackness, both physical and cultural. Many of the African Americans born in Grand Rapids were of visibly mixed racial heritage, which, in a racist society, automatically gave them higher social status in the internal politics of African American life. While many Southern-born blacks shared this legacy of mixed racial heritage, the vast majority of Afro-Southern migrants were brown- and black-skinned people who shared an even lower status in a cultural atmosphere of white supremacy. Across America, physical blackness was often associated with poverty. To many whites as well as blacks, this impoverishment meant that Afro-Southern culture was impoverished as well. However, to Afro-Southerners who began to migrate into Grand Rapids by World War I, just the opposite was true. The Afro-Southern traditions of Protestant worship, folklore, and a strong sense of community self-reliance—that is, not being totally dependent on "white folk"—shaped what the unlettered often meant by self-respect and respectability. The experiences of African American Southerners who came to Grand Rapids often conflicted with the sensibilities of Northern-born community leaders and old settlers regarding color, social behavior, public decorum, and social attitudes toward the larger white communities.

In this mix of Southern-born and Northern-born African Americans, the question arose: In a world where being black resulted in intense stigmatization, how could blacks arrive at a constructive social and commu-

nal identity? Community leaders often thought that by simply addressing unjust social policy, they could thereby affirm positive communal
attributes. However, such strategies failed to fulfill the need within the
African American community to be properly respected as a community
of people, a community with a constructive history worth remembering as integral to the larger American past. Historian Nathan Huggins
states the matter succinctly in his study of the Harlem Renaissance:
"The challenge to find a black identity within the American cultural
context was made more difficult because the stereotype which defined
Negroes for most Americans was the obverse of the Protestant Ethic,
that convenient measure of deserving character. Laziness, slovenliness,
and excessive sensual appetite deserved no reward except poverty and
dishonor."[15] The search for respectability among African Americans in
Grand Rapids, particularly within the leadership class, was inescapable
when a Calvinist Protestant culture heavily defined the character of the
city and racial stereotyping defined the nation. It should come as no
surprise that African Americans were filled with the same status anxieties as their Euro-American counterparts. The ideology of racial uplift,
which characterized the rising black middle class, cannot be adequately
comprehended without an explanation of the driving Protestant ethos
that supported it.[16]

Gaining respectability also meant gaining political power.[17] However,
the great interlocking barriers of race and limited social-class mobility
prevented African Americans in Grand Rapids from amassing the kind of
political power that black community leaders dreamed of commanding.
The public face of respectability became the struggle for civil rights, led
by a frustrated middle class. It is important to note also that local politics eventually (and inadvertently) played an important role in achieving
the goal of black political empowerment. In 1910, the Grand Rapids city
charter was revised through electoral maneuverings, which weakened the
duties of mayor and ended partisan ward elections. These changes in the
city's charter, in effect, limited black voters' ability to build an effective
political base as their numbers increased through migration. Without a
partisan base in city politics, blacks in Grand Rapids had little chance of
gaining political power as an ethnic block in exchange for black votes.
This electoral marginalization stymied local black politics, moving it
away from politics that supported communal self-interest toward a civil-
rights politics that emphasized protest and interracial cooperation.

This lack of political empowerment created yet another issue that
troubled African Americans in Grand Rapids. They could not sustain
and build a middle class without political incentives. Affecting the

community's sense of respectability meant they lived in the shadow of larger black communities in the region: Chicago to the southwest, where meatpackers, industrial workers, blues singers, and jazz musicians filled the air with a cacophony of black voices; and Detroit to the southeast, where automobile manufacturing, the UAW, and other forces drew African American Southerners into a working-class community and laid the groundwork for Motown Records, large-scale urban unrest, and even large-scale urban segregation. In between these two great metropolises, both of which had large African American communities, lay the city of Grand Rapids. The African American community there had neither the population strength to threaten the existing city political structures nor the numbers to foster great cultural or middle class institutions like its sister cities. The shadows of Chicago and Detroit were simultaneously a source of inspiration for what black Grand Rapids could be if it had a more diverse middle class and a source of fear because the African Americans in the larger cities had much more despairing ghettos.

Blacks and whites lived in relative harmony in Grand Rapids because the population base of African Americans remained small until the 1950s. However, as the population of Grand Rapids grew, local black middle-class leaders feared the possibility of large-scale ghettoization and its incumbent threat to African American worthiness and respectability. It is the theme of respectability that ties African American urban history to the larger discussion within the field of urban history with regard to the formation of an ethnic identity. This study hopes to link African American history to other "white" ethnic communities wrestling with their own respective integration into American Protestant culture. Looking at the story or Grand Rapids from the angle of respectability tells us more fully what African Americans wrestled with ideologically in a Northern urban context as they struggled to construct a positive communal identity, gain citizenship rights, and forge economic opportunities throughout the latter half of the nineteenth century and the first half of the twentieth century.

To paraphrase the words of the French writer Jacques Rancière, the dignity of African Americans during this period was not to be found in their membership in a wage-earning category but rather in the stories of how they simultaneously tried to fit in with and dislodge themselves from a society and a city that showered heaps of indignities upon a small community.[18] This, then, is a tale of how a community worked for collective power and individual freedom.

———————

There are two divisions in this book. The first half—chapters 1–3—covers the formation of the African American community in Grand Rapids from 1850 to 1915 and describes the formation of the community and its struggle against racial and social exclusion. The second half of the study follows the changes and the growth of Grand Rapids' African American community in the aftermath of World War I and that community's continued struggle to achieve social recognition and political power through local efforts aimed at gaining civil rights, building civic associations, and creating economic opportunities. Unlike other studies, the present analysis attempts to view these periods as continuous rather than separate. Following historian David Katzman's lead, I see the latter half of the nineteenth century as foundational both culturally and socially to the actions and reactions of blacks in Grand Rapids in the first half of the twentieth century.[19]

Finally, a note about changing ethnic designations to describe African Americans: this study attempts to be faithful to the terms African Americans in the past have used to describe themselves. From chapter to chapter, I will use various terms such as African American, Afro-American, colored, Negro, and black according to the historical context of the discussion at hand.

AFRICAN AMERICANS IN THE
FURNITURE CITY

1 *"The Negro, North and South":*
Racial Stigma in Nineteenth-
Century Grand Rapids

On April 2, 1872, the *Grand Rapids Eagle* reported the election of William J. Hardy as the county supervisor of Gaines Township, a farming community south of Grand Rapids. In the typical partisan fashion of the local dailies, the *Eagle* observed that the township had "redeemed itself from the indiscretion committed last year of electing a Democratic supervisor." The article stated that "this year the Republicans elect William J. Hardy, one of the most highly respected citizens of that town, who a few years ago, was challenged by the Democratic Party at the polls in a district school meeting because of African blood in his veins. As there is not the slightest question of his fitness and capability for that position, the electors have done a good thing, the right thing, at the right time in choosing him for Supervisor."[1] Hardy's election was quite remarkable. Unlike black officeholders in the Reconstruction South who depended upon a plethora of freedmen to gain political office, Hardy's election depended on good fortune.[2] The *Eagle*'s boast about Hardy's good standing could not hide the fact that his election was an anomaly.

In the 1830s, Alexis de Tocqueville observed the existing racial sensibilities in the United States. He outlined the contours of American life by comparing slavery in antiquity and in nineteenth-century America, noting that the "fact of servitude is most fatally combined with the physical and permanent fact of difference in race."[3] He observed further that in the North, racial animus appeared "stronger in those states that have abolished slavery than in those where it still exists, and nowhere is it more intolerant than in those states where slavery was never known."[4] Tocqueville's understanding of slavery in America led him to conclude that whites in the North had no other means of controlling the social mobility of free persons of color than by ostracizing them. "In the South," he reflected, "the master has no fear of lifting the slave up to his level, for he knows that when he wants to he can always throw him down into the dust. In the North the white man no longer clearly sees the barrier that separates him from the degraded race, and he keeps the Negro at a distance all the more carefully because he fears lest one day they be confounded together."[5] One region Tocqueville clearly had in mind when he wrote of the North was Michigan.[6]

Nearly thirty years after Tocqueville's trenchant observation about slavery and race, the *Grand Rapids Enquirer & Evening Herald*, a Democratic daily, echoed a similar sentiment as an apology for the decency of Southern slavery. The editorial, titled "The Negro, North and South," declared:

> In the South, no lady or gentleman considers it a compromise of character to ride in a car with a "person of color." So says the Richmond *South:* They treat their Negroes, at the South, with a great deal more equality than we do at the North. No northern lady would think of riding in a rail car, with an aromatic negro wench for a companion, but at the South, the wench has just as good a seat as her mistress. There is far more equality between the black and white races in the South, than in the North. This can be seen in the church, in the car or stage coach, in business transactions, and in the household. The blacks of the South are better treated in every respect, than the blacks of the North; they have more attention and consideration; more care and kindness; better religious privileges; and are happier and healthier. The Southern negro is a prince compared to the kicked, cuffed, and despised Northern negro. These are facts, though our readers may not believe them to be facts but, nevertheless, they are facts and can be seen by any one who will look at Southern life just as it is. If our abolition friends have any tears to shed, let them be shed for the Northern negro, who as general rule, is the most degraded being in our midst.[7]

The editorial's suggestion that African Americans were better off in the South expressed local opinion well. The North was demarcated as free, which meant white; therefore, black people in the North were on the periphery of society. Race as an ideology was one of the determinative features of African American life in the nineteenth century.[8]

Therefore, individuals like William Hardy lived their lives fettered by it, experiencing the dynamics of racial stigmatization through both formal exclusion (political disenfranchisement) and cultural subordination (informal resentments and cultural ridicule) before and after the Civil War.[9] Although racial stigma was structured into everyday life, this stigma did not prevent individuals such as Hardy from challenging the prevailing barriers and making life choices within and without the socially acceptable boundaries of the day.

———————

William Hardy was born on January 9, 1823, in New Jersey to parents who were slaves. Subsequently, his parents, Mary and Henry, relocated to Seneca County, New York, where William spent his earliest childhood.[10] The Hardy family moved west in 1827, following the migration of New Englanders and New Yorkers across the Erie Canal into Michigan's Washtenaw County, where the earliest Afro-Yankees settlers clustered.[11] Henry Hardy soon died, leaving Mary to raise William alone. At age six or seven, William was bound out as a farmhand near Ann Arbor.[12] As a bound servant, he spent years laboring to pay off the terms of his indenture and thereafter trying to earn enough money to establish himself as an independent farmer. In 1844, William married a free woman of color named Eliza Watts, whose family had migrated in the 1830s from Pennsylvania into Washtenaw County's Pittsfield Township.[13] By 1846, he had earned enough money to purchase two tracts of land through a state land patent in Gaines Township, due south of the city of Grand Rapids.[14]

Shortly thereafter, William and Eliza began their family. The 1850 census lists the Hardy family as including William, age twenty-seven; Eliza, age twenty-eight; and three children, all born in Michigan: Alice, age four; Eugene, two; and Asher, four months.[15] By 1870, the household had grown with the birth of more children: Lloyd, born in 1856; William, 1858; and Mary, 1859.

When Hardy moved to the Grand Rapids area, the village was a boomtown gone bust. Initially, the region experienced a population surge from the East with the opening of the Erie Canal in 1825; however, the village's economic prospects had diminished due to over-speculation and an economic depression. By 1838, according to one local historian, the village had been in existence only "twelve years, mostly troubled by the financial chaos of the time, hidden some winters in deep snow, and much of the time slithering in mud."[16] Between 1838 and 1850, the county, although beset with financial woes, grew steadily with the assistance of state land grants. In 1850, the total county population increased to 12,016, and the city's numbers grew to 2,686. From 1850 onward, Grand Rapids expanded rapidly.

The Hardy family settled in Gaines Township southeast of the city. Township land, though inexpensive, was still difficult for many settlers to attain. An 1881 history of Kent County described the earlier settlers of Gaines as "poor, having barely means enough to enable them to purchase their lands of the Government for $1.25 an acre, yet their families and households, through the wilderness, gained a foothold on their farms." The author claimed that the township residents used persistent energy "to work, and the heavy forests began to disappear. It was soon found to be one of the richest tracts in the vicinity for agricultural purposes, and at the present day is one of the best in the country."[17] Although we may exercise a degree of skepticism at the author's civic boosterism, Gaines Township did in fact grow, and so did the fortune of the Hardy family. From an economic standpoint, the Hardy family migration into the area was timely.

Race, however, continued to hinder the family. The Hardys lived in what anthropologist Victor Turner would call a liminal state.[18] They were racially categorized in the census as mulattos. Their "racial" mixture is evident from all written accounts of them. They possessed neither black nor dark brown skin and exhibited limited Negroid features. Their cultural identity could best be described as Afro-Yankees.[19] It should come as no surprise that they shared some of same cultural traits as their white neighbors.[20] Notwithstanding their genetic and cultural blending, they could not formally blend into the society in which they lived. Their lives were in limbo, both politically and culturally. Their census categorization, though biologically fictive, was a millstone around their necks.[21]

Although the Hardys were one of the first African American farming families in the Kent County area, they were not the first people of African descent to enter the region. As early as the late 1700s, there were single men who were traders and assorted laborers in the Great Lakes region.[22] In the town of Lowell due east of the city, one trader is identified as having settled in among the native population, where later his son Cobmoosa ("the walker") became the chief of the Flat Water Indians.[23] In another instance, in 1835, one of the city's founding fathers, Lucius Lyon, had in his entourage an African American, John Scott, who served as cook to the men building the village's first canals.[24]

The Hardys' migration into western Michigan coincided with that of other African American settlers in adjacent towns and counties. Ottawa County attracted both free people of color from the east and runaway slaves from the South. The town of Grand Haven became a primary stop on the Underground Railroad in the 1850s.[25] In 1847, Hezekiah Smith, a free man of color, purchased land from the state in Spring Lake, Michigan. Smith planned to establish a colony of freed people. Because of threats by neighboring whites, Smith disbanded the colony in 1850. In the 1870s he resumed farming on his land, where he lived out the remaining years of his life.[26] All of these traders and settlers in the Grand Rapids region, like the Hardys, lived with the burden of race —what Tocqueville called the mark of servitude.

Antebellum Michigan was racially stratified by custom and by law.[27] When Hardy's parents arrived in Michigan in 1827 from New York, they were faced with the new law, passed by the territorial legislature, entitled *An Act to Regulate Blacks and Mulattos, and to Punish the Kidnapping of Such Persons.* This act, David Katzman explains, although ostensibly designed to protect African Americans from slave hunters, required all African Americans in the territory to have a valid court-attested certificate of freedom and to register with the clerk of the county court. The stiffest provision of the act required Negroes immigrating into the territory to file a bond of five hundred dollars guaranteeing good behavior.[28] Incidents such as the Blackburn riot in Detroit in 1833, where the African American community overran the jail to protect a runaway slave from being seized by slave catchers, typify the turbulent times and searing realities of Hardy's formative years.

Sectional strife over slavery ran high in the local newspapers as the Hardy family settled onto their farm in the 1850s, and Hardy could have taken little consolation from news reports that, for example, California had been admitted as a non-slaveholding state—but only because of an accompanying concession to the Fugitive Slave Act—or that in 1851 the Iowa legislature had prohibited free Negroes from entering the state (as Michigan had attempted to do in 1827).[29] Indiana also prohibited free African Americans from settling in the state or being hired for contract.[30] Throughout the upper Midwest and the Great Lakes region, the Hardy family and many other free families of color faced *de jure* and *de facto* racial exclusion in all aspects of civic life.[31] If this were not enough, William Hardy had yet another and perhaps a more ubiquitous hardship to face: a constant barrage of printed and staged cultural mockery.

───────────

Throughout Grand Rapids, newspapers constantly characterized African Americans as either deserving of slavery or incapable of managing liberty.[32] Numerous uncomplimentary depictions of African Americans as buffoons appeared in the newspaper.[33] Columns reinforced ideas set in motion by the advent of the minstrel show. African American cultural styles were co-opted for their entertainment value, thereby marginalizing African Americans politically and demeaning their personhood through crude humor. Although slavery had no economic role in Michigan as a state, slavery, as Tocqueville recognized, set the cultural and ideological parameters of the dominant society.[34] Even the private reflections of Grand Rapids diarist Rebecca Richmond captured the sentiment and popular attitude about African Americans prevalent in 1863.

> Rain. "The Black Swan," alias Miss Greenfield gave a concert this eve-
> ning at Luce's Hall. Mother, Father, May and I rode down. The hall
> was quite filled when we arrived and it was some time before we could
> obtain seats but were finally ushered into some that had been reserved
> but failed of being sold. The program consisted of music of the highest
> order, which the colored lady rendered with much evident taste, refine-
> ment, and expression. Her voice is quite pleasing, sweet and melodious,
> and of remarkable compass. In the lower register it has much more the
> character of the male than of a female: indeed, so striking [were] the
> changes that, where she sang one stanza in the middle register and the
> second one a octave below, I thought for a moment that her pianist, Dr.
> Kress, must be singing. In her appearance, I was disappointed. She is pure
> African of the homeliest kind—short, thick, black, awkward. A bright
> pink silk dress made low in the neck and with short sleeves displayed to
> the best advantage her ebony skin. A wreath of red roses sat evenly on
> her wooly crown; and her white-kid gloves were of the most perfect fit.
> A great portion of the audience evidently attended from pure curiosity,
> and were apparently disappointed with the style of music, not looking
> for that of so high a tone. She sang not one Ethiopian melody.[35]

Richmond's observation confirms the argument of Eric Lott that in the North's "rowdy theatrical spaces an emergent racial politics was both registered and created, and that the racial feeling underlying and shaping but [at] times eluding the official narratives of race in these years began to appear."[36]

All aspects of African American lives were subject to cruelty and crudeness of racial stereotypes. In March 1859 the *Enquirer & Herald* reported a domestic dispute between two well-known African American barbers; the subheading for the article read "Grand Rapids Not to be Outdone by the Federal Capital!!" The story told of how Mr. Wilsen, the "Sable Saint," as the paper referred to him, was having an affair with the wife of his fellow barber, Mr. Highwarder. The paper noted how Mrs. Highwarder had planned to abandon one of her children in Toledo in an elaborate scheme to run away with Mr. Wilsen. However, the scheme failed because a letter Mrs. Highwarder had intended for delivery to Mr. Wilsen fell instead into the hands of Mr. Highwarder because the person carrying the letter, in the words of the newspaper, "could not distinguish one letter from another." Highwarder's discovery of the infidelity caused a thunderous uproar that ended up in civil court. Like an afternoon television soap opera, the story of the Highwarders and Wilsen provided great entertainment for its white readers. The writer noted, "We await with breathless anxiety the *finale* of this dark affair."[37] Two years later the press again reported about the disputes at Highwarder's barbershop.[38] The interesting thing about this portrayal of the Highwarders is that the African American population between 1840 and 1870 was numerically insignificant (0.7 percent of the city's total population). Yet, as one can gather, this small segment of the larger community served as significant source of entertainment.

The editor of the *Enquirer & Herald*, the Democratic daily, acknowledged as much in an 1859 editorial column while trying to justify black inferiority.

> Residents of the extreme North come in contact with so few of the negro race; they cannot really appreciate what the latter consist of and amount to, when gathered in considerable numbers as residents of any particular locality. It was our fortune to reside for about a dozen years in a city of one of the more Northerly of the Southern States. In that city were several thousands of free darkies; and yet, of all that number, there were not as many "respectable" individuals as there are among the very few colored inhabitants of Grand Rapids. Left to themselves, they seem to deteriorate in morals, mental and physical condition and numbers. But when they are only a few of them, surrounded by a white population, they are rendered infinitely better as citizens and individuals in every respect.

Free people of color in Grand Rapids as well as in "Canada West," in the opinion of this column, proved to be problematic as independent agents. In Canada, he noted, a grand jury of Essex County, Ontario, had "alluded to the 'great prevalence for the colored race among' the occupants of the jail." It is ironic that the editor of the newspaper observed that African Americans living amid whites would make better citizens. Citizenship, however, as a result of the majority opinion in the United States Supreme Court in the Dred Scott decision (as well as the political actions of Michigan's legislature), was not available to free people of color in Michigan.

The question arises as to why newspapers even bothered to report the domestic matters of such ordinary persons as the Highwarders. Their life troubles, it seems, served the larger community as a source of humor, fulfilled stereotypes, and reinforced Negro inferiority. As scholars of race have observed, blackness as a status fostered whiteness as the ideal of American citizenship.[39] In the antebellum era, free persons of color in the North, like their soon-to-be emancipated siblings in the South, were a bellwether for the ills of American economic class structure. Race trumped class status. The cultural subordination that stereotypes provided further eroded the status of families like the Hardys.[40]

Notwithstanding the misconstrued stereotypes, African Americans in Grand Rapids lived real and complex lives. For instance, many individuals lived within the town—like the butcher, Samuel Bryce, who was married to a German woman. There was also Mr. Highwarder, the barber who struggled to hold together his family and business. On the other hand, there were farmers like the Hardys who resided in the rural areas surrounding the city, and like the Vond family, who migrated from Vermont. There were also the Minsees of Pennsylvania who lived with the Hardy family until they established their own farm, and David Roberts, a horse trader who lived in the city but whose work took in both towns and rural areas. These men and women, having made their way from New York, Ohio, and Pennsylvania, had commonplace lives just like their neighbors.

In order to survive the racist patterns that dogged their existence, these people clustered together and developed networks of kin and mutuality. They worked diligently to forge community. These were the individuals whom Frederick Douglass idealized in a speech given in Grand Rapids in 1868 entitled "A Self-Made Man."[41] Douglass's Victorian promulgation regarding the self-made man should have resonated with people like the Hardys, Minisees, Vonds, Highwarders, and Bryces, those independent farmers and entrepreneurs who worked hard to attain property, goods, and respectability. Yet they remained largely invisible in the grim social realities of white supremacy.[42] Free people of color in Grand Rapids throughout the nineteenth century were found largely in the labor pools of servants and physical laborers. At the time there was not much difference between the laboring status of blacks and their white counterparts. Both were struggling to stay alive, feeding on the bottom of the food chain in an ever-expanding urban setting. The earliest records found in the local Directory of Grand Rapids list the vast majority of African American men as porters, cooks, and assorted laborers. In this regard, there was constant scrutiny on local African American women as to their middle class probity. The role of women in the rough-and-tumble culture of the laboring classes spoke volumes about the social well-being and the general morality of the African American community. The local press paid close attention to "Mama" Sarah Walker who ran "a house of ill-fame."[43] An *Eagle* reporter observed the following during a raid on her house: "Last evening was a most unfortunate one for the domicile known the State over, as A Nigger Mammy's house, on LaGrave Street, and certainly one of the most loathsome and degraded of houses of prostitution in the city. Strange [as] it may seem, it was a favorite resort of both white and colored girls, and judging from the popularity it enjoyed in one sense of the word the frequenters of the place were as equally divided in color as the inmates."

Although acknowledging the popularity of Walker's house, the reporter seemed unable to describe her in anything but the most unflattering, racialized terms. "First and foremost appeared the notorious head centre of the *posse*, no other than 'Nigger Mammy,' whose rightful name is supposed to be Sarah Walker. But 'not for Sarah' this time; in other words, she made a voluntary appearance, for the purpose no doubt, of keeping her watchful eye on the flock. A queer specimen of humanity is the decidedly unprepossessing in appearance. . . ."[44]

What the reporter missed was that Sarah Walker was an entrepreneur, albeit in an unsavory business. She made her money by providing services on the underside of Victorian prohibitions. She worked! In the domestic ideology of the nineteenth-century in which all women were to appear virtuous, the violation of middle-class probity was doubly burdensome on the African American community. Women were the standard-bearers of hearth and home, the idealized image of gentility and civilization, which meant that the role of African American women was all the more on the margin of proper laboring culture. If a distasteful incident involved a woman in the African American community, the woman was viewed with even more contempt.[45] This furthers what historian Deborah Gray White offers as a typology of slave women—the image of "Jezebel," the stereotype of wanton and libidinous women, associated not only with enslaved women but also urban free women of color.[46] Sarah Walker, however, achieved her own sense of respectability. Within her own community, she was a founding member of the African Methodist Episcopal (AME) Church in 1874.

The Grand Rapids dailies often made it appear that all vice and crime were synonymous with Afro-American life.

Serious Affray Man Stabbed: A drunken and disgraceful row at an Irish shanty, near the depot, last night, in which one man got a fearful stab in the abdomen. It appears that four or five men laborers in and about the depot among whom was John Carroll, an Irishman, and a colored man named Wm. R. Nelson, got to drinking whiskey, or some other miserable liquid, and thereby got into a dispute and row, the result of which was that Carroll was stabbed pretty seriously by Nelson, in the left groin, or side, letting the intestines protrude. Though the wound is a severe and dangerous one, the attending physicians think it will not prove fatal. Nelson surrendered himself to the authorities this morning, and the examination of the case is being had before Justice Leffingwell, as we go to press.[47]

Nine days later, the *Enquirer & Herald* characterized the rift between these two railroad workers in this fashion. "The negro, Nelson, who was arrested on Wednesday of last week, for his murderous assault on one Carroll, has failed to obtain bail, and now lies in jail to await the action of the Circuit Court."[48] The paper did not give the full context of the story. Nelson and Carroll inhabited the world of countless laborers who frequented the same taverns where men and women often engaged in a variety of passions that sometimes ended in bloody disputes.

Although the daily newspapers exaggerated the extent of vice among Afro-Americans, these stories also served as evidence of the interchange between black and white laborers. As the population of Afro-Americans slowly increased, the level of white anxiety also increased.[49] The newspapers drew considerable attention to any work gained by or any employment opportunities for Afro-American men. "Colored Laborers: The Toledo Commercial says: AA Railroad Company in Michigan has lately made application to the Freedmen's Bureau for 400 negro laborers to be employed in the construction of a new line of road in the State. They offer to pay such laborers 87½ cts. per day and board them. The proper officers of the Bureau are now engaged in collecting the required number of blacks, and it is probable that they will be dispatched thither during the month. We wonder what Railroad they are to be employed on."[50]

Before the railroad companies began inquiring of the Freedmen's Bureau about black laborers, black men of the region had already established themselves as railroad laborers. In Grand Haven, Michigan, black male workers were employed by the railroad and demanded timely wages. An *Eagle* reporter stated that the "*colored population*, employed about the freight depot of the D&M Railroad, at Grand Haven, are up to the times. They have had a great strike and their employers have *come down* with an advance in wages."[51] African Americans were recruited statewide as inexpensive labor.

In 1872, C. C. Comstock, the former mayor of Grand Rapids, built a barrel-making plant on the Grand River. The *Grand Rapids Eagle,* referring to Comstock enterprise to build accommodations for Negro workers, announced on August 9 that "the Hon. C. C. Comstock's *Hotel de Afrique,* on North Canal Street, is about finished. It is 240 feet long, and will accommodate 20 families."[52] John Wesley Lowes, a native of Ontario, Canada, in search of work in the post–Civil War expansion of Grand Rapids, was one of the workmen who built Comstock's Row. Lowes described the barrel-making factory in a June 1872 letter to his wife Sarah Benson Lowes. He wrote: "I got work again. For the next day about fifty yards from Johns to help build a negro factory (you will say what kind of a factory is that well it is a building two stories high twenty four feet wide & two hundred and forty long divided into eighty rooms for the purpose of making and raising young negros curious factory) that it will take a few weeks to build and I expect to get work at it while it is finishing."[53] Comstock, like other Michigan entrepreneurs, wrote the Freedmen's Bureau inquiring into the availability freedmen to work in Michigan.[54] Like the railroaders seeking cheap labor, Comstock hoped that by building an operation that housed families, he would give freedmen an incentive to work in his plant. The barrel-making plant attracted many freed people who were born in the South and others, who escaped slavery, from Canada. The *Eagle* reported that the "demands for rooms in the Ethiopian Hotel on the upper end of Canal [S]treet had been so great" that Comstock contemplated expansion. If the tenants did not work for Comstock, they held other assorted laboring jobs.[55]

Life in Comstock's Row quickly became synonymous with wanton living.[56] The Grand River district where the Row was located attracted other laboring people who worked in sawmills as railroad workers and in the burgeoning furniture industry. Still, the press failed to give the fuller context in which these interactions took place. The supposedly loose morals among African Americans occurred in interracial and working-class environments such as taverns, gambling establishments, and brothels. The people of Comstock's Row were no more or less moral than their overall community.[57]

A despised minority rarely has a chance of winning political power through the exercise of brute force. From the formation of the United States as a separate entity from England in the eighteenth century, free people of color developed a civic tradition of protest in freed communities throughout the United States, particularly in the North. Region, culture, circumstances, and populations dictated how this tradition was employed. In Grand Rapids, African Americans joined with other small African American communities throughout the state and openly carried out civic protest in their moral appeals to gain citizenship rights.[58]

In 1860, David Roberts, a horse trader, and E. H. Wilson represented Kent County at the statewide meeting of Afro-Americans to petition the state legislature for the right of suffrage,[59] yet little came of these protests until the passage of the Fifteenth Amendment.[60] As Michigan historian Willis Dunbar observed, white politicians rarely disguised their contempt for black enfranchisement. In 1850, when suffrage legislation came before the voting populace of Michigan, it was defeated by a vote of 32,026 to 12,840.[61] Despite the defeat, African Americans in Grand Rapids, like their compatriots throughout the state, continued to resist political exclusion long before the social reordering brought on by the Civil War.

The Civil War provided the seismic eruption that destroyed Southern slavery and modified Northern racial segregation. As the war commenced, African Americans and white supporters formed a militia composed of black men, an effort rejected in 1861 by Michigan governor Austin Blair. Later, when pressed, Blair offered grudging support for African Americans who wanted to fight on behalf of the Union Army. In a speech given in Adrian, Michigan, Blair, using the familiar racist language of the day, supported the use of Afro-American troops. He declared, "I am utterly unable to see why it is not proper to use a rebel's sacred nigger . . . I am entirely unable to see, too, why Sambo shouldn't be permitted to carry a musket."[62] Blair's backhanded support of African American troops was consistent with the stereotypes and language of daily life. The black men were menial laborers and "dandies," not soldiers.

Despite the political opposition, African Americans statewide continued pressing for their chance to fight in the Union cause. This effort paid off. In 1864, African Americans from around the state formed Michigan's First Colored Infantry. At least thirty men from Grand Rapids and adjacent townships and counties participated in the Civil War, with a good portion of these men joining the First.[63]

The First Colored Infantry was modeled on the society at large: it was a segregated unit led exclusively by white male officers, and black soldiers received poor combat preparation and unequal pay. Once organized and attached to the 102nd United States Colored Troops, the First Michigan Colored Infantry fought bravely throughout South Carolina and Florida.[64] Although the unit was formed in the context of racial inequality, one historian viewed the formation of the unit as a hopeful sign for the demise of racial segregation. For white supporters, the organization of the regiment was proof that African Americans were fully capable of military service and therefore deserving of civil rights. To blatant white supremacists, the regiment represented a threat to the superior social position of whites. However, "[t]o the black community in Michigan, [the regiment] was the vehicle by which they could demonstrate their loyalty and courage, and thus hopefully procure equal rights as citizens."[65]

The defeat of Southern secessionist did not automatically mean that Afro-Americans received full citizenship in Michigan. The Civil War brought the end of slavery, but the cultural legacy of racial stigma clung powerfully in the day-to-day interactions in the city,[66] and the issue of suffrage continued to serve as a lightning rod for white fears. The *Grand Rapids Democrat*—whose logo read "White Man's Paper"—urged its readers not to support an extension of suffrage rights to African American men. The editor of the paper contended that African American interests were safe in the hands of the dominant race, much safer than they would be in their own hands. The *Democrat* further suggested that the expansion of suffrage rights would bring about the demise of white laboring opportunities.[67]

Nevertheless, African Americans in Grand Rapids and around the state continued to advocate for their citizenship rights. On January 29, 1863, following the issuance of the Emancipation Proclamation, African American delegates from around the state met and called upon the electors of Michigan to end racially segregated politics.

> At such a time as this, when our beloved country is writhing beneath the throes of political devastation, every man, of whatever race or color, who at all values the endearing name of American citizen, should be called upon and required to do his duty in upholding the General Government, and putting down the most infamous rebellion that ever distracted a country in the history of the world. Whatever may be required of others should be required of us, and we feel willing and stand ready to obey our country's call, in summons to arms in her defense, or in any other just capacity in which we might be required. But as residents of Michigan, we cannot feel willing to serve a State while it concedes all that is due to others, and denies much if not the most is due to us. Therefore, in view of all these facts, we appeal to you as fellow citizens of the same State, and having one common destiny, to use your influence by petition and otherwise, to have the word *white* erased from the State Constitution, and to repeal all laws and statutes which make a distinction between us and other citizens of the State.[68]

Tellingly, this appeal did not ask the state to make them citizens; rhetorically, they already claimed it in the appeal to vote.

Even though the *Grand Rapids Eagle,* a daily linked to the Republican Party, advocated for the rights of African Americans in the South, they were at a loss as to why the people of Michigan had not accorded the same formal citizenship rights to its own denizens. The *Eagle* explained: "In Michigan, although a colored man cannot, as yet, wield the ballot, yet, in all other respects, he stands before the law as equal of any other citizen. His natural rights are all secured by the same laws that secure those of his white neighbor. The black citizen in Michigan, and in all the Northern states, is secure in his rights of person and property."[69]

If equality existed as the *Eagle* claimed, then it should have been easy for the larger populace to accord political privileges to all. In 1867, when Michigan voters took up the issues that had burdened the Reconstruction-era Congress regarding citizenship rights, they rejected the referendum that permitted African Americans the right to vote. The *Eagle*'s judgment was that the 1868 changes to the state's constitution, which dropped the "color" provisions, resulted in nothing more than a "Negro" suffrage bill. The newspaper argued that the new constitutional changes were good because they extended democracy.

> But in this canvass we shall strenuously object to calling it a negro suffrage instrument. It is precisely because we are *not* in favor of negro suffrage, yankee suffrage, white suffrage, black suffrage, Irish suffrage, or German suffrage, that we like the suffrage article of the new constitution. It is because we are in favor of democratic, *citizen* suffrage that we like it. We are glad the convention had the wisdom to say "citizens," not white, nor green, nor yellow, nor black-haired, flaxen-haired, or sandy-whiskered, nor kid-gloved, nor leather mittened citizens, but simply "citizens" or "inhabitants," possessing certain qualifications by reason of residence, virtue, and an interact in the common welfare, such as all who take part in making the laws should possess.[70]

Of course, the newspaper was correct to a degree. Ironically, the *Eagle* never mentioned that the Colored Convention of 1863 had asked for the same legal color blindness: the paper simply forgot that the people of Michigan had rejected this earlier request. The political openness that the newspaper trumpeted could not suppress white fears about the status of African Americans.[71] In spite of the reluctance of the mass electorate, the Michigan legislature ratified the Fifteenth Amendment in 1870. The Legislature accorded the vote to Afro-American men as a political debt owed to their fellow Republicans in the Congress. Any moral commitment to them as citizens was secondary to supporting the larger Republican cause.[72] The state legislature's moral motivation for according the right to vote to the African American male population appeared to be of little concern to the African American community itself, so long as they received the power to exercise their vote.[73] The *Eagle* commented: "We are glad to learn that quite a number of colored men have registered and are prepared to exercise the right of suffrage, for the first time, at a general election, tomorrow. It has come to be admitted, we believe, that colored men are human beings, and that the color of skin is not a just and fair standard by which to measure out political rights and franchises. One fact cannot have escaped attention, which is that these men put a high value upon their newly attained rights and privileges."[74] With the power to vote, Afro-Americans at once set out to gain office. From the northern county of Manistee and throughout the western half of the state, Afro-Americans engaged in the political process.[75]

William Hardy's election to the Kent County Board of Supervisors demonstrates the point clearly. Hardy eagerly employed his new voting privileges and became involved in township politics. He ran for a seat on the local school board in 1870 and lost. In spite of this setback, Hardy remained involved in local Republican politics. In the spring of 1872, he again sought a position on the Kent County board of supervisors; this time he won. What made his victory an anomaly was that Gaines Township was a Democratic stronghold.[76] While the city of Grand Rapids proper was thoroughly Republican, many of its outlying townships were Democratic.

Although he did have "African blood running in his veins," Hardy's social standing was that of a good farmer and neighbor,[77] affording him a modicum of freedom that Afro-Americans in the city lacked. He derived his status in part by arriving in the township while it still was the frontier—frontier societies sometimes maintain a rough form of egalitarianism[78]—and in part from being relatively prosperous. Perhaps, too, it was his decency that allowed other farmers to overlook his tainted ancestry. Whatever the facts were, he won the Republican caucus and defeated the incumbent Democrat Aaron Brewer in the general election.[79]

Franklin Everett, a local historian and Hardy's contemporary, lauded Hardy's election.

He had no advantages in early life, and the soul-crushing disadvantage of belonging to a despised and slighted race. But, with the thought that a negro may be a man, he educated himself, until he ranks among the well-informed. By his moral dignity and sterling good sense, he won respect, until he was allowed his place among the leading men in town. He is, so far as known, the first colored man who held office in Michigan. He has served his town in various public positions; in 1872 as supervisor. The people have forgotten that he is black, and no one is above visiting

the family, which he has educated as gentleman and ladies, or of respect-
fully any of them as equals. The example of Mr. Hardy may show what
any one who has native talent, ambition, character and perseverance can
do; that respect can be *commanded*; and that humble origin need not be
followed by humble life.[80]

Everett celebrated Gaines Township because of Hardy's election, because
"she was the first town in the State to show that manhood was to be
respected for its worth, and not its color. For this conquering of deep-
rooted prejudice, all honor to Gaines."[81] Here was the paradox of Everett's
pronouncement: as an individual, Hardy was a well-respected man with
an upstanding reputation in his farming community; however, his personal qualities were not enough to secure his reelection in 1873.

In Gaines Township, Hardy had two strikes against him: he was both
a racial and a political minority. The *Democrat* chronicled his defeat.

At the Republican Caucus in the town of Gaines, Wm. J. Hardy received
on several ballots a majority of the votes cast, and should have been the
nominee for Supervisor, but the Republicans, seeing that Mr. H. would
not voluntarily take the hint and withdraw his name as a candidate
went to him and told him that they thought he ought to withdraw, for
they feared he could not be elected; not because he had not been an able
Supervisor, but the novelty of a colored man on the board having become
somewhat stale, and Mr. Hardy having been treated by the Democratic
members of the board the same as any other Republican, no political
capital could be made of the election. The action of Mr. H., who immediately withdrew his name from before the Caucus, was unlike what
would been done by his fairer skinned political brothers, but very much
like them he went to work quietly and by his influence defeated his competitor in the Caucus, at the polls. Whether he will hereafter be termed
a traitor, copperhead, or rebel, remains to be seen.[82]

It would have been truly revolutionary for race not to factor into Hardy's
reelection bid. Personal character may have caused some aberration in
the racial hierarchy, but individual good character was not enough to
redefine local culture and politics.

Yet Hardy did not retreat without addressing his own interest. Sizing
up his chances for another possible run for office and the needs of Afro-
Americans around Grand Rapids, he spoke in gratitude to the Republican
Party. In response to the *Democrat*'s charges, he wrote:

I notice in the weekly issue of the *Democrat* . . . an article regard[ing]
. . . the Republican Caucus in Gaines, in which my name and the course
I took at the Caucus and at the polls are discussed. The writer in the
Democrat says that I went to work quietly and by my influence defeated

my competitor in the Caucus, at the polls. In this, he is mistaken. My competitor in the Caucus, W. B. Pickett, and myself are mutual friends; and I voted for him at the polls. Although I might have thought that the nomination belonged to me, the Republican Party has done too much for me, and for my race, to go back on it for the first thing that looked a little shaky. The *Democrat* is right in saying I was treated as any other Republican on the Board. I was treated gentlemanly by every member of the Board, and received, perhaps, more consideration than I deserved.[83]

He knew that racial politics played largely in his not being re-nominated, but in his world he had few political options. The Republican Party, the (slim) ruling national majority at the time, was the party that led the fight against slavery and had been the party in office as Afro-Americans became full citizens. However, much of the local politics throughout the state were still controlled by Democrats who continued to be averse to black political participation. Hardy pragmatically chose to continue his alignment with the Republican Party.

The Civil War and Reconstruction ended slavery in the South and legal racial exclusion in Michigan. However, the use of race as a powerful ideological tool in politics and within local culture remained constant. Hardy and the local black community were tolerated as individuals but loathed as a people. The *Grand Rapids Morning Democrat*, commenting in response to Negroes being enfranchised, wrote the following opinion:

> We speak of the negroes. We have reference to the pure African, that human being without one drop of white blood in his veins. Is he equal to white men? Did God Almighty design him to be equal, in all, or any one element that makes the man? Is the race of life equal? Can it be equal? With equal advantages can the pure Ethiopian ever reach the level of the Caucasian in intelligence, in refinement, in manhood? Then why make him of different color with a different physical structure, with a different constructed brain, with blood even chemically different. If the same thing was meant, if the same object was sought, why this so greatly different structure of machinery? Time has proved the African the inferior race. The history of the race is before the world and it is not a matter of conjecture which is the inferior and which the superior. What has been gained, in civilization, has been the work of the white men. He who doubts this is an insane bigot.[84]

While the *Democrat* spoke the sentiments of the minority political party in Grand Rapids, it was the popularly held view of the majority of citizens.

Racial stigmatization in nineteenth-century Grand Rapids was a part of the Northern ideological landscape.[85] Although African Americans comprised only a tiny fraction of the population, they were observed in a panoptical fashion. The local community was constantly scrutinized, given advice, and derided. It is no wonder that at the turn of the twentieth century, W. E. B. Du Bois reflected on the two-ness of the Negro and being seen through the eyes of others.[86] Hardy's life reflected the regional dimensions of the DuBosian dilemma. Remarkably, African Americans in Grand Rapids continued to create spheres to make life livable outside the judging gaze of white Protestants.

The contours of African Americans as an ethnic community were to be found in the travails and limitations of living life as racially stigmatized persons.[87] American slavery served both the North and the South, although differently, as the basis for African Americans' being prohibited from political and economic competition with Anglo-Americans and subsequent European immigrants. While slavery swelled in the South until the mid-nineteenth century, in the antebellum North racial segregation became the bedrock of American life. In his study of Jim Crow, historian C. Vann Woodward notes that American race relations developed the pattern of formal racial stratification found in the North prior to the Civil War. Woodward claims that during Reconstruction and on into the 1880s, there were forgotten alternatives between blacks and whites throughout the South. By this he meant that the relationship between blacks and whites was more fluid politically and offered the possibility that different kinds of outcomes might have occurred other than the hardened race relations that arose in the formal laws in the South, which became known as Jim Crow. Of course, there is a great deal of merit to this point of view. The story of American race relations after Reconstruction was fluid for a short and contested period, and Hardy's life in Grand Rapids serves as a testament to this fleeting period in the North. The forgotten alternatives of American race relations that Woodward keenly observed existed in the South after Reconstruction were always limited by the structure of racial segregation entrenched in the North.[88] What made the South's later version of racial segregation far more brutal and violent were the numerical strength and political threat African Americans posed throughout the South. Racial segregation followed emancipation in the North as it would follow the abolition of slavery in the South.[89] These forgotten alternatives were temporary, and as soon as possible, African American office holders were voted out of office in the North in the same way they would later be dislodged throughout the South.

There is no question that the marker for the decline in social status

during this period was any association with black African-ness. Symboli-
cally, slavery and then racial segregation became signs of social pollution and danger.⁹⁰ The editor of the *Eagle,* in criticizing the local Democratic newspaper, aptly summarized the social contamination of the day:
"Take up any Democratic paper today, and you find it filled with nigger. They have but that string to their fiddle, and they saw away on that
from morning till night. You can see Cuffy's thick lips in every whistle
they make to keep up their courage, and see his long head at every kick
at liberty and humanity. Every word they write is steeped in nigger, and
every sentence is woven full of his woolly hair."⁹¹

Racial stigma as a sign of cultural pollution and political inferiority
became one of the defining features of daily African American life in this
era. It affected the ethnic formation of African American communities
throughout the country. Whether in the North or the South, slavery and
then racial segregation functioned to adjudicate the shifting social order
in the United States.

For Hardy's family, life under this stigma was often unbearable.
Eugene Hardy, William and Eliza's oldest son and the first black male to
graduate from a Grand Rapids High School, was quoted by a neighbor as
saying that he would never bring a child into the world to lead the life
of "a Negro." Only one of the six Hardy children had any children.⁹²

In addition to the pressures of living in a racialized world, the economic transformation in the wider country affected the family too. They
lived in an era that witnessed the transformation of American farming.
At the time of William Hardy's death in 1888, his farm had shrunk and
his children had gone to seek their fortune and their freedom in the growing city.

The men and women of William Hardy's generation had lived in a
slaveholding society, and the blemish of that society had disfigured their
lives with the mark of servitude, as Tocqueville predicted. However,
what Tocqueville's aristocratic vision overlooked was the agency and
strength of African Americans to resist the fetters placed on them.⁹³ His
French version of America saw African Americans as mere pawns. African Americans fought valiantly to relinquish stigmas attached to them.
They won their citizenship rights through struggle—a struggle that had
been born in opposition to American slavery and through the bloodlet-
ting of the Civil War. The achievement of citizenship rights, however,
did not abolish the racial hierarchy or the cultural stigmas associated
with their lives. The struggle for social and political recognition in the
city was to be long and hard.

William Hardy's generation gained the formal freedoms in the civic sphere but was ineffectual in combating the enduring cultural and political power of racial stigma that evolved over the course of the nineteenth century. At the time of Hardy's death, Jim Crow laws throughout the South were evolving and solidifying the political domination over the lives of Afro-Southerners; by contrast, the formal laws of racial exclusion in Michigan had been legally banned. Nevertheless, the ingrained culture of white supremacy that followed Hardy all the way to the grave continued in both the North and South—and remained alive in the city where his bones rest.

2 *"In Colored Circles":*
The Shape of African American
Civil Society

In the years following William Hardy's death, a cluster of African American urban dwellers evolved in Grand Rapids. One local newspaper article entitled "In Colored Circles: A Horrid Scandal Kicked Up in Comstock Row" identified this network, in this way: "John Weathers, of this city, by Alexander Hamilton, his solicitor, has commenced divorce proceedings in the circuit court against his wife, the famous Josephine Weathers of police court renown. Complainant charges that defendant has been in the habit of coming [home] nights in a beastly state of intoxication. Also that she has taken his watch and chain in order to obtain liquor." As though his readers had not already known this particular fact, the reporter noted that the parties are colored people.[1] Divorce, even by late-nineteenth-century standards, was not something so unusual that it warranted this type of publicity. The dailies normally placed divorce notices at the bottom of the page and listed them with the other routine matters occurring in the local courts. The Weathers' case, however, was different because Josephine, an African American woman, earned notoriety in the city as an infamous drunkard.[2] The personal travails of Josephine and John Weathers did not matter to the reporter. They were a caricature. The world she and her husband occupied was one filled with alcohol abuse—which, incidentally, became the scourge of many communities, not just black ones.

Although the intent of the column was to entertain its readers with yet another funny story of African American life, it also inadvertently acknowledged the existence of a separate civil society that had a continuum of social relationships within it. African Americans in Grand Rapids developed a layered social ecology[3] with four components: cultural nationalism rooted in Protestant Christian faith; organized political affiliation and party activities; membership in local democratic civic associations and churches; and a functional network of kith and kin developed throughout Michigan and Ontario, Canada. One vital aspect of civil society this African American community lacked was a collective economic base. This deficiency, which resulted from a numerically small population and widespread racial exclusion, weakened the formation a strong Afro-American civil society. As a result, the ambitions of community leaders were frustrated, the growth of middle class expanded at a snail's pace, and political gains were infrequently achieved.

The cultural nationalism of Grand Rapids' African American civil society was infused with Protestant Christian sensibilities, constructed on memories of enslavement, and seen ritually in civic expressions such as Emancipation Day celebrations, various commemorations, and written histories. These collective expressions are central for understanding the African American community in the late nineteenth century.[4]

The celebration of Emancipation Day, August 1, was a prime holiday for all Afro-Americans in Michigan,[5] commemorating the day the British emancipated slaves in the West Indies in 1834. It became an annual holiday in Grand Rapids sometime in the early 1870s. In the years following emancipation in the United States, Afro-American communities in Michigan continued to use Emancipation Day celebrations to define freedom, bond the community, and delineate a shared past.[6]

The Emancipation Day celebrations in Grand Rapids were shared experiences between African American communities in Battle Creek, Kalamazoo, and other parts of southwest Michigan. Citizens of these respective cities joined each other via rail connections to celebrate the remembrances of overcoming slavery. Each year the celebration alternated between cities, a rotation that allowed Afro-Americans living throughout southwest Michigan to feel numerical strength within their respective communities, allowed each community to avoid the yearly strain of planning and hosting their own separate annual celebrations, and helped to build community.[7] In addition, the changing venue facilitated a trip away from home to visit friends or family, and it made a way for the single person to meet potential suitors. The ritual observance of Emancipation Day was filled with "dance and drink alternated with prayer and speech."[8] The significance of the day was always given in a recitation of the grand progressive Afro-American narrative from slavery to freedom.

On August 1, 1883, Eugene Hardy, the son of William J. Hardy, recited this kind of narrative in an Emancipation Day speech. Hardy stood before five or six hundred people and directed his words to people who were born in slavery,[9] such as the lawyer Alexander Hamilton,[10] prominent barber J. C. Craig,[11] and Joseph C. Ford.[12] He stated:

> I see around me today many subjects of the emancipation act of 1863, and if it were possible to convert this assemblage into a sort of class meeting or conference, if you please, that each might relate his or her experience in a life of slavery and a life of freedom, it would set forth far more brilliant than can be portrayed by the most eloquent orator, the fact that human slavery is the greatest evil that ever befell any race or nation on the globe, and that the event of the emancipation of slaves in this country was the most important event in the history of this Nation.

Hardy continued, saying, "the Emancipation Proclamation was not made for the sake of the Negro but for the sake of the country. God made it a political necessity." Referencing the escape of the Hebrew slaves from Egyptian oppression and Moses' leadership, he stated that "God had made a like demand down here in the nineteenth century through the abolition workers to this Nation, which refused to obey until they had to sacrifice hundreds of thousands of their noblest sons in civil war." God's providence, Hardy charged, "allowed the colored man to wage war on his own against slavery and help preserve the Union." Consequently, "the Union was preserved," he proclaimed "and the chains were melted from 4,000,000 human beings in the heat of war. The Thirteenth, Fourteenth and Fifteenth Amendments were added to the Constitution and gave to the colored race their rights under the United States law."

Looking over the past horrors of the Civil War, Hardy told his audience, "We stand to-day upon an eminence, which overlooks a century of National life, a hundred years, crowded with peril, but crowned with success." The success, he was quick to add, had come with a great deal of suffering and pain. "Think," he said, "of the incidents pertaining to slavery, the chains, the whips, the thumbscrews, the chain gangs, the slave pens, the bloodhounds and the auction block, with its attendant horrors, evidences of which are still extant, and can be seen in the scars of the emancipated bondmen and women." Not simply wanting to indict the old South, Hardy continued by saying, "Think of the slavery as it was beheld in the North. Who has forgotten the Oberlin rescuers, the abolitionists clubbed and dragged through the streets; the Fugitive Slave Law and its attendant horrors; colored men excluded from railroad cars, hotels and public schools." The Civil War and Reconstruction politics, in Hardy's words, laid the legal foundation for all citizens, "black or white—throughout the American Union."

African Americans, now free from slavery, Hardy opined, were soldiers in the "grand army of human progress." It was up to them to take advantages of the freedom that divine Providence had provided. Following the lead of Frederick Douglass and foreshadowing the emphasis of Booker T. Washington, Hardy continued by observing that African Americans were not in a position of strength as a people. "We are placed among them to become learners, and show them that we are their equal in industry, intelligence and moral standing and our civil rights will be respected." Civil rights, he acknowledged, were violated by color caste. However, this was not God's will. "Black is not a color despised by God or man. Four-fifths of the human race are black. Black appears to be the favorite color with the Lord for humanity, and is a favorite color with man everywhere else except in the human face." The barrier for African Americans, however, was not the color of their skin but, rather, the dishonor associated with its color. Hardy continued, "[Color] is despised in this country because it has become a badge of poverty and ignorance. If it were a badge of wealth and knowledge, how different would be our standing in the Nation." The issue was not color but power. Hardy succinctly stated, "What we want is not another color but power." The way to power, he believed, came through attainment of formal knowledge. "Finally, our great safeguard against danger," he said, "is to be found in the general and thorough education of our people, and in the virtue that accompanies such education."[13]

Although commemorative memorials were never as large as the Emancipation Day celebrations, they, too, were civic rallying points for African American collective identity: remembering notable abolitionists and social reformers like John Brown, Charles Sumner, Sojourner Truth, and Frederick Douglass was yet another way local people formed themselves into a community.[14] These commemorations rallied the community to engage in the political life of the city, reminding them that there could be no rewards materially or socially if they did not become a part of the political process. Remembering those who fought against slavery taught the community that liberty was not guaranteed without sufficient political organization.

Written history of African Americans in Michigan also served and formed collective identity. Natives joined with others throughout the state to produce written documentation of black people's accomplishments. In 1899, A. A. Owens and Harvey C. Jackson, working on behalf of Michigan's Bureau of Labor, began to compile data to tell the story of Afro-Americans in the state. Their rationale was: "First, That this is the first action taken by the State Labor Bureau to embody in its annual report any official statistics of Negroes in the State of Michigan; and second, that by reason of such action, the State hereby recognizes sufficient importance in that class of citizens to warrant giving their status in a statistical report." They stated, "It is our purpose and intention in this report to give their present standing, and compare it with that of other citizens. Also to give the facts about Negroes as far as can be obtained, setting forth the causes and conditions which placed them in their present position in the State."[15] Owen and Jackson, rather than give a bland statistical profile, went on to describe the rich activity of Michigan's Afro-Americans as a whole. Sixteen years later, the compilation begun by Owen and Jackson would be developed into a commemorative volume celebrating the progress of freemen.

In July 1914, Governor Woodbridge Ferris appointed a commission led by Charles Warren to plan and celebrate the Lincoln Jubilee and the half-century celebration of Negro freedom to be held in Chicago in the summer of 1915. Warren wrote to African American leaders throughout Michigan requesting that they petition the state legislature to finance and create a commission to organize an exhibit showing inventions, handiwork, science, and art of African American life in Michigan. In addition, the commission would "prepare a manual showing the professional, political, and religious achievements of citizens of this state in whole or in part of Negro descent." On March 2, 1915, the legislature authorized the commission; on April 14, Governor Ferris, a Democrat, signed the act sanctioning the commission's work.

The publication was entitled *The Michigan Manual of Freedmen's Progress*. The committee appointed to compile information in Grand Rapids consisted of the Reverend Henri Browne, Grace Sims, Thomas Jefferson, and Mabel Perkins. The information gathered about the area showed the Afro-American community at its best. The *Manual* pictured local small-business owners, socialites, clergy, and activists. Its intent was to show the progress of Afro-Americans from the Civil War to the New Century—how a new people, having grown from slavery, possessed the capacity, if given a chance, to rise in society. The *Manual* recast the image of Michigan Afro-Americans by portraying them as industrious and

determined people. This compilation of images fits well with what literary scholar Henry Louis Gates calls the trope of a "New Negro." Gates
explains that given the virulent racism of the time, African Americans
had no choice but to carefully shape their public image. He states that the
"Public Negro Self, therefore, was an entity to be crafted."[16] The intent
of the *Manual* was to craft a respectable image and build cultural pride,
recalling, like Eugene Hardy's 1883 Emancipation Day speech, the grand
narrative of slavery to freedom.

The cultural pride exhibited in the commemorative history of the
Emancipation Day celebrations and *The Michigan Manual of Freedmen's
Progress* stemmed from a strong sense of cultural nationalism that can
be best summed up in what historian Wilson Moses calls assimilationist
black nationalism. Moses contends that between 1890 and 1920, both
"integrationists and separatists often accepted without question many of
the Protestant, middle-class prejudices of the Anglo-American bourgeoi-
sie. In accepting these values uncritically much of this nationalism placed
the emphasis on Negro Improvement or racial uplift on Afro-Americans
themselves." He argues that "the idea common to separatists and integrationists was that the prime responsibility for the improvement of the
status of black people rested with black people themselves." Furthermore,
he states, if black people "intended to survive in the modern world and
to command the respect of other peoples, they would have to dedicate
themselves to self-improvement."[17] According to this way of thinking,
self-improvement was a sure way to gain social recognition in an ethnically competitive and racist world. The goal of self-improvement was to
win ethnic, social, and political power. Late-nineteenth-century black
cultural nationalism was not merely a compensatory reaction to social
exclusion, it was also a positive expression of communal self-regard.[18]

African Americans wanted to assimilate into the larger society on
terms that gave their community respect. No doubt there is ample evidence of individuals' ambivalence about their racial identification, but
there is also substantial evidence to suggest a sense of solidarity *as a people*
ran strong in cities like Grand Rapids. Emancipation celebrations, commemorative celebrations, and written histories reminded Afro-Americans
why and how they had become a people. They had been forged in American
slavery and struggled toward citizenship rights. They viewed themselves
as unique contributors to the history of the city and the nation.

African Americans' collective identity was grounded in an idea of
historical progress derived from Protestantism. Religious historian Laurie
Maffly-Kipp observes that African Americans during the "four decades
preceding World War I" had been in the process of developing "a histori-

cal consciousness that was at once thoroughly Protestant and thoroughly African-American." According to her this consciousness was

> [s]ynthesized in a new way by a new generation of middle-class black Christians [and] took into account a temporal sweep measured in centuries rather than decades, evaluated by providence rather than human means. This sweep frequently allowed for both the ultimate forgiveness, and also for an unyielding commitment to a historically specific collective destiny embodied in the suffering and future triumphs of the Negro race. Neither assimilationist nor separatist, inspired by Euro-American philosophy and African American cultural unity, this worldview was articulated in the only form that could fully represent its dependence on a linear and progressive notion of time: chronological narrative.[19]

The collective identity of African American civil society steeped in this historical consciousness came through the biblical narrative. The Bible had taught them that although at one time they were no people, now they were God's people.[20]

A collective sense of self automatically fostered the local black community's political ambitions. The community was highly politicized, and this was particularly true of men. It did not matter how small the group was, African American men everywhere organized politically to receive the spoils of partisan elections.[21] Partisan political loyalty rarely paid off in the manner in which many hoped, however. The brunt of their frustrations was directed toward the Republican Party.

The national issues that discouraged African Americans were with regard to the national Republican Party in the Compromise of 1877, the abandonment of the Civil Rights Act of 1875, and in the Jim Crow laws of the 1890s that were allowed to grow steadily in the Southern states virtually uncontested. In Grand Rapids, the rewards of being loyal Republicans on the local level held few benefits. Local political activity was more often than not a vehicle for expressing grievances than for electing candidates.

In the city election of 1894, local frustrations fueled a small rebellion against the party of Lincoln. "A movement is on foot among the colored voters of the city," the *Grand Rapids Democrat* reported, "to organize action which will ensure them some recognition. They have been talking for several years and twice before have been given promises, but that is as far as they ever got, and now they propose to get things 'dead to rights' before casting a vote." The newspaper quoted an unidentified African American community leader as stating:

There are about 600 hundred colored voters in this city and we own at least 100,000 dollars worth of property. Year after year we have walked up to the polls and voted the Republican ticket. After the war, every colored man was a Republican, and the white folks seem to think we can't be anything else but Republicans. We are strong in numbers and have been doing a heap of thinking lately. Our 600 voters can change the results of the election here in the spring and we can elect the whole [D]emocratic ticket just as well as the Republican. We have always been good Republicans, but what have we ever got out of it? If it was any other element, we would have received recognition long ago, but they think that because we are colored we must continue to vote with them and get nothing for it. A year ago Mayor Stuart promised to give us something, but as soon as he was elected he forgot all about it. We have good men in our race as well as other people have and they are capable of holding office. The prosecuting attorney promised to give Mr. Robbins, the colored lawyer, some of his work to do, but he has never done it, and Sheriff Lamoreaux agreed to put a colored man on his force but he has not done it yet. The only time a colored man has been given any political recognition in this city was when Mayor Uhl appointed Louis Henry as poundmaster. We don't demand pie, but we do ask that we be given a few crumbs that fall from the table. There are several places where a colored man could be worked in to good advantage and we going to see what there is in it before we caste a single vote this year. Our 600 votes will turn the city election either way, and we shall make 'em come and see us this year.[22]

This reaction demonstrates several ideas worth analyzing. First, it reflects the steady rise of a comfortable working class and middle class— people who were property owners and did not wish to be taken for granted in patronage politics. Black community leaders were more than willing to work under the terms of patronage politics; however, their pleas to enter this arena were consistently ignored. This political affront to the Afro-American community must also be seen in terms of gender. Politics of the nineteenth century was mostly a male affair, and political exclusion was an insult to Afro-American "manhood." Politics was the arena in which men competed with one another. Instead of entering into competition against white males, Afro-American men often competed against one another for political standing. For example, Jack Adams, a leading Republican in the black community, responded to his fellow citizens by denouncing their move away from the Republican Party. Adams alleged that "the whole thing was stirred up by John W. Robbins, the colored lawyer, who imagines that he would make a good assistant prosecuting attorney, and John B. Bell, who wants to be janitor of the city hall." He insisted, "[T]he colored people would not be hoodwinked." Adams then proceeded to promote himself for a political appointment by couching his plea for a job in terms of American nationalism: "What I am after . . . is the Republican nomination for poor director—not because I am colored man especially, but because I am an American citizen. The colored man has never been recognized by the Republican Party in this city, and I think it about time some member of the race should receive recognition."[23] Patronage politics rarely paid off, however. The African American population was numerically too small and economically too marginal to bargain in the coarse arena of white-ethnic patronage politics. The concessions the African American community received were miniscule compared with their desires.[24] Although the local community did not have success in patronage politics, it did find success the creation of democratic civic associations.

———————

Local civil society was highly democratic, and this democratic culture ran throughout all the institutions and associations in the city.[25] There were all types of clubs for social beneficence, enrichment, and entertainment. The associations ranged from Odd Fellows, Masons, and Mystic Shriners,[26] to the Order of True Reformers, the Bennington Club, the Colored Knights Templar, the Married Ladies Nineteenth-Century Club, and the Grand Rapids Study Club. Many scholars have emphasized the self-help dimensions of these associations to such a large extent that they have overlooked the democratic culture that extended through them.[27] These organizations operated by parliamentary procedure, produced bylaws, and formed constitutions. They served as small-group forums for debate on culture as well as public policy. They splintered among themselves over issues of religion, social class, and gender, constantly reconstituting themselves into new democratic organizations.

The Masons were one of the strongest black civic associations in Grand Rapids. The Michigan Colored Masons organized in 1872, in part because the members felt unnecessarily restricted by the National Lodge. Although the Colored Masons never stated that racial exclusivity was one of the reasons for their break with the National Lodge, their decision to be autonomous reveals much about the racism of the time and about the democratic culture. The Colored Masons' explanation for their break from the National Lodge directly imitates the Declaration of Independence. Jacob Highwarder (see chapter 1), a local barber, served on the committee that composed the resolution calling for a new association representing Afro-Americans. In the document, the committee made several assertions: first, the National Lodge had robbed them of their choice of officers; second, the assessments and expenses imposed by the National Lodge were unduly burdensome; third, the National Lodge was an innovation in Masonry; fourth, the National Lodge violated rules of local autonomy inasmuch as "the Grand Master and Grand Lodge are supreme in their own districts"; fifth, the National Lodge violated the power of the local Grand Lodge, which "has the power to finally determine all points of law for the government of its own jurisdiction"; and sixth, the National Lodge violated a precedent established in England in 1717 giving local Masons the right to be autonomous from centralized rule. Using this Masonic precedent set in England, the Colored Masons charged that "any rite of Masonry acknowledging a higher power than a Sovereign State Grand Lodge is irregular; and any State Grand Lodge acknowledging the so called National Grand Lodge, place themselves at the mercy of the so called National Grand Master, to do as he wills—his will being the laws."[28]

The Colored Masons joined hands with their compatriots in Ontario, Canada, on September 23, 1872, to form their own lodge. This lodge gave them the right to participate in a democratic association where they could exercise their own leadership and decision-making.[29] Given the era in which the Colored Masons organized their lodge, it would be easy to attribute the founding of their association solely to racial conflict, but according to African Americans members of the time, the differences were also about democratic principles. They disagreed with their Anglo-American masons about constitutional powers, believing that the National Lodge had usurped and centralized power to the extent that regional orders could not exercise any autonomy. Democratic participation mattered to the Colored Mason and they fought for the right to have their vote count, even in a civic association.

Civic associations such as the Colored Masons served as tutors to the black community in the rudiments of democratic political organization. They voted, debated complex issues, changed rules, ratified new association rules, and campaigned for office within the organization. The lessons learned in the Masons were in effect a training ground for black political and civic leaders.[30] Not only did the Masons provide avenues of civic training, they also provided a physical space, a hall, in which African Americans could have social space to gather, entertain, and socialize.

Women were equally a part of these democratic associations.[31] They, too, were Masons, Knights Templar, Women's Christian Temperance Union members, and members of social clubs.[32] They, too, struggled against the racial exclusion and for regional autonomy, but unlike male counterparts, women's associations were often confined to the domestic sphere.[33] Women's activities were focused on the church, family, education, and charity. Historian Darlene Clark Hine calls this period the era of domestic feminism. Women were to keep hearth and home together and leave the more formal world—the public sphere—to males. This type of feminism, Hine observes, was transformed through "private and civic work" and "many of the distinctions demarcating male and female spheres of influence" were later blurred.[34] In this setting, women's civic associations worked on two fronts as democratic change agents. They worked for the well-being of the Afro-American community as a whole as well as for the specific empowerment of women. Historian Wilson Moses noted that it was "impossible for middle-class Afro-American women to separate their concerns as women from their concerns as black people. To have done so would have been unrealistic since they were victims not only of sexism, but of racism as well."[35]

Two of the more important women's organizations in the late nineteenth century and early twentieth century were the Married Ladies Nineteenth-Century Club and the Grand Rapids Study Club. The Married Ladies Nineteenth-Century Club was founded in 1894 and later changed its name to the Nineteenth-Century Club of Colored Women. This Club was never purely a social organization; as one of its members stated, they "found so much work to be done that it was turned into an organization for the diffusion of knowledge and the uplift of the race." From their inception, the women's organization sought to defend the reputation of its community. As the keepers of the hearth and home, these women sought to dispel the image of women that Josephine Weathers had displayed. Instead, they focused public attention on a proud legacy of African Americans.[36] Mary Robert Tate, president of the Nineteenth-Century Club, stated in a newspaper interview that:

> [M]y race has many Booker T. Washingtons, Mary Church Terrells, and Lucy Thurmans. If they were but known. We deplore the "social equality scare" with regard to the race question and we feel that if white people would but think seriously, they would find their social pleasures among their own people—the English, German, Italian, Hollanders, etc., have their own churches, clubs, and societies. Why should colored Americans be different from the rest? They are not. They have some refined homes here in this city, which compare favorably with those of the white citizens. In common with other races we have our more cultured class, and people of this class do not want recognition. We want simply a fair showing and we feel that as we have accomplished much in forty-two years of our freedom, we expect to do more in the next forty-two years."[37]

In 1904, the Grand Rapids Study Club came into existence, succeeding the Nineteenth-Century Club. The Study Club began as an association for young single women and evolved into the most dominant social club for black women in the city. Like its forerunner, the Study Club was a democratic organization for selected women—generally, women who met particular class and respectability requirements. The Study Club's motto was "Rowing Not Drifting"; its objective, "to unite all efforts towards individual home and community betterment through study and civic cooperation in all which pertains to the advancements of all groups." This democratic forum for women sought the advancement of women and their race.[38] The 1912 annual of the Study Club demonstrates the diverse topics these women discussed: "Benefits of Home Nursing," "Negro Book-Makers and Sketches of their Lives," "Which Is the Most Beneficial to the Race: Josephine Silone Yates or Mary Church Terrell?" and "The Religious Side of Eugenics."[39] These women's associations, like their male counterparts, operated regionally and nationally.[40]

Not all civic associations enhanced middle-class ideals, however. Male club life was commonplace in this era, and Afro-American men founded clubs in which to drink and gamble. Unlike the Masons or the women's clubs, these clubs were deemed undesirable; however, they did provide space in which working-class individuals could exist without the judgment of middle-class mores.

Economic and employment opportunities were additional factors influencing the formation of local civic associations.[41] Interestingly, men's baseball clubs were the most distinguished of these groups during this period. Local city historian Richard Harms has traced the story of Jess Elster, a prominent Afro-American baseball player and one of the chief architects as player and manager of the Grand Rapids Colored Athletics Baseball team. Elster, a Kentucky native, came to Grand Rapids in 1904. By 1914, Elster, along with Stanley Barnett, an Afro-American businessman, formed the Colored Athletic Business Association (CABA). Harms argued that the Association was "formed to provide financial and moral support for the team, most notably jobs for players."[42] Associations such as these were part of the bedrock of a highly democratized ecology of the black community, representing a broad spectrum of people and interests. The most enduring of these associations, however, were churches.

Religious scholar Benjamin Mays considered black churches to be the most "democratic fellowships" within black community life.[43] Historian Evelyn Higginbotham has written that churches of this era had a twofold and interrelated sphere. The first sphere was an arena where white domination of black life was contested. The second was a discursive sphere where democratic debate took place concerning issues of gender and race.[44] The democratic culture in which these churches were organized was part of a wider religious tradition that arose in the United States. African American congregations were born in an atmosphere where, according to historian Nathan Hatch, church leaders shared "a relentless energy and . . . went about movement-building as self-conscious outsiders. They shared an ethic of unrelenting toil, a passion for expansion, a hostility to orthodox belief and style, a zeal for religious reconstruction, and a systematic plan to realize their ideals." No matter the theology or organizational structure, the democratic emphasis within these churches all "offered common people, especially the poor, compelling visions of individual self-respect and collective self-confidence."[45] This democratic tradition of American Protestantism, led by Methodist and Baptist, infused local African American churches.[46]

From 1870 to 1915, there were at least five churches organized in the Grand Rapids Afro-American community: Zion Methodist Episcopal Church in 1868 (which later became African Episcopal Zion Church);[47] African Methodist Episcopal Church in 1874;[48] Messiah Baptist Church in 1889;[49] Old Time Colored Methodist Church in 1907;[50] and St. Philip's Episcopal Church in 1911.[51] Each of these churches represented various religious, class-interest, and familial schisms within the community, and they saw one another as direct rivals for members and status. As members became frustrated with a church, they either joined one of the others in the community or formed another one more suitable to their interests.[52] The entrepreneurial religious spirit of revivalist Protestantism galvanized most of these churches in camp meetings, revivals, and mission outreach.[53]

More important, in a community comprised primarily of the laboring classes, the church was the institution that promoted idea of respectability more than any other civic institution. A respectable life was to be attained through religious duty, marital fidelity, sobriety, and honest work. But the standards preached by the church were often contradictory, centering on individual personal salvation *and* collective responsibility of the congregation, responsibility to the self through acquisition of wealth and material goods *and* self-sacrificial duties to the common good. Though the religious culture moved in many competing directions and at times sent mixed messages, local congregations informed the class identity and aspirations and reached into the private and public lives of the African American community like no other institution on a consistent basis.[54]

The most important church in this regard was the African Methodist Episcopal (AME) Church.[55] In Grand Rapids, the AME Church went by various names in the second half of the nineteenth century. First, it was known simply as the AME Church; upon moving into a new building in the 1880s, it changed its name to the Spring Street AME Church. In 1899, it changed its name again to Arnett Chapel, in honor of the AME Bishop of Michigan, Benjamin Arnett.[56] The Spring Street Church was one of the chief social centers for the comfortable working class and aspiring middle class, and it was significant in Grand Rapids for two reasons. First, the African Methodist Episcopal Church as a denomination was one of the most important institutions for African Americans in the nineteenth century.[57] Beginning with its sixth bishop, Daniel Alexander Payne, the AME Church sought—to paraphrase author David Wills—to domesticate the spirit and tutor African Americans into a Christian middle-class culture.[58] In fact, through Payne and a highly structured bishopric, the denomination was able to pool its meager resources and develop churches, schools, colleges, newspapers, and journals. Nationally, for a better part of the nineteenth century, the AME Church was the church of the African American leadership class. This was true in Grand Rapids as well. The small leadership cadre in the city attended the AME Church, which hosted concerts, May Queen festivals, and lectures by Lucy Thurman, Frederick Douglass, and Booker T. Washington. The values promoted by the church were religious piety, personal decorum, education, sobriety, and hard work. In other words, being Christian meant being respectable, and being respectable meant being Christian.

The Christianity that these churches preached not only saved souls but also fostered discipline.[59] According to the *Grand Rapids Press*, Rev. A. P. Miller, pastor of AME Zion Church, offered this assessment in his 1902 lecture titled "The Black Man's Burden."

> [Rev. Miller] asserted that two things were responsible for the black man's burden, the prejudice of the whites and the ignorance and weak moral standard of the blacks. The speaker, while denouncing the methods of the whites in dealing with the negro, did not spare his people and freely pointed out wherein they had proved themselves unworthy. Their low moral condition he attributed to the brutalizing effects of human slavery in this country. Lynching he denounced as being only meted out to the black man, while the white man yielding to the same lust went unpunished. He held that the negro must create more respect for himself, seek better education and acquire property rights. This would do more to help on the race than blind obedience to a political party which had freed the slaves more than forty years ago.[60]

Miller's lecture reflected a growing disenchantment with the Republican Party and revealed his own irritation at the slow development of middle-class values within the African American community.[61] While greater emphasis might have been placed on moral rectitude and economic well-being at the end of the nineteenth century, this was a continuous theme in African American religious history. In the early years of the American republic, Richard Allen, founder of the AME church in Philadelphia, placed the same emphasis on values and self-sufficiency that Miller did some eighty years later.[62] What had changed was the social condition of living in an increasingly urbanized environment and its incumbent challenges. Thus, we understand Miller's exhortation for the Protestant work ethic to be replicated in the lives of local African Americans was born of his desire to see the community achieve enduring respect.

If the Methodists were strong in inculcating moral seriousness, so were the Baptists. In 1899, Rev. Robert Gillard of Messiah Baptist Church forbade the popular turn-of-the-century dance, the Cake Walk, believing it to be a frivolous waste of mental energy. He suggested, instead, that his members read "literary figures, which have plenty of humor of the right and wholesome kind, but nothing on the vulgar order."[63] The moral behavior of Afro-Americans in Grand Rapids, as it related to the community's economic well-being, was always of concern to members of the clergy.

Female leaders of the community were also concerned about the moral behavior of the African Americans in the city,[64] and they led the efforts to build churches in Grand Rapids. They put on socials, baked cookies, and organized countless events not only to keep the church doors open but also, literally, to put the doors onto the church. Sarah Walker (see chapter 1), the well-known brothel owner, put up money to establish the AME congregation and allowed initial charter members to meet in her house.[65] Moreover, Catherine Carter's driving determination helped forge the Messiah Baptist Church. Through the determined efforts of these women, the church buildings, which served as the primary social center of African American life, were constructed. These women used their influence within the context of the church to promote bourgeois civilities, joining with the preachers to demand family stability, sobriety, and moral guidance for the youth. They did this by teaching Sunday school, putting on pageants, and raising funds for the minister's salary.

Although churches were supposed to be the center of propriety, they did not always succeed. Members of Messiah Baptist Church had only been worshipping a year when they dismissed the church's first pastor, Rev. J. W. J. Johnson, for misappropriating funds.[66] Three months later, prominent members of the Spring Street Church were involved in a fracas over funds, which turned from insult to assault. The *Grand Rapids Evening Leader* reported the incident:

> The audience in police court this morning was a large one, and composed entirely of colored people. It seemed as if the whole colored population of the town was there, from the aged grandaire to the giddy young belle of darktown. The occasion was the trial of J. J. Adams for assault upon Mrs. Minnie Robison [*sic*], both prominent members of the Spring Street African Church. The assault occurred last Wednesday evening a week ago, and it made a great sensation in colored circles. It seems from the evidence that Mrs. Robison [*sic*] was chairman of an entertainment committee and solicited money for an entertainment. Adams is the chairman of the board of trustees. A week ago, the coal was getting low and it was suggested that the entertainment money be used for coal. A few evenings previous to the row, at a meeting when they were preparing their "annual reports for the quarter," the subject was brought up and Mrs. Robinson was asked for a report, but she refused. After services on Wednesday evening the congregation was divided into groups and Adams threaten to call a meeting to "settle her case." She resented his threat by calling him a "nasty black nigger." The evidence differs here, the complainant swearing that he struck her in the face so hard as to raise a swelling. Other witnesses also swore that he kicked her in the chin or high as her chin anyway. The defendant says she struck him first and then he "let her have it." He admitted kicking at her also, but the congregation interfered and separated them.

Lawyer Alex Hamilton defended Adams in the case. After hearing all parties to the case, the judge dismissed it.[67]

These two stories make important points. The case of Adams demonstrates the strong influence women held in area congregations. In this situation, the male trustees had run out of money and were unable to take care of the basic operations of the church. Unreasonably, these trustees, instead of consulting the churchwomen, demanded the money that the women controlled. In addition, the story of the misappropriation of funds at Messiah Baptist Church points to the relative impoverishment of these churches. The clergy were a part of the laboring classes just as their congregants were, and they had very little formal training or personal wealth. The temptation to steal money under these circumstances was a greater burden than some could bear. However, despite their economic burdens, most local clergy were faithful to their religious commitments. The economic impoverishment of the churches was unfortunately reflected in the black community at large.[68] The theological and moral message of the churches provided hope and ethical direction for its laboring members, but this alone was not enough to generate a moral society in which their members might have adequate wages to live as they were called to do.

Although the local congregations lacked large economic resources, the churches continued to exercise influence in the lives of local people. Each local church was part of a denomination with statewide and national connections. Even more than the Women's Club movement and the Masons, the church was an association whose boundaries extended internationally.[69] For example, the state AME district covered Michigan and Ontario, Canada. Its meetings included such guest speakers as Bishop Henry MacNeil Turner, who advocated migration of African Americans to sub-Saharan Africa.[70] This exposure to larger networks informed the local communities about the struggle of Africa and African Americans all over the country and the world. Social trends in the larger culture, such as changes in fashion, behavior, and thought were often mediated for African Americans through national church connections.

———————

Family life was the cornerstone of the black community, providing networks of mutual aid and stability. The limited number of black or brown families in Grand Rapids meant that these families generally knew one another—and were known to the larger white community. Therefore, a family's name could be harmed if a rebellious child's behavior defied the normative standards of the day. Families used their names to gain employment, do business, and appeal to white leaders for assistance. A family's name often carried weight in establishing an individual's reputation. The old Afro-American families of Grand Rapids took great pride in being Fords, Johnsons, Joneses, Husos, Weekleys, Craigs, and Burgesses. A family name could help people gain acceptance in all the local associations and could give family members standing in a church. Organizations such as the Study Club or the Masons accepted individuals easily if they had a good family name and demonstrated responsible behavior. In a world where skin color meant wholesale judgment of one's humanity, a good family name was often a mediating factor against indiscriminate racism. One historical study of African American kinship in Monroe, Michigan, points out that black families used their sense of kinship for cooperation and care from the vicissitudes of the times. Further, this study shows that African American families in Monroe created interlocking family systems—that is, families married into other local families and cared for non-family members as family.[71] In Grand Rapids, interlocking families permeated the black community. The Minisee family intermarried with the Joneses, the Glenns married the Weekleys, and the Burgess family was related to the Beverly family. These families then married other families throughout the region, caring for one another's children and elderly relatives.[72] Interlocking families laid the foundation for black civil society and tried to stave off the social and economic effects of living in a racist society.

Laborers—railroad porters, cooks, waiters, and gardeners—formed the basis of Afro-American civil society in Grand Rapids. Both men and women worked long hours and at hard jobs. An ex-slave and veteran of the Tenth U.S. Cavalry Regiment, Alexander Hamilton had the wherewithal and good fortune to become an attorney. However, because he was constrained by finances, he could not fully enjoy the status of his profession, often supplementing his law practice by being an entertainer.[73] On the other hand, Joseph Ford attained a comfortable life through constant work as a railroad porter, Michigan Senate cloakroom attendant, and hotel doorman for over forty years.[74] Moreover, a number of men and women ensured their futures through domestic work in Grand Rapids.[75]

Others, like J. C. Craig, a prominent barber, and John J. Johnson, a mover, even managed to establish small businesses and make them profitable.[76] A few men, such as Enoch Pettiford, who was a brakeman and, later, an office superintendent in the Grand Rapids train depot, advanced in railroad companies.[77] For a short period, Grand Rapids even supported two Afro-American physicians, Eugene Browning and William Jordan. As a few churches grew in numbers, a few ministers were able to gain a comfortable existence as full-time clergy.[78] However, these individual achievements did not translate into good fortune for the entire community. Having access to a middle-class lifestyle necessitated capital. And in those years the capitalist, if one dare call in anyone in the black community by that name, was the man or woman who lived on the margins of respectable society.

Leading business people like as Stanley Barnett, owner of the Stanford Hotel for Colored People, made comfortable sums by allowing gambling at his establishment. When Sarah Walker discontinued her trade as a brothel owner, others picked it up and carried it on at the House of All Nations.[79] Vice, which was one of the few businesses in which black entrepreneurial energies had room to excel, supplemented the meager wages of domestic and physical laborers.

The chief vice that carried away the troubles of hard labor was the consumption of alcohol. Both men and women drank to ease their toils;

much of male socialization outside of work centered on consuming alcoholic beverages.[80] If religion did not fully alleviate the burdened heart, it seems that whiskey did. Yet the heaviest burden of this addictive behavior was placed on the women. When churchwomen in Grand Rapids called for prohibition, they were driven not by simple-minded Victorian respectability but by their desire to protect women and children who suffered abuse at the hands of drunken spouses.[81]

Economics are at the foundation of any civil society. Although community leaders touted the material accumulation of the black community, the vast majority of the people remained at the lower end of the laboring classes. Karl Marx recognized by the mid-nineteenth century that civil society (as promoted in European political philosophy of the eighteenth and nineteenth centuries) obfuscated the realities of laboring people. He thought that placing so much emphasis on civil society and the rule of law was a sham used to disguise the power relations that capitalists had over laborers in terms of access to the means of production.[82] To an extent, he was right. Grand Rapids' African American civil society was weakened because it did not control any means of production or dominate any labor market. This economic weakness of the community retarded its population growth and the development of middle-class civil society.

What emerged in Grand Rapids, therefore, was an African American working-class culture that sometimes contradicted the aims of community leaders who envisioned a respectable community. The story of Josephine Weathers and John Weathers was a source of embarrassment for those who held those aspirations. The Weathers's story, nevertheless, was a part of, but not the entirety of, communal reality. Within colored circles life was often weighed down by the twin struggles of fighting racial stigma and working against economic inequality.[83] Even though middle-class growth was impeded, it is also true that locals acquired cultural habits of the middle class: acquiring property and being politically active citizens. In Grand Rapids, African American leaders never let city officials forget these facts.

———

Overcoming economic and racial marginality was a formidable task—one so great that it led Gilbert Osofsky to write despairingly of the period, "[T]he essential structure and nature of the Negro ghetto have remained remarkably durable since the demise of slavery in the North. There has been an unending and tragic sameness about Negro life in the metropolis over two centuries."[84] Economics, however, is just one aspect of human motivation. Faith is another. The "unending and tragic sameness" was not what individuals fully believed about their community. They believed, by faith, that they were progressing. What kept them on the battlefield on behalf of their community was a sense of divine Providence; many held to the belief that God had not intended for the community to remain in dishonor. This belief drove the community's politics, formed its sense of identity, and gave it strength to withstand its subordinate social position. It was this communal faith, founded in the slavery and emancipation that wearied but did not falter and directed the community's energies in the face of despairing odds.

Eugene Hardy. Courtesy of
Grand Rapids History and
Special Collections Center,
Archives, Grand Rapids
Public Library, Grand Rapids,
Mich.

Black and white lumbermen, date unknown. Courtesy of Grand Rapids History
and Special Collections Center, Archives, Grand Rapids Public Library, Grand
Rapids, Mich.

Edward Mabin, a Civil War
soldier. Courtesy of Grand
Rapids History and Special
Collections Center, Archives,
Grand Rapids Public Library,
Grand Rapids, Mich.

Reverend Samuel
Graves. Courtesy of
Grand Rapids History
and Special Collections
Center, Archives, Grand
Rapids Public Library,
Grand Rapids, Mich.

Charles C. Comstock. Courtesy of Local History Department, Grand Rapids
Public Library, Grand Rapids, Mich.

Comstock Row. Courtesy of Grand Rapids History and Special Collections Center, Archives, Grand Rapids Public Library, Grand Rapids, Mich.

Cosmopolitan Restaurant. Courtesy of Grand Rapids History and Special Collections Center, Archives, Grand Rapids Public Library, Grand Rapids, Mich.

The Objects of the Home

1. To protect the girl on coming to the city in search of employment.

2. To raise the standard of domestic service, and recognize it as a profession.

3. To bring our girls together that they may realize their worth as a true woman.

4. To provide suitable accommodations for lady transients.

MRS. GOGGINS, President.

As the years come and go,
There is work for all to do.
Labor for the weaker brother;
Lend a hand to help each other.

Mabel Groggins. Courtesy of Grand Rapids History and Special Collections Center, Archives, Grand Rapids Public Library, Grand Rapids, Mich.

Booker T. Washington (circa 1911). Courtesy of Chicago Historical Society.

3 "Thirteen Races and Nationalities": The Politics of Race Relations in the Age of Booker T. Washington

The December 20, 1908, feature-section headline of the *Grand Rapids Herald* newspaper read, "Teach Young Ideas of Many Nations: Thirteen Races and Nationalities Represented in the Roster of South Division Street School—Bright and Interesting Little Cosmopolitans." The reporter, Abe Gelhof, wrote,

> The South Division Street School is a typical Ellis Island in miniature. Practically every nationality represented in the population of Grand Rapids is represented in this school. There is the slanted-eyed Chinese lad who will some day be a rich purveyor of chop suey; there is the representative of darkest Africa, whose ambition at this primitive stage in his life extends even as far as the wearing of the full dress suit of a hotel waiter; there is the dark haired olive skinned little beauty from Italy; the fair haired little miss from Stockholm or the land of Macbeth and Hamlet; the rusty-topped lad from Erin; the lass from bonny Scotland, in short, children of all nations.

Gelhof claimed that the diverse ethnic population of the South Division School studied together in "perfect harmony."[1] This depiction of the South Division School highlighted that African Americans in Grand Rapids lived in the midst of a large and ethnically diverse community. In 1908, the city had no geographic racial ghettoization. Whites and blacks shared neighborhoods, similar religious values, and public schools; on many occasions they intermarried (even though this was strongly frowned upon by both races). This shared civil society was inescapable in a city where the African American population was less than 1 percent of the total population. African Americans were one ethnic group of people living among various European ethnic communities. Because blacks and whites shared a civil society, they interacted with one another on many different levels.

The description of the South Division School as a miniature Ellis Island was accurate. Foreign-born European immigrants came to the city in great droves between 1880 and 1915, causing a population boom and increasing the pool of low-wage laborers.[2] They were integrated into the local industrial order relatively peacefully, and social relations among ethnic communities within Grand Rapids, as compared to other nearby major cities, were relatively tame.[3]

African Americans in Grand Rapids lived as the city's most visible racial ethnic community. As such, African Americans were pitted against white ethnic communities in competition to establish an advantage in the city's economic and cultural order. What made African Americans different than ethnic whites in the city was their constant need to advocate against the inequities of Jim Crow practices.[4] Race relations in Grand Rapids did not consist of one simple, monolithic relationship (white over black). Rather, a closer analysis reveals that many factors such as ethnicity, social class, and religious affiliation mediated the views of how whites and blacks dealt with one another. The ideology of white supremacy that dominated American thought had many different shadings and meanings in Grand Rapids.

The African American community's response to the protracted racism of this period was not a single response, either. The black leadership class chose to align itself with the white Protestant establishment in terms of philanthropy and cultural identification. Their strategy was to protest racial inequity—in writing letters to the editors of local newspapers, seeking out political office, and creating organizations for interracial cooperation. Although African American leaders realized that white civic organizations and businesses did not completely back their causes, they could not politically forsake this paternalistic alliance, given the realities of ethnic competition and black economic disadvantage. African American civic organizations regularly received assistance from white philanthropists and churches to keep their own organizations solvent. White philanthropists and church leaders also were financially supportive of some Southern, church-related, African American educational institutions. In addition, the white Protestant elite laid claim to an abolitionist legacy as a way of reminding African Americans to hold their grievances to minimum. These white elites believed that the legacy of having fought on behalf of the North during the Civil War—or having anti-slavery sentiments, or having been charitable to former slaves—was a sign of their support for the African American causes. The paradox of this position was that the white elite supported racial exclusion in the industrial order while adapting a positive paternalism to African Americans in general. This stance left African American leaders feeling betrayed. Nevertheless, the social realities of the time left local black leaders aligned with white elite. Working-class white ethnics rarely sought alliances with African Americans in any mutual causes. They were trying to integrate into American society themselves— many times at the expense of African Americans.

African Americans who did not share the burdens of leadership—day laborers, cooks, maids, porters, petty vice dealers, and drifters—contested their social situation through other means. They contested white privilege and unfairness in the ordinary struggle of living. Some literally fought with their white counterparts in the neighborhoods they shared. Still others chose to live their lives out quietly, using their daily labor, religious conviction, and earnestness to give them dignity in a racist world. Yet another segment of the community continued abusive vices: strong drink, like religion, was one of the opiates for all working classes.

Although the African American community was small, the white working classes sometime perceived it to be an overwhelming threat— one consistently expressed as sexual anxiety about the number of interracial relationship and marriages, particularly between African American men and white women.[5] Interracial sexual encounters—in addition to a real economic threat in the workplace—kept ethnic whites jealously guarding their social status and laboring position in the city's social hierarchy. White workers regularly used race to exclude African American entrance into various occupations, especially those guarded by unions. This employment exclusion, joined with the industrial paternalism throughout Grand Rapids industries, gave African American workers limited opportunity to excel economically. As Gelhof stereotypically depicted, the best job an African American could attain in the city was attired in "the full dress suit of a hotel waiter."

The early history of Grand Rapids was a reflection of upstate New York and New England.[6] A sizable proportion of the early settlers had migrated from those two regions and many of them had brought anti-slavery and abolitionist sentiments into the state.[7] As early as 1858, the Universalist Church proclaimed its abolitionist beliefs. According to the *Enquirer & Herald* newspaper, Rev. Hayward outlined the following principles of the Universalist Church:

> [T]he practical universalist labors for the abolishment of slavery everywhere, and universal brotherhood; also for the abolishment of capital punishment. He also labors to prevent war and bloodshed between nations, and does not countenance war under any circumstances. He further remarked that the Universalist Church does not flourish in the Southern States; that you would find a society there, and if you did it was a small one, made up of New England Men. He said that a true Universalist was an Abolitionist, but that all Abolitionists were not professed Universalists. Again he said, go where the people were oppressed and down-trodden, and where the aristocracy rule, and Universalism found little favor, but in Massachusetts, where the masses are the most intelligent and free, you would find Universalist Churches and Societies numerous; and that it was revealed in God's Word that Universalism would ultimately be the religion of the whole world.[8]

This type of abolitionist sentiment infused the upper echelon of the Yankee religious establishment in numerous area churches. Individuals such as Rev. James Ballard (1803–81), an organizer of the downtown Park Congregational Church, arrived in the city with Puritan rectitude, anti-slavery thought, and abolitionist views. Ballard, for instance, was a devotee of William Lloyd Garrison, the famed Massachusetts abolitionist, before his arrival in Grand Rapids in 1837.[9] He distinguished himself first by preaching against slavery in his congregation and, later in his career, by moving to Texas and Mississippi to join with freed men and women in their education. While serving in the South, Ballard occasionally wrote letters to the *Grand Rapids Eagle*, apprising readers of his work there.[10]

Ballard was not alone in his willingness to head south to teach ex-slaves. Thomas Creswell, another Grand Rapids native, had also spent considerable time teaching in Tennessee during Reconstruction.[11] Creswell, like Ballard, wrote to the local editor of the *Eagle* newspaper, informing readers of the progress of freed people in the South. Both Creswell's and Ballard's letters were used to encourage local support for their respective missions with ex-slaves. The local Congregational church and other churches in the Grand Rapids area supported the work of Ballard and Creswell. Leading religious figures in the city saw the South and education of ex-slaves as a great opportunity for Christian mission.[12]

Another founding father in the abolitionist legacy of Grand Rapids was Rev. Samuel Graves (1820–95) of the Fountain Street Baptist Church. Born in New Hampshire and educated in Vermont, Graves was called to be the pastor of Fountain Street Baptist Church in 1870. Ill health and social conviction led Graves to resign his well-established congregation to become the second president of the Atlanta Baptist Seminary (later known as Morehouse College). Graves served as President of Atlanta Baptist Seminary from 1885 until 1894.[13] Graves, like Ballard and Creswell constantly solicited and informed the Grand Rapids community about his mission to educate African American Southerners.[14]

While individuals like Creswell, Ballard, and Graves wrote to inform the Grand Rapids community of their work in the South, we must remember that others were also writing attacking the "Negro progress." These attacks largely fell along partisan lines and were usually printed in the Democratic newspaper. Despite the partisan attacks, the Grand Rapids newspaper informed readers about events occurring throughout the South following the Civil War.

Ballard, Creswell, Graves, and others built the foundation in Grand Rapids of what historian James MacPherson termed the "abolitionist legacy."[15] That is, they represented the generation of individuals who advocated ending slavery and supported the Union's cause during the Civil War. These individuals invested themselves heavily in the political reform efforts of Reconstruction. What is more, they engaged in the mission to educate former slaves, viewing their work as an extension of their Christian mission. They hoped that with proper schooling African Americans would reach the standards of education, work ethic, and moral rectitude of upper-class white Yankees and Yorkers. They believed it was their job to support African American institutions in this effort of extending Christian civilization. The precedent they set of supporting anti-slavery and abolitionist causes continued throughout Grand Rapids in the established downtown churches, through local philanthropy, and in local Republican politics.

Philanthropically, the abolitionist legacy worked through financial donations by local business leaders to support African Americans in their efforts to construct their church buildings. The local AME Zion and the AME congregations consistently sought the contribution of local white leaders in their early years. Individuals such as Delos A. Blodgett, a banker and lumbermen, regularly aided these churches in staving off mortgage foreclosures.[16] Messiah Baptist Church received steady support from the Grand Rapids Baptist Association and the Fountain Street Baptist Church, a leading church of the Protestant establishment, in organizing and paying the debt on its first properties.[17] Although African

Americans received financial assistance from white philanthropists and churches, those congregations did the lion's share of the work to make their churches survive during the hardest times.

Another feature of the abolitionist legacy in Grand Rapids was the support that some ex-slaves received in coming to Grand Rapids. For example, Alexander Hamilton (1852–94), the city's first African American attorney, received encouragement after the Civil War from Grand Rapids area natives (like A. J. Howk) to move to the city to attend high school and study law.[18] Added to this were the number of ex-slaves who migrated to the city from Ontario, Canada, and the South. Grand Rapids' newspapers frequently published articles about the lives of ex-slaves living in the city. Grand Rapids was also a stop on the touring lecture circuit for notable African American and abolitionist lecturers. Frequently within the city, public forums discussed the progress and plight of Southern ex-slaves. City residents knew of Sojourner Truth, who lived south of Grand Rapids in Battle Creek. Frederick Douglass lectured and campaigned in Grand Rapids at least five times after the Civil War.[19] Blanche K. Bruce, the Reconstruction senator from Mississippi, discussed the predicament of African Americans throughout the South on at least two occasions.

In addition to white religious leaders having gone to the South to teach, African American student choirs from the South toured Grand Rapids in fundraising concerts to generate income for their schools. The Congregationalist network was particularly strong in and around the city. Student choirs from Talladega, Fisk (Nashville), and Hampton (Virginia) toured the city on numerous occasions.[20]

Troubling to local African Americans was that the attention focused on the South detracted from local issues of race. For those in the white Protestant elite, white racism was a Southern regional problem that needed the largesse of northern intervention. The Grand Rapids' newspapers reported that the real problem was the lack of education of Southern African Americans. If they were educated and prepared, the race problem might soon diminish. Of course, there was much truth to this claim that the race problem was something peculiar to the South. In fact, the majority of African Americans resided in the South and needed educational opportunity.

By the 1890s, the largesse of Reconstruction-era politics waned. As many historians have established, the court of public opinion had shifted by 1877, slowly pushing the legitimate political interest of African Americans aside in favor of sectional peace with the South.[21] Racial justice receded to the background as labor and economic concerns moved forward.[22] African Americans, like all people in the country, emphasized gaining access to education and property. No one represented this better than Booker T. Washington.

———————

Booker T. Washington was loved and respected in Grand Rapids. Washington first visited the city eleven months after the death of Frederick Douglass and four and a half months after his famous "Atlanta Exposition Speech."[23] When he arrived in Grand Rapids, Southern conservatives had already pronounced him a safe leader. Washington's national ascendancy marked (in the minds of white Southern business and religious elite) an end to the Civil War. And, likewise, the elite whites of the North "were in search of a black leader who could give them a rest from [the] eternal race problem."[24] In an editorial in the *Grand Rapids Democrat*, the editor wrote that Frederick Douglass had "outlived the days of hatred and oppression; at the same time, he was not so great a success as a politician as he had been as orator and agitator, and some of the brilliancy of the prestige was lost in the fields which required greater discretion and ability than were demanded in the exciting times when he won his greatest reputation."[25]

Washington came to the city already crowned by the local press as the new national African American leader. On January 24, 1896, he addressed seven hundred people at the Park Congregational Church on the subject "The New Negro of the South."[26] The speech was a modified version of his famous Atlanta Compromise Speech given in September the previous year. By the time he spoke in Grand Rapids, Washington had already constructed the themes he would later publish in his 1903 autobiography, *Up from Slavery.* Washington projected himself as a mythic Horatio Alger figure who rose above the impoverishment of slavery through education and hard work to become an American success.[27] His ideals were a perfect fit for Grand Rapids, which by 1896 had reached its zenith as the country's leading furniture-manufacturing city.[28] He told the audience that the "great hope of the Southern Negro is a material and industrial fund [based on] intellectual and religious training and they are determined to take advantage of every opportunity to attain it." Moreover, as was typical of his speeches, Washington lauded the great virtue of patience among Negroes in their efforts to achieve full equality.

Washington received overwhelming support during his first visit to the city. There was little criticism of his address. The one exception was Rev. Thomas W. Illman, as reported in the *Grand Rapids Democrat.* "The Rev. Thomas W. Illman was interviewed regarding his opinion of the lecture given in the city recently by the noted Negro orator,

Booker T. Washington of Tuskegee, Ala. Mr. Illman endorsed the colored man's system of elevating the Negro race, but when it came to
admitting that as a race they are constitutionally possessed of a greater
amount of patience and forbearance than are Anglo-Saxon he said it is
all a fiction, and that if the Negro possesses the virtue of patience over
and above other men it is because of the same reason that women are
patient—just because they have to be."[29]

Washington's idealization of business and industry was a mirror
image of the ideology that the leading businessmen of the city promoted.
Through his words, they heard their own values—Christianity, hard work,
a belief in industry, and the Republican Party.[30] More important, Washington represented to them the continuation of their own efforts to safeguard their abolitionist heritage.[31] His gradualism was perceived by local
businessmen to be sensible, and his careful direction in cultivating industrial education for African Americans was seen as forward-thinking.[32]

Washington returned to Grand Rapids five years later in 1901, again
reporting on Tuskegee Institute's effort to prepare students through industrial education.[33] Upon his return, he was unquestionably the most well
known African American political figure in the United States. Local audi-
ences enthusiastically received him; in fact, area newspapers reported
that the audience stood on their feet and applauded for five minutes
before he could give his address, "Industrial Conditions in the South."
His speech, filled with classic Washington rhetoric, carefully avoided the
issue of civil rights, emphasizing economic gains and African American
self-improvement.[34] Locals, both black and white, took up some aspect of
his mantra of industrial training and wealth-building. Some accepted his
counsel that the African Americans should avoid political confrontation
in the South.[35] Everyone heard something from Washington that resonated with his or her own viewpoint on the peculiar problems of African
Americans. He set the tone for much of the local discussion about race
relations.

Reverend Robert W. McLaughlin (1866–1936), pastor of Park Congregational Church in 1904, gave the best articulation of the "Negro problem" from the perspective of a local white Protestant elite.[36] On Sunday,
February 28, McLaughlin preached a sermon on understanding race relations before the Men's Sunday Evening Club, which was organized as
an evangelical outreach for "men twenty-one and over who attended no
other church home." The Club brought in national lecturers and hosted
contemporary discussions and musical programs.[37] One of the initial lectures given before the club and later published was McLaughlin's sermon
entitled "The Negro Problem."[38]

McLaughlin contended that the vital question was if "the negro [is] a man possessing normal possibilities of manhood, which if developed, will equip him for usual privileges of citizenship in our democracy." This moral and intellectual question could only be answered by African American deeds. Looking at material prosperity, the rate of literacy, labor history, educational gains and the quality of leaders like Washington, McLaughlin thought, the facts were undeniable as to the full humanity of African Americans.[39] He drew two conclusions from this point. The first was that the African American "has a place in our democracy, and should be recognized on the basis of manhood as other men are recognized." Second, he said that "having the possibilities of normal manhood, it becomes the duty of the church to assist the state in developing the same." Here he acknowledged "the devotion and sacrifice of noble men and women from the North who have given of time and substance to lead these backward people on" from the Reconstruction era. The work begun by the abolitionist must continue "for the sake of this race, for the sake of our common country, for the sake of the Master himself." In conclusion, he said, "the struggle will be long and weary, the first flush of success has passed and henceforth the work will proceed more slowly."[40]

The abolitionist legacy continued in Grand Rapids primarily through the mission of the church, just as McLaughlin had suggested. In particular, Grand Rapids' downtown congregations provided aid to African American educational institutions throughout the South and continued forums on race relations.[41] In 1912, Rev. Henry Beets, a local Christian Reformed Church pastor and the editor of his denomination's magazine, editorialized about the injustice in African American education. Beets compared the efforts of Northern states to incorporate immigrants with that of the South. He wrote, "in the North all this effort is being made to provide education for these foreign people, many of whom are merely sojourners in this country, and will return in a few months to their homes in Europe, it is only natural that the Negro in the South should feel that he is unfairly treated when he has, as is often true in the country districts, either no school at all, or one term of no more than four or five months, taught in the wreck of a log cabin, and by a teacher who is paid about half the price of a first class convict." Beets urged the eradication of the educational inequities throughout the South.[42] Some years later Beets visited Tuskegee Institute and urged his denomination to become involved in the Southern Normal and Industrial Institute in Brewton, Alabama.[43]

Recent historical studies have shown that churches and religious personalities continued in dialogue about racial reform in post-Reconstruction America. This scholarship corrected earlier histories that sug-

gested white churches paid little attention to racial reform in the Social
Gospel era of the late nineteenth and early twentieth centuries.⁴⁴ This
newer history persuasively argues that racial reform remained an ongoing dialogue among black and white Christian leaders. Certainly, the
interaction among black and white Christian leaders in Grand Rapids
supports this revision. It is to the credit of the men and women of Grand
Rapids that abolitionist legacy continued through religious institutions.
However, what of the political realities in the city?

The moderating force of religion also contributed to the views of local
leaders. In February 1904, Grand Rapids school superintendent William
H. Elson visited Tuskegee Institute and Spellman College while attending the National Superintendents' Association meeting. Elson reported
in the *Grand Rapids Press* that Tuskegee was "a great trade school" and
"would be a good thing for white students in the North." He also took
note of "the negro public schools of Atlanta," observing that "they were
taught by negro teachers." African American teachers, he learned, were
"paid less than the white teachers, although some of them are just as
capable and do just as good word [*sic*]." Elson ended his interview stating
that he "saw some negro teachers that I would be glad to have in Grand
Rapids schools as far as their ability is concerned."⁴⁵

Another notable example of the abolitionist legacy was United States
Senator William Alden Smith (1859–1935). Smith was born in Dowagiac,
Michigan, in Cass County. Cass County and the town of Dowagiac held a
special place in Michigan history because of the settlement of free blacks
there in the 1830s. According to one historical study, Cass County was
a somewhat progressive place for Negroes to live and farm in the nineteenth century.⁴⁶ Smith, therefore, took special pride being from Dowagiac and having grown up in a county where blacks thrived.⁴⁷

In many ways, the life of Smith paralleled the life of Booker T. Washington. Smith had struggled in his youth, worked, and became a wealthy
lawyer and a successful politician. Like Washington, Smith had a limited
education, having completed only the eighth grade. Smith also showed
a remarkable amount of tenacity in achieving his goals. In 1883, the
Grand Rapids courts swore Smith into the practice of law after his having apprenticed and studied law in a local law office. By the late 1890s,
he had become the part owner of two railroads that traveled through the
city. He also served as the area's congressional representative until 1906,
when the Michigan legislature elected him to the U.S. Senate. Smith,
like Washington, had pulled himself up by his bootstraps with tenacity, business acumen, and political guile.⁴⁸ They were men of the same
generation—archetypal self-made men of the nineteenth century—or

so each promoted. Smith's background helped him to empathize with the plight of African Americans, but equally important to him was the political support he could garner from being perceived as friend of African Americans.

The year Smith became a United States senator was also the year he became owner of the *Grand Rapids Herald* newspaper, which became an editorial vehicle to promote his own ambitions and those of the Republican Party. The *Herald*'s editorial often commented on the race problem in order to promote African American loyalty to the Party.[49] In 1909, Smith made great news, particularly in the *Herald,* by defending Robert Pelham, a former resident of Michigan who worked in Washington.[50] According to the *Herald*'s report, Smith left the chambers of the Senate to defend a falsely accused Pelham against charges of disorderly conduct by the Washington, D.C., police. Pelham appealed to Smith because he could not afford legal counsel, and a conviction would have meant the loss of his job. Smith promptly took the case and exonerated Pelham. The *Herald* noted that "the incident bids fair to become as famous as the Booker T. Washington dinner at the White House, with Senator Smith in the role of Roosevelt." The paper made one more point about Smith and the case as it closed the article: "So earnest was Senator Smith that he gave up important morning engagements, made his way early to the courthouse in a torrential rain. He sat among the negro onlookers for at least an hour and a half before his case was called. In the meantime, he studied, with increasing surprise, the rough and tumble way in which negro prisoners are dealt in Washington police court practice."[51]

The *Herald* often self-servingly portrayed Smith as a contemporary abolitionist.[52] Smith exemplified his goodwill to the African American community with his invitation to Booker T. Washington to be one of the speakers in 1912 at the city's Lincoln Day Banquet.[53]

Smith used the banquet to cover all his political bases. Washington, an African American, would sit on the same dais as Senator Albert B. Cummins of Iowa, Congressman Caleb Powers of Kentucky, and the Honorable Doctor J. Louden, Minister from the Netherlands. Interestingly, in the newspaper article about the event, the photographs of Cummins, Powers, and Louden are displayed on the front page of the article; however, photographs of Smith (with two local Republican Party officials) and Washington (alone) appear elsewhere in the newspaper. Nevertheless, in Smith eyes, and by the racial etiquette of the day, it was a progressive act to invite "the leader of the Colored Race."[54]

In fact, the political policies of the local Republican Party downplayed the infectious racism and violence that spread like cancer across the South. When the local press did address the issue of racial reform, it was often in the form of commentaries that focused on the racist behavior in the South, contrasting it with the enlightened race relations in Grand Rapids.[55] This line of thought was used by Republican politicians to deflect any legislative agenda enforcing or calling for civil rights in local and national politics. One could cynically view William Alden Smith as befriending African American causes so long as they were Republican causes. On the other hand, given the era, Smith's paternalism was generous. Here was the community's political dilemma: Smith was a local friend; simultaneously he was also a part of the racist social system that went long with African American subordination.

On the night of banquet, the *Herald* reported that Smith introduced Washington with these words: "Of all the men who have begun life under a handicap, none has begun more humbly than he. Born humbly a slave, he has lived to be the guest of kings and queens, to whom the flags of all nations have been dipped; a man who has never sought public office but who has lived to do a work which has the benediction [*sic*] of God. It is no small honor to sit in the presence of the foremost man of his race in all the world. I take pleasure in introducing to you Booker T. Washington."[56] Washington delivered his speech, "The Proclamation: Forty-Eight Years Afterward," with great aplomb.[57]

Local African Americans were excited about Washington's presence in the city. The *Grand Rapids Herald* described his meeting with the black community in the city council chambers as overflowing with "colored people." Washington noted that the Dutch minister, Dr. Louden, "was proud that he was coming among his people." He observed that ethnic pride was essential to progress. Appealing to black pride, he stated: "No people can amount to anything unless they are proud that they possess the blood of their race. You must be proud that in your veins flows the blood of the negro. I am proud of it. I am black, and I am proud of my ancestors. We must all be proud of our race and of our blood." Acknowledging the ethnic and immigrant competition the black community faced, especially from the Dutch, Washington said, "Here in Grand Rapids you are thrown into competition with the sturdy and thrifty Dutch. If you lose out you will come to me and tell me they drew the color line. I will tell you it is nothing of the sort. The white man does not draw the color line in business unless you yourself draw it. You draw the color line by inefficiency. It is not the white man who does it." Washington told the black community to avail themselves of the opportunities of education and in business that came to them. Casting the issue of racial discrimination as solely a matter of individual behavior, Washington urged the local black community to live upstanding and frugal lives. "When I hear of Senator Smith starting with a few sacks of peanuts I say no colored man has the right to think a small beginning is too small for him. But you must work. You must educate your children. You must live moral lives. You cannot create a demand for your services; you cannot be efficient in any undertaking if you spend half the night at the gambling table, in the saloon or in the den of vice. Next day your work is not good and this man from Holland here will have your job, as he has a right to have it because he goes to bed decently and lives a moral, frugal life and is the efficient workman." Although the newspaper quoted some of Washington's comments extensively, there were no comments recorded from the audience on how they felt about Washington's views.[58]

———————

Political realities made the proprietors of the abolitionist legacy unreliable allies for the African American leadership class. Leaders could ill-afford to alienate supportive friends in the established centers of power, for they needed allies in the establishment to win civil rights victories, gain employment opportunities, and benefit from philanthropy. Yet, as a proud people, they could not afford to be quiet about the daily social inequities they suffered. These individuals walked a tightrope. On the one hand, they had to be critical of their own for not accepting the prevailing bourgeois values of the day. On the other hand, they had to hold whites accountable in some way for their acceptance of racism. Reverend A. P. Miller, pastor of St. Luke AME Zion Church, delivered a lecture at the Park Congregational Church entitled the "Black Man's Burden" in 1902. His lecture balanced his attack on white prejudice with the flaws of "his people." Miller could not present an invective against the prejudice and brutality of the time; he had to be deliberate and careful in his judgments.

The affront of the color line was too great a burden for even the most moderate of leaders to bear. One of the city's longtime community leaders was Joseph C. Ford, affectionately and pejoratively known as "Senator" Joe. Ford had been born a slave in Fredericksburg, Virginia, around 1852. The *Grand Rapids Herald* reported that, during the Civil War, "he served in the Confederate commissary and recalled holding the horse of Gen. Stonewall Jackson." Ford came to Grand Rapids in 1872 and found work with the Grand Rapids and Indiana Railroad Company. For forty-six of his forty-nine years of employment, he served the Railroad Company as their head porter. In addition, Ford worked in Lansing as the attendant in the State Senate cloakroom for fifty-two years. During the same time, he attended all of the National Republican Conventions with the Michigan delegation, taking care of their "headquarters."

While the newspapers saw Ford as the genial porter known as "Senator Joe," African Americans recognized him as a leader.[59] He had been involved in the Michigan Equal Rights League and was an important member and trustee in the AME Church. In 1916, Ford was elected mayor of Idlewild, Michigan, a summer resort area for African Americans.[60] Ford used his congeniality to accomplish things in the community, and his leadership earned the ear of local Protestant elites. Yet the color line got the best of him as well. In 1902, he wrote a letter to the local newspaper in response to a letter by a Mr. Bogert, who claimed that African American men were not fit to be firemen.

> After reading communication in The Press the other evening I would be very much pleased to say that if a man who possesses any intellect would be as low as to say that colored men as a whole are shiftless, cowardly, and unfit for a position such as firemen in the Grand Rapids fire department it would be a blessing for him to go to such cities as Chicago, Indianapolis, Columbus, O., and Pittsburgh, and other cities of the first class and note the record made by those gentlemen, and taxpayers who pay millions in taxes feel proud of them, and their integrity. Furthermore, it can be shown that the colored people of this city pay more taxes per capita on real estate than all such characters as this Mr. Bogert. When in this part of the country where he saw so many shiftless illiterates, why could he not see there were no schools to teach pupils as we have in the North? Now in regards to cowardice, I dare say he will never face a flag to fight for his country when it is in need of able-bodied men to fight the foe. I suppose the black man would be good enough to fight fire in time of war but not eligible to fight fire in time of peace.[61]

Six years later, Ford again wrote a letter to the editor of the *Herald* newspaper regarding his frustration over the racial discrimination against a visiting clergyman in a local restaurant owned by J. A. Bauman. As Ford describes the incident, Bauman sought to charge Rev. McDaniel one hundred dollars for an ordinary meal because he was black. Ford's letter questioned the Christian basis of the city:

> But perhaps Rev. McDaniel has a mistaken idea of Christianity, which he represents and of which Grand Rapids so proudly boasts, for this is not a country nor a city wherein one can love his neighbor as himself, if his neighbor happens to be a colored man, even though the Holy Bible gives the command. We have outlived the day when man should do unto others as he would that men should do unto him. No wonder Christianity is on the wane when such conditions prevail. . . . No wonder that anarchy, lust, and pollution [are] crushing the very life out of American

traditions and institutions. No wonder that the teachings of Jesus Christ, George Washington and Abe Lincoln have given way to the teachings of Lucifer, Ingersoll, and Emma Goldman.[62]

Racial discrimination was doubly irksome to individuals like Ford—people who worked closely with those in the business elite by serving as porters, maids, and butlers. This proximity allowed them to see the ways of their employers and the unfairness perpetuated by racial injustice. Men and women of Ford's stature did their best to behave in a manner befitting respectable bourgeois culture, yet they continued to feel the sting of racial subordination. Mary R. Tate, president of the Colored Nineteenth-Century Club, believed that the racial discrimination in Grand Rapids was emblematic of the North's acquiescence to mandates of white Southern culture.

> The north has reached the point where it is ready to echo almost anything the south chooses to assert. The result of this activity had been such that in many instances the negro in the north now finds himself deprived of the facilities for moral and intellectual improvement, which he once enjoyed. He is denied the right of becoming a member of the Y.M.C.A., and in some places churches, schools and restaurants are closed to him. So far, the north unites with the south to make criminals out of the race and then unite in blaming it because it becomes criminals. Money talks and the south knows it. It has obtained its foothold and proposes to use its power to carry out its mission to keep the negro down, push him into the brothel, keep him an inferior, and make him a criminal.[63]

The stranglehold that Jim Crow laws began to have throughout the South and the *de facto* culture of Jim Crow in the North were constant in the lives of all black people.[64]

Rev. S. Henri Browne, the minister of Messiah Baptist Church during the early twentieth century, cultivated a deep and careful understanding of the African American community in Grand Rapids. Browne possessed a cultural and educational background that few in the black community had at the time. The *Grand Rapids Press* reported that Browne, who was born in Haiti, received his formal education in England, where he earned a doctorate in divinity.[65] In his seven years in Grand Rapids, Browne earned a reputation as a fine preacher, delivering sermons on topics such as "The Longing of a Sinner's Heart" and "Are the Claims of Christianity Too Exacting?"[66] In addition, Browne personally experienced the petty and hurtful acts of racial discrimination. One local newspaper recounted the refusal of a local merchant to allow Browne to make a shoe purchase because of his race. Browne, therefore, brought personal and academic experience to the article he published in the *Grand Rapids Press* on April 6, 1913, titled "The Negro in Grand Rapids."[67]

Browne explained that the city's African American population had grown to 665, of whom only 264 were voters. Though the black community was not large, Browne acknowledged it had a functioning civil society—filled with associations, churches, and clubs. He attributed the small population of African Americans to a number of factors within the city, lamenting specifically the lack of education within the community. He wrote that of the 104 African Americans in the area schools, only four were in high school. Browne complained that there had only been one black person allowed to teach in the area school system: "The unnecessary delay and the manufactured excuses on the part of the School Board have tended to act as a determent to others, who would like to take teaching as a profession."[68] Grand Rapids' only black teacher, Hattie Beverly, taught at the Congress Elementary School from 1899 to 1902.[69] It would be seventeen years until another African American teacher, Theola Ford, entered the city's schools.

Many African Americans, Browne argued, saw high school as useless because even with a diploma in their possession, they found all but the "most menial" jobs still unavailable to them. Therefore, if the job opportunities were limited even for the educated, then it made little sense for the average person to obtain a formal education, which appeared to possess no value in the marketplace.

Despite the inferior social status of African Americans at the time, Browne argued that they were no more criminally disposed than "the dominant race." Defending African Americans against the charge of criminality, he used African American motherhood as an example, stating that "mothers have strong love for their children; if one should lose her husband, leaving her with two or three children, she would never think of putting them in the Home, but [would] work to care for them, and in many instances to give them a good education." Browne used the mythic strength of African American womanhood as a representative image of his community's respectability. He also used statistics from the Poor Department showing that few African Americans had the need for welfare assistance. He also pointed out that of the 3,295 people arrested in 1912, only 57 were African Americans.[70]

In Browne's opinion, the most pressing social condition for African Americans was housing, because slums fostered crime. He believed that landlords and real estate agents rented or sold their homes at more expensive rates to blacks than to other ethnic communities in the city. He also believed that blacks' limited success in Grand Rapids was due to inadequate wages. "We are denied as [a] rule," he said, "all lucrative employments; our men and young men must be railroad porters and waiters or hotel waiters; and it must be presumed you are fully aware of the small pay. And in face of all this to accumulate this amount of property seems marvelous." Although African Americans had been—and would continue to be—heroic in the face of the odds against them, Browne concluded, "We are a dependent race."[71]

Browne further delineated the struggles of African Americans by underscoring slavery: "When your forbears and their children were holding conversations with Milton, Shakespeare, Socrates, Plato, and Cicero or sitting at the feet of some far-framed old masters, or listening to the muses with their enchanting songs you were doing as these and more besides. At the same time, the Negro was being bought and sold; [he was] used to fill your coffers; the negresses were being used to satisfy the salacious propensities of their vicious owners, under the most inhuman duress, for 250 years. This is a matter of history."

Slavery, Browne believed, enshrined African American inferiority, especially in the nineteenth-century Dred Scott decision written by United States Supreme Court Chief Justice Roger B. Taney. "The Court," Browne wrote, "[in] the sweeping language of the Declaration, that all men are born free, had no application to Negroes, because at that time they were generally regarded as inferior, that they had no right which the white man was bound to respect." He observed that the effect of the decision "remains ever true."[72]

Browne concluded by offering thanks to the white community for its past benevolence and abolitionist legacy—and for its continued work for race relations in the future:

> We are fully aware that many of you are cultivating the spirit of Charles Sumner, William Lloyd Garrison, Wendell Phillips and others, who emphasized the brother-hood of man and the Father-hood of God. We need your help yet; instead of erecting a Chinese wall in our pathway, remove them and give us a helping hand. No race has a patent right on virtue, morality, culture, and education. You need these and so do we. Have patience with us. If we are—Children crying in the night, Children carrying for the light, With no language but a cry—then give us the Light.[73]

Black community leaders such as Henri Browne knew well the realities of living in Grand Rapids. It was not solely a matter of *Southern* racial prejudice; the color line was drawn in their city, too.

———

Race relations among the laboring classes in the city can also be viewed from another perspective. African Americans clustered in neighborhoods that they did not numerically dominate. Historian Oliver Zunz explains the concept of dominance "as the threshold at which the geographic concentration is significant for a given group in a given an area." He argues that there is a "complex interplay of the variables which caused geographic concentration and dispersion."[74] Locally, Dutch settlers fit this model.

The first Dutch settlers came into the area in 1847 and settled about forty-five miles southwest of Grand Rapids on Lake Michigan in the village of Holland. The reason for Dutch immigration into the area is two-fold—religious and economic opportunity.[75] Dutch immigrants who came to the Grand Rapids area were overwhelmingly Protestant. This migration encouraged a conservative subculture.[76] By 1890, immigrants from Holland comprised 14 percent of the city's total population.[77] From Booker T. Washington's first visit to Grand Rapids until his death in 1915, the native-born population of Hollanders in western Michigan grew rapidly. Perhaps more than any other ethnic group, the Dutch would stamp their peculiar character upon the city.

Although the Dutch community was significant in Grand Rapids in terms of concentration, it was not entirely dominant. Earlier in its history, the city had experienced immigration from Prussia, Ireland, and—later in the nineteenth century—Polish-German immigrants. These groups met native-born whites and blacks as they arrived. Up until the 1890s, there was marginal interaction between ethnic communities. All the neighborhoods that Negroes were clustered in had majorities of white residents. This intersection of whites and blacks fostered interracial relationships at every level.

Interactions between African Americans and their neighbors were widely varied. On one hand, African Americans reacted with a degree of nativism toward new immigrants, as the surging numbers of immigrants pushed blacks onto an economic precipice. In 1890, African American leaders in the city asserted their loyalty and their equal citizenship with native-born white Americans in comparison to other European immigrants.[78] Or, in another instance, Assyrians and African Americans allegedly "rioted" in 1912 over the ill treatment of black customers in an ice cream shop. Ostensibly, this incident—and the resulting tensions in the African American community—prompted Booker T. Washington to make his final visit to the city. On the other hand, African Methodists found commonalities with Dutch immigrants because of their shared Protestant values; indeed, the Spring Street AME Church rented the Dutch schoolhouse for Sunday morning worship until their church was built.

As the furniture industry reached its zenith in the 1890s, the city's racial dynamics began to change. The sheer number of Dutch and Polish immigrants placed them in an advantageous position, both politically and as laborers.[79] In addition to numerical strength, Dutch, Polish, and other ethnic whites were racially preferred by employers. Up until the 1890s, African American men played a prominent role as barbers with a multiethnic clientele. By the 1900, these barbers served ethnic customers exclusively. Before the 1880s, Black laborers worked alongside whites in the dangerous sawmills and as lumberjacks. Just a few decades later, however, blacks and whites rarely worked together.[80] The demographic changes occurring in the labor force, accompanied by an ever shifting racist ideology, relegated African Americans to the domestic and menial realms. African Americans were resentful of these social trends and the racial advantages that the white laboring classes enjoyed. African Americans lived with the newcomers despite their resentments: they had little choice.

During this time, the perpetuation of black stereotypes also continued to make life difficult for African Americans. The derogatory minstrel-show images of blacks abounded in newspapers through advertisements and comic strips. Added to this were local newspapers' nostalgic and idyllic stories of the Old South, with the lore of loving black mammies and dutiful slaves. These depictions unwittingly represented to the readers of the dailies that most African Americans were harmless children.[81] More important, though, was that these stories continued to define African American life for the white community, disguising the political brutality of the South and making a joke of the African American struggle for human rights and cultural dignity.[82] The net effect was that the lives of ordinary black people were circumscribed by the ubiquity of cultural stereotypes. As middle-class aspirations grew among African Americans in the city, so did hypersensitivity and hypercritical attitudes toward one another. Fearing that they could never overcome the pervasiveness of these images, they often blamed one another for behavior that confirmed the stereotypes. African Americans knew that whites looked for stereotypes among black people, in the newspapers and on the streets—and they always found what they were looking for.

African American entertainers, however, used these depictions to get the last laugh on whites. Black minstrel entertainers and notable entertainers like Bob Cole and J. Rosamond Johnson learned that creative stereotyping was quite profitable.[83] Local athletes, especially baseball players, used their image to make money and gain status the same way that heavyweight boxing champion Jack Johnson had, taunting challengers to beat the black boys at bat.[84] While this might not have been sanctioned in respectable society of Booker T. Washington, the use of negative images, in the end, paid those who could transform them from hackneyed forms into an art.

Booker T. Washington's last engagement in Grand Rapids was on October 16, 1912, when he was invited by a union of the downtown churches. As was Washington's usual pattern, he was fundraising for Tuskegee Institute.[85] At the Park Congregational Church, Washington gave a speech discussing how Tuskegee was advancing the education of African Americans. Although Washington again avoided addressing the topic of civil rights in his speech, he did assert his great pride in being black.[86]

Washington also spoke to an all-black audience at the Arnett Chapel. Unfortunately, there are no records of what Washington said there, nor is there any record of what members of the community asked him.[87] Although whites heard from Washington about the value of hard work, African Americans in Grand Rapids saw their deepest aspirations in him, desiring the type of respectability that Washington espoused. Because Washington was, as his biographer Louis Harlan asserts, from "the last generation of black leaders born in slavery in the Old South," many residents of Grand Rapids—once slaves themselves—related to him, desiring his level of success and respectability.[88] They wanted farms, businesses, and stable families, but they struggled to put what Washington preached into practice, especially when the forces of culture and economics were aligned against them.

Booker T. Washington's unexpected death in 1915 was a source of sadness for white religious leaders and African Americans alike. The editor of the *Grand Rapids Herald*, in an article entitled "Another Washington," wrote:

> In the death of Booker T. Washington, the country loses a leader who has occupied a niche peculiarly his own. It was niche, which he carved for himself with his own hands. It was a niche, however, to which millions of people will come with wreaths of respectful and appreciative memory.

His skin was black; but his heart was white—and the human service which he rendered in his fruitful life-time will measure with that of any educator of this or any other time. Born in slavery, he lived to lead in a great movement that has sought to complete the emancipation from bondage, which began when Lincoln struck the iron from the shackles of the negro race. Booker Washington will live in his works for decades to come. Grand Rapids entertained him once at a Lincoln banquet. We know of his personality and purpose—and it is in the light of this knowledge that Grand Rapids will join in doing honor to his memory.[89]

On Sunday, January 9, 1916, at the Fountain Street Baptist Church, an interracial tribute was held in memory of Washington's life. The tribute featured keynote speaker James Dooley, principal of the Southern Normal and Industrial Institute. After Dooley's presentation, prominent local white clergymen paid tribute to Washington. The pastor of the Burton Street Christian Reformed Church, Rev. Henry Beets, set off a lively discussion in his remarks. Beets, the newspaper reported, tied his comments about Washington to his own exoneration of the Dutch involvement in the transatlantic slave trade. His argument was simple: the Dutch did not introduce the slave trade to the Americas; indeed, the "Dutch and the Christian Reformed Church aided the cause of the Negro."[90]

Not to be outdone by Beets's defense of the Dutch, the other clergymen sought to defend their own ethnic and denominational heritages regarding race relations. Reverend G. F. Francombe, a Methodist minister, defended the English and the Methodists as abolitionist. Reverend A. W. Wisehart of the Fountain Street Baptist Church made it known that Abraham Lincoln's mother was a Baptist and "claimed that the Baptists could be said to have been as great an aid to the Negro as any other denomination."

Once again, local newspapers did not report the comments of African Americans about Booker T. Washington, even though African American clergy officiated at the service; nor did they report the words of tribute given by Rev. Louis Pettiford of the AME Church, who presided over the event; or the prayer of Rev. W. H. Bixley, pastor of the AME Zion Church; or the scripture lesson of Rev. W. H. Hill of the Messiah Baptist Church. The article did not quote T. E. Benjamin's poem or list the songs the Dooley family quintet sang.

It is also evident from this interracial gathering that Protestant Christianity played a defining, mediating role in race relations in Grand Rapids during that time.[91] Protestant churches were the foundation on which blacks and whites in Grand Rapids could build a common civil society. The Protestant religious ethos, that all people are equal before God, placed limitation upon the most virulent racist attitudes in the city. The religious ethos did not remove racism, but it did soften it. Religion fostered racial paternalism and politeness.[92]

By 1915, race relations in Grand Rapids had an ongoing tradition of interracial cooperation and civil discourse among the aspiring and respectable middle-class blacks and whites. This discourse, however, was constantly strained because of the hypocrisy of (white) racial social privilege. And among the working classes, tensions continued to flare up over jobs, neighborhood interaction, and social intermingling.[93]

Booker T. Washington died fifty years after the end of the Civil War. In that half-decade, African Americans acquired limited educational opportunity, sought political office, purchased homes, and articulated their own aspirations. They progressed. But it was also true that fifty years after the end of slavery, African Americans in Grand Rapids, like those throughout the United States, were still struggling against the effects of the law and culture of Jim Crow.

There was one change at the time of Washington's death that went unnoticed in the local news media. The unreported words of the local leaders at Booker T. Washington's tribute service represented the last time in Grand Rapids where whites alone would dominate a discussion about African American concerns. A new generation of leaders, no longer laboring under the guise of white paternalism, had arrived.

4 Making Opportunity: New Negroes and the Struggle against Jim Crow

On December 18, 1925, a short column appeared in the *Grand Rapids Herald* with the heading, "Colored Organization Hears Woman Lecturer." The article noted that a Miss Hallie Q. Brown of Wilberforce, Ohio, had addressed the closing night of the local National Association of Colored People (NAACP) membership drive at the Messiah Baptist Church. Brown charged her audience with stirring words: "We are here to discuss not gifts but opportunity . . . Abraham Lincoln, John Bunyan and Booker T. Washington made great achievements because they grasped opportunity. If our race is to come into full freedom there must be a well trained and educated leadership, who realize their obligation. We must sacrifice good times and frivolity. Would to God that every young man of my race would say, 'I will make opportunity.'"[1]

Brown's words that evening were not merely the positive rhetoric of racial uplift. Veiled in her speech was the deliberate strategy of an African American civic leadership to end the custom segregation in public accommodations. By attacking the legal basis of racial exclusion, these men and women could put an end to the dishonor imposed on their community by racist custom; they could work to fully integrate African Americans into the mainstream of city life.[2] Their specific goal was to be recognized as middle-class Americans in both status and lifestyle. To this end, the leadership's fight centered on the attainment of higher education, availability of employment opportunities, and access to public accommodations.

The practice of racial segregation in Grand Rapids was not legally codified as it was in Southern cities.[3] Michigan had a civil rights statute, formalized into law by 1885 and amended in 1919, forbidding discrimination on the basis of a person's race, creed, or color in all public accommodations.[4] However, the practice of relegating African Americans to seats in theater balconies, using separate restaurant entrances, and enduring various other kinds of public humiliation took place with impunity throughout the city and the state.[5]

Brown's address to the NAACP served as a rallying point for a community whose formally educated and professionally trained leadership had come of age and was prepared to challenge Jim Crow. Her speech was linked with the actions of the civil rights lawsuit filed against one of Grand Rapids' premier theaters, the Keith.[6] Three days before Brown's speech, court documents alleged that on Monday, December 14, 1925, Emmett Bolden, a local dentist and native of Grand Rapids, had been refused equal access to the theater. Bolden's attorney, Oliver M. Green, explained in his complaint that his client was offered seating in the theater's balcony while other patrons were permitted to buy seating on the theater's main floor. Green's initial brief in Grand Rapids Superior Court noted: "The Civil Rights Act is violated where, after a person has bought a ticket entitling him to a particular seat in the theater, he is deprived of the right to occupy it on account of his race or color, although hs [sic] is offered another seat."[7]

Green's appeal simply stated the obvious. Both he and Bolden knew that the use of exclusive seating in the balcony for Negroes, pejoratively known then as "Nigger Heavens," was a violation of the state's civil rights statute. They further understood that their lawsuit, legally known as *Bolden v. Grand Rapids Operating Corporation*, was not the first local effort to end the *de facto* practice of public segregation. Throughout the city's history, African Americans waged a political struggle to gain equal protection under the law and end all forms of racial discrimination. This fight, however, was led by a more self-consciously rebellious group.

Green and Bolden's generation called themselves "New Negroes." In Grand Rapids, as elsewhere, they created a new urban cultural identity that no longer felt the need to cajole and accommodate white leaders as, say, Joseph Ford and other local leaders who came before had done. They had stepped out of the shadow of slavery into the light of formal education and professional training. These New Negroes melded the fight for civil rights, the search for a constructive Negro history, and urban middle-class culture into a new weapon with which to wage war against white supremacy.[8]

The assessment that Rev. Henri Browne made in 1913 article, "The Negro in Grand Rapids" (discussed in chapter 2), was an eloquent plea for desegregation. However, he too had felt the sting of customary Jim Crow in Grand Rapids when his right to buy a pair of shoes was denied by a storeowner solely because he was black. The irony and perhaps the bitterness were not lost on the African American community, as this incident occurred on the same day his report was published in the newspaper.[9]

Despite the history of living in close proximity to whites and having extensive interaction with them, African Americans lived with the daily humiliation of being segregated. Their struggle against segregation was one that the community, more often than not, fought alone. This is not to say there were not noble white allies in the fight against segregation. However, the primary burden of social change lay in their sometimes feeble, sometimes ingenious, and often courageous self-initiatives. In the fight to end segregation in everyday life, Negro leaders articulated the viewpoint that achieving respectability meant achieving full desegregation, for only desegregation could ameliorate their social resentments at being excluded and stigmatized by law and custom.

By 1904, a group of African American men organized a league to protect their constitutional rights in the face of persistent racial discrimination. In a *Grand Rapids Post* article, William Gaines, a plumber, described how racial discrimination operated in Grand Rapids: "If a colored man comes into some of the restaurants here and asks to be served, the proprietors will tell him to go way back in some dark corner. In some places they will come out plainly and tell him that [they] do not wish for his patronage and they will not entertain him. In saloons it is the same. The barkeeper will tell him that he has had enough when the colored man probably has not had even a drink."[10] Although this group vigorously protested such discrimination, their actions failed in any significant way to change it.[11] Even judicial appeals in Grand Rapids failed.

In the fall of 1908, Felix D. Booker and Wesley McCoy, two second-year students of the Grand Rapids Medical College (a local veterinary school), were not readmitted, based on their race. In circuit court, the students' attorney, Martin Carmody, charged that the college was a quasi-public institution and therefore could not discriminate solely on race. At issue were three things, Carmody believed. He reasoned that the college was a quasi-public institution because it was exempt from taxes, because it was under the administration of the state board of education, and because its diplomas were accepted in lieu of examination by state board of veterinarians. The circuit court judge, Cyrus Perkins, upheld Carmody's claim and ruled in favor of the plaintiffs. The judge determined that although the college was privately funded, its favorable treatment by the state made it a quasi-public institution of learning; therefore, it could not discriminate. Judge Perkins ruled: "All citizens according to the court's findings are entitled to the privilege of education in public institutions of learning, and the drawing of the color line is an unjust discrimination."[12] However reasonable, impartial, fair, and legally correct this decision might have been, it did not fare well among the college's students or in appeal to the Michigan Supreme Court.

Four days after the circuit court ruling, junior students vehemently and violently protested Booker and McCoy's presence at the college. Thirty-four students walked out of their classes, shouting, "This is a white man's school" and "lynch 'em if they don't keep out." In the college's lobby, the white students created an effigy of a Negro and carried it out into the streets, doing a "lively war dance around" it. The press reporter noted that "a large percentage of the students of the college [were] from the Mason and Dixon line" and were determined to prevent any attempts by "coloreds" from ever entering the college. Despite the intimidation, Booker and McCoy were determined to remain at the college.[13] Months later, however, the court barred them from the campus permanently.

On January 12, 1909, the law firm of Hatch and Raymond entered an appeal on behalf of the college to the Michigan Supreme Court, contending that Judge Perkins's ruling against the college was unconstitutional. Specifically, the college's attorneys asked the high court to reject the lower court's determination that the college was a quasi-public institution. They enjoined the court to note: "Private institutions of learning though incorporated, may select those whom they will receive as students, and may discriminate by sex, age, proficiency in learning and otherwise; and the arbitrary refusal to receive any student, in the first instance, would not violate any privilege or immunity resting in positive law protected or guaranteed by the Federal or State Constitutions."[14]

The college's status as a private institution, they insisted, permitted it to discriminate as it pleased. The lawyers for the college also argued that the Medical College was not obliged to allow Booker and McCoy to remain as students, since they had passed one term, and there was no contractual stipulation that guaranteed they should be accepted for another. The lawyers concluded that the presence of two African Americans irreparably disrupt the decorum of total campus life.[15] The Michigan Supreme Court overturned Booker and McCoy's initial circuit court victory because the civil rights statute as they interpreted it could not compel a "private institution to perform its obligations resting in contract with an individual . . . . The apparent hardship of a particular situation is not a good reason for departing from the rule."[16]

The ruling against Booker and McCoy was consistent with other judgments handed down that same year on civil rights. In *Meisner v. Detroit Isle and Windsor Ferry Company*, the court ruled that theaters, circuses, racetracks, private parks, and the like were private enterprises, and as such, proprietors could refuse anyone they chose.[17] Unlike the blatant Jim Crow practices in the South, Michigan's Jim Crow customs were often disguised in arguments about free enterprise and the freedom of association. But the effects of racial exclusion, whether based on theories of racial inferiority or free enterprise, netted the same results. In 1919, Michigan's civil rights statue was amended to define clearly the intent of the law in public accommodations, but it was not until 1927 that the issue of customary segregation in public facilities was legally settled in Grand Rapids.

African Americans waited eighteen years before another legal challenge to the practices of local segregation was mounted. In the meantime, they continued to lodge their complaints in the daily newspapers and through church-related forums. Reflecting national trends, the city developed a small but articulate college-educated middle class, many of whom were influenced by the writings and activism of W. E. B. Du Bois. In 1917, Du Bois came to Grand Rapids to give an address to the Sunday Evening Club, an evening forum organized by Park Congregational Church. The editors of the *Grand Rapids Press* offered a cool reception to his speech "The World's War and the Darker Races,"[18;] Du Bois's comments raised troublesome questions about the war, race, and the European colonial powers. However, it emboldened many local African Americans to view their struggle for civil rights in a wider global movement for democratic freedoms.[19]

World War I brought a wave of patriotism as well as ample concerns about American race relations. Local dailies covered African American men who joined the Army, and the *Grand Rapids Herald* consistently wrote editorials about the necessity to resolve racial problems in the United States.[20] The patriotic rhetoric of democracy filled the newspapers and political pronouncements.

Daniel Boone Lampkins found this rhetoric of democracy useful in his candidacy for the city commission. According to newspaper accounts, Lampkins was a porter in a downtown barbershop who had attended Earlham College in Richmond, Indiana, for two years before he ran out of funds and subsequently came to the city for work. He was a committed member of the Republican Party, having developed his local political reputation as the spokesman for the Colored Republicans club. In this capacity he was a stout critic of President Woodrow Wilson; he criticized the Wilson administration for its blatant racial discrimination at the same time it was preaching democracy. In 1917, Lampkins joined the war effort, serving as a YMCA worker in France and providing entertainment and relief to African American troops. His exposure to the war quickened his resolve to exert pressure locally for democratic inclusion of African Americans. In 1918, he told the *Grand Rapids Herald* that he had "the utmost faith in the American people. I am an American. Our forefathers, when they founded this nation, decreed that we should either dig in or dig out. I have preferred to dig in." He believed the time had arrived "when one man who is aiming to do something great and good for humanity will observe that I am seeking to do the same and that, therefore, things equal to the same thing are equal to each other. Then the fact that God saw fit to give me a black skin will not count. The world will look at us all from the inside instead of the outside, and it will not be who are you or whence you came, but what have you got that will count."[21] Lampkins lost his race for city commission, but his willingness to enter the campaign signaled a new readiness in a small segment of the community to challenge everyday exclusion of blacks in civic life. The establishment of two institutions signaled this group's readiness: the local chapter of the NAACP and a local newspaper, the *Michigan State News*.

On January 3, 1919, fifty people gathered with Rev. Robert Bagnall, the Great Lakes district organizer of the NAACP, to charter the Grand Rapids chapter.[22] The National office of the NAACP granted a charter to the local chapter twenty-two days after the submission of their application. The officers of the branch were Thomas E. Benjamin, a railroad porter, who served as president; Basil Ray, a waiter, was appointed vice president; George M. Smith, a printing superintendent, was the group's secretary; and J. Ed Jones, a custodian, became treasurer.[23] Each charter member paid one dollar and received a subscription to *Crisis* magazine.

The organization of the chapter in 1919 was a part of the larger expansion of NAACP branches all over the country. A historian of the NAACP noted that, at the time of the 1919 national conference of the NAACP in Cleveland, "there were 220 branches and 56,345 members, and the circulation of the *Crisis* stood at 100,000." The organization proclaimed in *Crisis* "that it was without peer, the greatest fighting force for Negro freedom in the world. . . . The Negro who is not a member of it finds himself on the defensive. The white man who does not believe in it does not believe in American democracy."[24] In 1919, at least fifty people went on the offensive against segregation as members of the NAACP.

Within a month of its formation, the Grand Rapids chapter of the NAACP began consulting with the national organization concerning troublesome local issues. On February 24, 1919, George Smith, the branch's secretary, wrote to the national secretary, John R. Shillady, concerning the formation of separate youth, parenting, and social clubs based on race. Smith expressed wariness over the lack of participation by African Americans in organizations that the public schools sponsored for progressive uplift. Some individuals within the Grand Rapids branch felt that the separation of public school activities by race might enhance the participation of colored citizens by allowing them to feel more "at home." Smith thought that any effort by African Americans to "self-separate or segregate" would further exacerbate the "wedge for future separation or segregation on the part of white neighbors." He added that the furthering of segregation by African Americans themselves was something the community would surely come to regret.[25] Two minds within the Grand Rapids' African American community were already evident from Smith's letter: one affirming integration and the other promoting voluntary ethnic segregation. As the most articulate spokesperson for the organization, Smith saw his view prevail: the Grand Rapids branch would fight any attempt at segregation, even among its own constituents.

In 1920, George Smith founded the *Michigan State News*, a paper modeled on the late nineteenth-century *Detroit Plaindealer*. The *State News* was dedicated to giving African Americans a statewide journalistic voice.[26] The motto of the paper was "Michigan's Race Paper." Although short lived, the *State News* articulated a viewpoint that helped to galvanize the fight against Jim Crow.[27] Smith's editorial policy stated: "The *Michigan State News* does not now, or never will, follow the lines of sensational journalism. Such news of a national character as we give to our readers will always be the kind that shows progress and advancement. We believe in movements that are constructive and not destructive. No article will ever be printed to create more discontent or unrest. We will, however, attempt to print as much news of a helpful and progressive nature as we can get hold of. Again—we are emphatically opposed to publishing of anything that will needlessly make conditions more unpleasant for any citizen of Michigan—black or white—Editor."[28]

In this policy, Smith not only reasserted his earnest commitment to integration but also verbalized his concerns about the race riots that were taking place throughout the country, especially the notorious Chicago riot in the summer of 1919.[29] In an editorial discussing the *Grand Rapids Herald*'s use of "red" journalism in sensationalizing a lynching, Smith expressed his deepest conviction:

> I have the honor of being a branch secretary of the National Association for the Advancement of Colored People, an organization composed of the better element of both your race and mine, who believe in America being a haven for justice in fact, as well as in name. We are teaching our people the majesty and sovereignty of American laws and ideals so that they may more fully appreciate all it means to be a citizen of this great country. I respectfully urge you to join us in helping to make this truly the greatest country in the world—not however by flashing the lawlessness of her citizens to the world, but by moulding public sentiment in the channels of justice and not in the path of hate.[30]

Smith's *State News* served as a statewide promotional vehicle for the NAACP. In the third issue of the paper, Smith covered extensively the visit of Walter White, the assistant national secretary of the NAACP, to Kalamazoo and Lansing.[31] The newspaper reported that the national organization's agenda was at that time focused on tenant farmers in the South, the needs of Southern migrants arriving in the North (and the racial tensions spurred by their influx), and legal challenges to "Jim Crow" laws.[32] The *State News*, in this way, bolstered the work of the NAACP and kept the local community informed about civil rights nationwide and encouraged the younger generation to constructively channel their resentment about the daily assault of institutionalized discrimination—which a small contingent of NAACP members in Grand Rapids did by voicing their opinions about Southern lynchings.

In the summer of 1920, Thomas Benjamin, the Grand Rapids NAACP chapter president, wrote to the local newspaper to deplore lynching and mob action in the burning of two men in Paris, Texas. His letter asked the readers of the *Grand Rapids Press* to support the rule of law. Benjamin stated: "What are we going to do about this leprous spot on our otherwise fair name? Is mob rule to reign supreme? Are we too busy in our particular line of endeavor so that we fail to perceive the danger to which our indifference is leading? When the sanctity and supremacy of law and order entirely are banished beyond recall, the objects that monopolized our thoughts, consumed our time and used up our energies, to the exclusion and negligence of repairing the breaches in the foundation of our government, will assuredly find themselves victims of the common destruction that the lawlessness, now unheeded, will precipitate."[33] The editor of the *Press* attached the following response to Benjamin's letter. "First reports of the lynching at Paris, Texas, published in the morning papers quoted the sheriff as in the above *Pulse* article. Later reports sent out to the afternoon papers by the big news agencies were to the effect that the guilt of the men had been established, one dispatch saying they had confessed before they were burned at the stake. Even though guilty, this did not justify the brutal exercise of mob law. It is stated simply that there may be no misapprehensions of the facts in the case."[34]

Blatant racism hovered over the Grand Rapids community in the early twentieth century. In 1915, the film *Birth of a Nation* stirred strong reactions throughout the country and in Grand Rapids, particularly for its depiction of African Americans. In a letter to the *Grand Rapids Press*, N. H. Beyley complained bitterly of the inaccuracy of the film, writing that Thomas R. Dixon, the author of *The Clansman* (the novel upon which the film was based), was an enemy to the Negro. Beyley had taken up the call of the NAACP's *Crisis* magazine, which urged Negroes to begin a counter campaign against the film.[35]

During this time, racist behavior and activities were public; one did not have to be a closeted confederate. For example, by 1919, the KKK had formed a "club" in Grand Rapids South High School.[36] The nefarious organization grew throughout the city and the state in the mid-1920s.[37] In 1923, the *Grand Rapids Herald* was offering its readers a history of the Klan that could have been penned by Thomas Dixon. The source of the editorial was *Harper's Encyclopedia of American History*. The editorial stated:

> During the days of reconstruction following Appomattox, when "carpet baggers" threw the Southern state governments into corrupt chaos and newly freed slaves officiously demanded immediate equality, the original Klan came into being. There are today no issues comparable with the ones the true Klan faced. Yet, although the original order proved effective in its extra legal way of remedying evils, a sort of Southern vigilante organization its leaders, two years later, became afraid of unwieldy size and unruly manner and ordered its disbandment. This was the end of the only authentic Ku Klux Klan."

The editor stated that the revival of the Klan in 1923 was reminiscent of 1869, when General Ulysses Grant subdued South Carolina. The editorial concluded: "The founders of the Klu [sic] Klux Klan had made the mistake of reporting their extra-legal methods, with the result a brutal decadence, through those who understood force alone, into partly organized lawlessness. No matter how the agitators for the so-called Klu [sic] Klux Klan there is no way to prevent such an agency from falling into similarly menacing decadence unless it discards its masks, opens its membership record, and accepts public responsibility for its public acts. Men who are proud of their principles do not hide their faces."[38]

In 1925, the Klan hosted a weeklong meeting of over three thousand members in Grand Rapids. Although there are no recorded acts of racial intimidation occurring during the meeting, the size of the gathering reminded the local African American community of its vulnerability as a minority. Further, the Klan's rebirth in Indiana and its growth throughout Michigan threatened black life all around the state. In the face of these threats, the local chapter of the NAACP stood as the city's sole advocacy group against racial harassment and injustice.

Integral to the founding of the Grand Rapids NAACP branch and the publishing of Smith's *Michigan State News* was the ascendancy of a new leadership class.[39] Grand Rapids native Emmett Bolden's completion of his dental education at Howard University in Washington, D.C., and his return to the city—where he had been a sports star at South High—to establish a dental practice were auspiciously announced in the *Grand Rapids Press*'s sports page in 1923.[40] Bolden was not alone; at least five of his peers were attending University of Michigan and receiving professional education in preparation to return to the city and establish their careers. These individuals were Oliver M. Green, an attorney; Floyd Skinner, who became Grand Rapids' most renowned attorney of African descent;[41] Albert Keith, the pastor of Messiah Baptist Church;[42] Cortez English, a dentist;[43] and Eugene E. Alston, a physician.[44] For the first time in the city's history, a college-educated, professionally trained male cadre existed.

———————

On September 30, 1924, Olivier Meakins Green, a native of New York City and veteran of World War I, was sworn into the practice of law in Kent County as the third African American attorney to do so.[45]

Like his predecessors, Green's legal practice faced racial limitations and financial hardship. Unlike his predecessors, however, Green's education gave him professional credentials others might have only dreamed of having. On February 19, 1925, the Grand Rapids Bar Association elected Green as its first African American member. On that same evening, the association also elected Julius Amberg—who soon became the chief legal counsel and agent of the Keith Theater—as a trustee.[46] Amberg, a native of Grand Rapids, had built a successful law practice in the city (and nationally), and served as Felix Frankfurter's assistant in Woodrow Wilson's wartime administration. Like Frankfurter, Amberg distinguished himself as a lawyer.[47] He was the president of the Michigan State Bar, assistant secretary of war in the wartime administration of Franklin Roosevelt, and a member of other local philanthropic organizations during the Great Depression.[48] Despite his progressive political credentials, Amberg defended the right of the Keith Theater to continue its practice of discriminating against African Americans. Throughout 1925, Green and Amberg opposed each other three times in court over the issue of racial discrimination.

To challenge the Keith Theater, the Grand Rapids NAACP devised a tried-and-true strategy: attempting to establish a consistent pattern of discrimination by sending individuals to the theater to determine if they would be excluded or segregated on the basis of race. The three suits that Green filed in 1925 each alleged that the Keith Theater discriminated in seating on the basis of race. On April 10, 1925, he filed the first two suits on behalf of William Glenn[49] and Roger Grant.[50] Although the suits were filed separately, the court required that they be heard as one case, *Glenn v. Grand Operating Corporation.*[51] Both men, porters at the Pantlind Hotel (today, the Amway Grand Plaza Hotel), charged that the Keith refused them admittance to the main floor solely on the basis of race. This discriminatory act, Green argued, violated Michigan's civil rights statute and caused his clients public humiliation. The NAACP probably chose Glenn and Grant as test cases because both came from families who were longtime residents of the city. Grant had been a city tennis champion from South High School,[52] and Glenn was the son of a well-established chauffeur for one of the city's wealthier businessmen.[53] Green held his clients out as exemplars of the colored race, noting their high school education and their employment at the Pantlind as a means to save for their college education. He asked the court to reward his clients one thousand dollars each for the "great mental anguish and pain" they suffered at the hands of the theater.[54]

Using a familiar argument, Amberg countered Green's complaint by stating that Michigan's civil rights statute violated his client's right to due process because it forced a private corporation to be non-discriminatory. He further contended that because the amended civil rights statute of 1919 was to be used only in criminal cases, the plaintiffs had "no right to recovery or damages in a civil suit." Additionally, Amberg asserted that both plaintiffs had willingly "accepted and occupied" seats in the balcony without complaint.[55]

In July, the two attorneys agreed to a stipulation that the case would be removed from district court to superior court. If it were necessary for appeal, each party would have the right to appeal directly to the Michigan State Supreme Court. It is not clear from the records how *Glenn v. Grand Rapids Operating Corporation* was settled. In a letter regarding the Bolden case to the national NAACP office, Green claimed to have won these cases. It matters little, however, because the Bolden case would fully settle the issues of racial discrimination in the Keith.

It seems evident that the leaders within the NAACP were not satisfied with the "win" in *Glenn v. Grand Rapids Operating Corporation*. They felt that only a win in the Michigan State Supreme Court would halt the practices of Jim Crow. The difference between the Glenn and Grant case and Bolden's was Bolden's professional status and the attention that the leadership felt it would draw to one of the African American community's best. Like Glenn and Grant, Bolden had also spent much of his life in Grand Rapids and had been a well-known athlete. Green and the NAACP felt that Bolden's high level of achievement would elicit community support for the case.[56]

Bolden's case was no different from Booker and McCoy's or Glenn and Grant's. The arguments were essentially the same: When could the state force a "private" corporation to end discrimination? The defense's case centered on the legal interpretation of the U. S. Supreme Court case of 1896, *Plessy v. Ferguson*, which formalized separate but equal public accommodations for whites and blacks; Amberg argued throughout the case that access to the Keith Theater was equal and seating was selected randomly. The court did not fully accept the argument that this pattern of seating was arbitrary, as Michigan law required.

Amberg's law firm took a different tack against Bolden. This time they kept the case stalled by having Green respond to motions. By taking this path, the law firm placed considerable cost and expense on Green and the NAACP—a cost that Green could hardly afford to absorb. This burden caused Green to waver and consider withdrawing from the case.[57] To add insult to injury, Green was beaten up by a police officer, Lieutenant Van Koughnet, for entering the front door of the police station in 1926. Green sued the officer but eventually dropped the case so as not to distract attention away from the Bolden civil suit.[58]

Despite the financial hardship and physical abuse, Green managed to keep the case open. However, Judge Leonard Verdier, who had earned a reputation for being anti-Negro, ruled against Bolden in superior court.[59] This was no surprise to many in the black community, since it was widely believed that Verdier, while in the Michigan legislature, promoted a bill against interracial marriages. Although no record of his stance on the matter of interracial marriages can be documented, his public statements in later years confirmed to some the judge's bias.[60] Verdier's ruling in the Bolden case followed the line of reasoning of earlier supreme court rulings, stating: "In view of the fact that a theater is not a public enterprise but is private property with the right to conduct business privately the same as any other private citizen transacts his own affairs, it is a serious question whether or not this act of legislature [The Michigan Civil Rights Statute] does not contravene the 'due process' clause of the constitution."[61]

A demoralized Green wrote to the national office of the NAACP; in a letter addressed to W. E. B. Du Bois, he appealed to the national office for their support in bringing the case before the Michigan Supreme Court. Green explained that in the case of *Glenn,* he had received seventeen dollars, a fraction of his total costs, and for *Bolden* he had not received any compensation. He complained that his opposing counsel offered him a job after winning the cases for Glenn and Grant in 1925. He further lamented that representing the Bolden case caused him to lose money he might otherwise have earned. Although frustrated by his difficult circumstances, he no doubt understood that Amberg was attempting to buy his silence.[62] Even though he needed the money, Green knew a well-paying legal job would not curtail the racial ostracism that he, Bolden, and many others experienced. If the case were to proceed, it would so with the assistance of the national office. He warned, "If the case is lost in the Supreme Court, it would mean that theaters in this state may seat colored people where-so-ever they choose to seat them." Despairingly, he observed that the Grand Rapids chapter of the NAACP had grown indifferent to the suit's outcome.[63]

What Green did not write in his letter, however, was that the Grand Rapids chapter of the NAACP was struggling to maintain a membership of fifty people—many of whom were working in low-paying jobs—making the organization incapable of funding Bolden's appeal to the Michigan Supreme Court.[64] Additionally, the weakness of black civic institutions and the relative powerlessness of the African American community in Grand Rapids made it necessary for Green to appeal to a wider audience.

Green's letter also reflected a fissure among African Americans along class, cultural, and ideological lines. The working class seemed more interested in their employment prospects than in obtaining access to the main floor of the theater. The indifference of newly arrived Southern migrants to this issue may have derived from the fact that they had lived with the pain of segregation all their lives—and Grand Rapids was, relatively speaking, much more congenial than the South. Established families in Grand Rapids, on the other hand, cared deeply about the issue of public accommodations. The discrimination was particularly injurious and insulting to them, since they had lived within a white community all their lives.[65] It is clear from the tone of Green's letter that the classes were at odds. Clearly, if one ties class divisions among African Americans to their ideological differences—civil protest versus an accommodating work ethic versus strains of nationalism—the fissure grows wider. It is obvious that those who brought the Bolden case amidst all of these fault lines had a relatively weak basis of support.

Fortunately, the national office of the NAACP responded immediately by urging the Detroit branch to assist Green and Bolden. On October 2, 1926, the *Chicago Defender* reported that the case had been appealed to the Michigan Supreme Court.[66] The NAACP's press release of October 8 stated that the Detroit branch, "the most powerful in the state, [was urged to] take leadership in fighting this case."[67] In November, the Detroit NAACP began raising funds for the Bolden appeal. By the end of November, the national organization, along with Green, had secured additional counsel for the appeal from the Grand Rapids law firm of Jewell, Face, and Messinger. The attorney assigned to the case was William Messinger, a law classmate of Green's at the University of Michigan. Through his involvement in this case, Messinger, a Grand Rapids native, continued the longstanding abolitionist tradition of interracial cooperation.[68]

Green and Messinger based their appeal on an 1890 Michigan court case, *Ferguson v. Gies,* wherein the court ruled against a restaurant for refusing to serve an African American male where other people were served. The court stated that this was a blatant violation of Ferguson's civil rights, and that he could be awarded damages for this public humiliation.[69] Green and Messinger prepared the appeal and submitted it to the supreme court on April 15, 1927.[70]

The Michigan Supreme Court decided the case on June 6, 1927. They agreed with Green and Messinger's appeal and found that the Keith Theater had violated the Michigan's civil rights statute. The court stated: "The act in question is usually called the 'Civil Rights Act.' Its purpose is apparent. While it applies to 'all persons within the jurisdiction of this State,' it cannot be doubted that it was enacted with special reference to those of African descent. It clearly provides against discrimination on the part of those conducting theaters by withholding from or denying to colored people the accommodations, advantages, facilities or privileges accorded to others."[71]

The court also ruled that Bolden was entitled to sue the theater for any damages he suffered.[72] Strangely, all of the Grand Rapids newspapers were silent about this outcome. The *Chicago Defender,* however, ran a story about the case on June 18, 1927. The headline read, "Court Rules against Jim Crow Tactics: Reverses Decision in Theater Case."[73]

Of course, the significance of this victory was not lost on Green. In his final letter on the case, directed to Walter White at the national NAACP office, he wrote, "Inclosed [sic] you will find a copy of the opinion rendered by the Michigan Supreme Court in the above entitled cause, which as you see, was a victory for the N.A.C.P. [sic] and greatly oblige."[74]

The struggle against Jim Crow in Grand Rapids places the efforts by the African American leadership class follows the national pattern of the NAACP's efforts to legally redress *Plessey v. Ferguson.* This small community's collective agency reflected the determination of African Americans nationwide to be free from the corrosive effects of racial segregation.

Bolden v. Grand Rapids Operating Corporation ended customary segregation in Grand Rapids. The Michigan Supreme Court ruling upheld the state's civil rights statute and assured Negroes throughout the state access to all public facilities. This victory, combined with the 1925 decision on behalf of Ossian Sweet of Detroit, gave the NAACP a singularly important voice on African Americans in Michigan, especially among the state's emerging middle and professional classes.[75] Doctor Bolden and Attorney Green were able to sit on the main floor of the Keith Theater. To them, the victory, though small, was sweet.

Although the court case was a victory for these professionals, daily racial discrimination continued. In an editorial that appeared on July 24, 1933, in the *Grand Rapids Herald,* the writer noted that big band leader Cab Calloway had given a performance in the city. The writer's observation on the matter read:

Cab Calloway, Negro musician, was in Grand Rapids last Tuesday night, playing an engagement at Ramona Gardens dance hall. That is scarcely news of importance to the editorial column. Those whom it concerned were there in large numbers. But this much is worth comment. Cab Calloway has made a fortune through his musical ability. He is an outstanding figure among dance orchestra leaders, commanding a considerable income. During the course of the Tuesday night dance we are told that many Grand Rapids Negroes proud of their racial brother, gathered at the rear of Ramona Gardens. During the intermission they called for "Cab." The successful musician didn't turn up his nose at his own people. Instead he took himself to the door and with a genial smile called, "How to do, folks. Glad to see you. How's everybody?" at the crowd outside. We don't know just how Cab's music rates with the critics of music, but this much seems evident, his success hasn't gone to his head. And that isn't so common as to be beneath notice.[76]

What did not occur to the editorial writer was what would have been immediately evident to Cab Calloway. He saw that African Americans were not dancing to his music at the Ramona Gardens. They could not dance because they were not welcomed into the club. Rather, they had to stand outside at the club's rear entrance, waiting to greet Calloway, one of their own. The legality of racial discrimination had been defeated, but the culture of racial exclusion prevailed.

The small cadre of professionals who led this legal battle against racial segregation did so amid the rising tide of Afro-Southern migration to the region. The increasing number of these individuals changed local culture and created greater class and cultural conflict within the African American community. Despite the community's internal conflicts, however, they shared a common foe, working tirelessly against the pervasive influence of racial segregation in their daily lives. Legal victories sustained the hopes of this leadership class, even as the shadow of the Great Depression hung over the entire city.

First Community AME Church youth choir. Courtesy of Grand Rapids History and Special Collections Center, Archives, Grand Rapids Public Library, Grand Rapids, Mich.

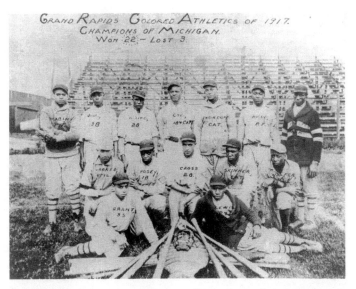

Colored Athletics, 1917. Courtesy of Grand Rapids History and Special Collections Center, Archives, Grand Rapids Public Library, Grand Rapids, Mich.

Attorney Oliver Green. Courtesy of
Bentley Historical Library, University of Michigan.

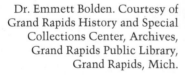

Dr. Emmett Bolden. Courtesy of
Grand Rapids History and Special
Collections Center, Archives,
Grand Rapids Public Library,
Grand Rapids, Mich.

Omega Psi Phi chapter, University of Michigan, 1923. Included in the photo are Floyd Skinner, Cortez English, Eugene Alston, and Robert Reed of Grand Rapids. Courtesy of Bentley Historical Library, University of Michigan.

Grand Rapids NAACP chapter, circa 1920s. Courtesy of Grand Rapids History and Special Collections Center, Archives, Grand Rapids Public Library, Grand Rapids, Mich.

Attorney Floyd Skinner. Courtesy of Local History Department, Grand Rapids Public Library, Grand Rapids, Mich.

Helen Jackson Claytor. Courtesy of Grand Rapids History and Special Collections Center, Archives, Grand Rapids Public Library, Grand Rapids, Mich.

Paul I. Phillips. Courtesy of Local History Department, Grand Rapids Public
Library, Grand Rapids, Mich.

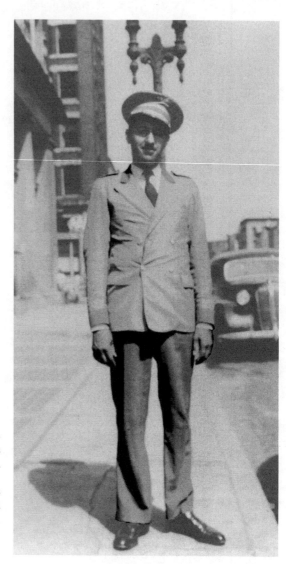

William Glenn. Courtesy of Grand Rapids History and Special Collections Center, Archives, Grand Rapids Public Library, Grand Rapids, Mich.

5 "Southern Negroes Flock to Michigan": Social Welfare and Northern Migration

On June 26, 1923, a short article, from the Associated Press wire service appeared in the *Grand Rapids Press*. Titled "Southern Negroes Flock to Michigan," the article said that a "report received by the state administrative board from L. Whitney Watkins, commissioner of agriculture, and Carl Young, labor commissioner, states that the influx of southern Negroes into Michigan is creating a difficult situation . . . southern lynching laws, the activities of the Ku Klux Klan and the unrest prevalent among young Negroes since the World War is sending them into Michigan industrial centers by hundreds. It recommended that the administrative board authorize a committee to proceed with a survey and the preparations to take care of the Negro population." According to the article, the report recommended "[T]hat Negro farm colonies be established in certain parts of the state. That immigration of the Negroes be discouraged. That some state body be authorized to keep in close touch with the welfare of Negroes." The article concluded by stating, "that some southern states are becoming alarmed at the departure of Negroes and the consequent effect it may have upon the southern labor situation."[1] The state report observed two salient features of African American migration into Michigan. It highlighted racial violence in the South as a factor. It also mentioned the heightened ideological militancy among Negroes in the wake of World War I.[2]

Afro-Southern migrants who settled in the city throughout the 1920s languished behind the great wave of European immigrants pouring into the city in late nineteenth and early twentieth centuries.[3] Although employment opportunities were not as great in Grand Rapids as they were in other cities from 1915 to 1945, the community's African American population grew steadily.[4] In 1910, the United States Census reported that there were 659 Negroes in the city, making up 0.7 percent of the total population. By 1930, the Negro population was 2,795. Over the decade of the Great Depression, the population decreased to 2,600, but by the end of World War II the population had tripled in size. Although the initial migrant population in the city was not large compared to the city's total population, it was sizable enough to transform the African American community.[5]

The arrival of new migrants exacerbated tensions between those who wanted social welfare programs and those who thought fighting Jim Crow laws and customs was paramount. The chief concern of some local black leaders, women leaders, and especially the clergy, was finding healthy social outlets for men, women, and children. They wanted an environment that stimulated the intellectual, spiritual, moral, and employment aspirations of ordinary black people. Given the general social and economic weaknesses within Afro-American civil society, this concern was extremely important. In a similar ideological vein as Booker T. Washington, these black leaders believed that the impoverished state of the blacks warranted that more attention be focused on the black community's internal needs. If the black community was going to be respected and have self-respect, these leaders theorized, the community must nurture individuals worthy of respect through institutions and agencies that trained people to be respectable. The badge of respectability was not defined through the lens of political economy but by behavior.[6] With the coming of Southern migrants, the debate between those focusing on the internal needs and those fighting exclusionary laws only intensified.

The dispute about social welfare had a range of meanings. The core of the debate focused on the meaning of urban respectability. What did it mean to live successfully in an urban environment? What were the proper protocols for city life? How could African Americans overcome the stigma of racial segregation and fully integrate into the various strata of the city? In essence, what were the best ways to assimilate the population into the life of the city? Was creating all-black institutions the best way? Would these institutions perpetuate Jim Crow practices? Underlying this discussion was a fear that African Americans would continue to languish as the working poor. Impoverishment was a source of shame and was associated with the servitude of sharecropping and the unhealthiness of underemployment. Those who looked internally at the black community felt that the only way to achieve communal social recognition was to modify the behavior of a poor community through social, cultural, and religious activities.

Afro-Southern migrants to the city found themselves trying to assimilate into an already struggling black community. The civil institutions created locally by African Americans in the nineteenth century were culturally important, but they were also economically vulnerable and politically weak. While many families purchased homes, there was no sizable, affluent middle class, no truly wealthy people inside the African American community. Nearly all of the black families in the city were in the laboring classes. At the upper end were the railroad porters, chauffeurs, gardeners, and maids of prominent white families. At the lower end were the day laborers, washerwomen, and vice workers. In 1915, there was only one African American professional in Grand Rapids—a physician, Dr. Eugene Browning. Like all laboring people in the city, African Americans were subjected to the vulnerabilities of underemployment, work slowdowns, work-related physical disabilities, and poverty. The increase of Afro-Southern migration, however, put even more pressure on a vulnerable community.

Although the "old timers" wrestled with the "ways" of Southern newcomers, they nevertheless responded to the needs of their kith and kin that trickled into the city. Most African Americans had a Southern heritage somewhere in their families, but they no longer embodied an explicit and open Southern culture. In fact, they perceived themselves as urbane and Northern compared to the Southern migrants who were arriving in the city. In the mind of the established black community in Grand Rapids, then, social largesse required them to protect and guide their newly arriving Southern kinfolk.

The first leaders who responded to the influx of the new population were women, whose efforts centered primarily on attempting to alleviate the difficulties faced by young women arriving from the South, the lower Midwest, and nearby agricultural counties (Cass, Allegan, and Ottawa) to take jobs as domestic servants in the city. In 1907, Mrs. M. R. Groggins, Eva McConnell, J. A. Crockett, and Allevia Wallace incorporated the Richard Allen Home for Colored Girls. Following the pattern set by churches, club women, and social workers all over the United States,[7] the Allen Home had four stated objectives: "To protect the girl coming to the city in search of employment; to raise the standard of domestic service, and recognize it as a profession; to bring out girls together that they may realize their worth as a true woman; and to provide suitable accommodations for lady transits."[8] Groggins and her cohorts organized the home because social agencies such as the local YMCA and YWCA, despite numerous complaints by black civic leaders, continued to unfairly exclude African Americans from utilizing their services. Like a character out of Thomas Hardy's novel *Tess of D'Urbervilles,* Groggins set out to meet female newcomers and prevent them from suffering the misfortunes of city life.

Many women activists believed that a community center would help put an end to the parochial resentments and brutish fights within the African American community.[9] Groggins had known this before the rising influx of Afro-Southerners into the city, and now the needs were even more pressing. She had recognized the problem both as a woman and a mother, and as a civic leader attempting to uplift her race. The welfare of children and families was a prominent concern for many women who worked outside the home.[10]

Long before the establishment of the Urban League in Grand Rapids,[11] women such as Grace Craig Simms, a registered nurse, began establishing a healthcare network for infants. In 1923, Simms and Dr. Eugene Browning founded the Lincoln Clinic at the First Community AME Church, where local pediatricians volunteered their medical services to African American parents. Simms served the clinic for fifteen years.[12] Women like Simms and Groggins worked to meet migrants with tangible and practical programs to enhance the life chances of their community; they viewed their actions both as civic responsibility and a religious duty.

For sixteen hundred dollars, the women also purchased, with the assistance of "white friends," the Richard Allen Home for Colored Girls, which had limped along for five years, beset with financial difficulties and ideological disputes that centered on segregation. The women discovered, however, that sustaining both the mortgage and the programming of the home proved to be difficult.[13] Some viewed the Allen Home as supporting racial segregation because it existed solely for the benefit of African Americans. To its supporters, however, the Allen Home was an agency of self-help and racial pride. In 1912, after considerable debate among community leaders, the Allen Home's board reorganized it as a social center. However, echoing the demise of other social work houses in the city (such as the Bissell House),[14] the Allen Home eventually failed.[15] Nevertheless, women leaders and clergymen in the city continued their advocacy for a social center.[16] As the population of African Americans grew, the pressure to find constructive outlets for children and adults also grew in kind.

In 1917, Rev. O. L. Murphy, pastor of the Messiah Baptist Church, estimated that the city's African American population had increased to twenty-seven hundred, and he speculated that this increase would result in "a large number of waste farms in Michigan" that would be "worked by Negroes on shares."[17] Although Murphy's prediction was hyperbolic, the arrival of Afro-Southerners did necessitate, at least in the eyes of the black community's leadership, the formation of centers that would assist these migrants in their adjustment to life in Grand Rapids.

It had long been perceived by clergymen and women activists that urban life, without strict guidance, might make children and naïve adults indolent and prone to vice. The temptations of the city could be over-whelming to those without a moral compass—the seemingly easy path of vice, they felt, was a great lure to the unsophisticated mind. Vices such as alcohol abuse and gambling lured the young and trapped them in worlds they could never escape. Community leaders, therefore, felt they needed a social alternative to the restless seduction of the alley and street corner—an alternative that stimulated the minds and developed the broader interests of community folk.

The rising migrant population increased the number of African American churches in Grand Rapids. At the beginning of the twentieth century, approximately four small congregations served African Americans in the city. After World War I, the number of churches doubled. In the 1920s, Afro-Christians founded True Light Baptist Church, Pilgrim Rest Baptist Church, Church of God, Saints of Christ Church, and other smaller storefront and house-based congregations.[18] Sarah "Sweetie" Glover, a Southerner who migrated to the city in 1922 and was a founding member of the True Light Baptist Church, observed that the few churches she visited were all staid. She said that people like herself wanted to "hear their churches in their own voices."[19] That is, Afro-Southerners wanted to have churches that reflected their social and religious sensibilities.

Reverend C. O. Murphy, the pastor of the St. Luke AME Zion Church, sought to capitalize on needs of migrants by seeking donations from white clergy to assist in building two large churches in the African American community. He contended that "Negroes should in the main, attend Negro churches."[20] And African Americans did, but not in the way Murphy suggested. Afro-Southerners built churches that represented many values in their lives: their class orientation, their particular Southern region, and their expressive worship style. While pastors such as Murphy believed that having two large churches would be advantageous to the African American community as whole, Afro-Southerners thought otherwise, creating many different churches that reflected their spiritual and regional values.

Even before the large influx of Southern migrants into Grand Rapids, African American congregations had been in furious competition with one another. By 1922, for example, at least two of the older congregations—St. Philip's Episcopal and First Community AME—had constructed new buildings with a block of each other.[21] In a 1928 survey of Grand Rapids conducted by the National Urban League (NUL), author R. Maurice Moss wrote that "the completion of First Community AME was contributed [sic] to many white supporters who hoped the Church would serve the entire Negro population." Warily, however, he cautioned that the "white supporters" had not taken into consideration the strong denominational loyalty among African Americans. Nor had they considered that the AME church was not in the same geographic blocks where the majority of African Americans were clustered.[22]

Messiah Baptist Church, which abutted the AME Church, completed their building in 1928. Less than a mile southwest of these churches, St. Luke AME Zion Church continued to seek out funds to complete its renovations. Not only did these churches try to serve new migrants— and longtime members—through building improvements, but they also attempted new mission congregations among Southern migrants.[23] The growth of these new church buildings and congregations caused both white and black civic leaders to be concerned.

In 1919, Rev. Henry Beets, editor of *The Banner* magazine, the denominational weekly of the Christian Reformed Church, described religious tensions between the old and new settlers within the African American community:

> It is said that within the last few years the Negro population of Grand Rapids has trebled. That brings various *problems*. For one thing, the old and newer colored populations of our northern cities do not mix easily. Socially they are quit different. And also religiously. The newcomers, from Southern country districts largely are used to shouting and strongly emotional exhortations called preaching, of the farmer-preachers of the South. Many of them appear to be ignorant and shiftless. At least the Northern Negroes accused them of this. On the other, hand, the Southern Negroes claims that the Negro of the North has lost his religious

fervor. This leads to the importation of some of the Southern preachers and the organization of rival churches.[24]

Beets understood that there were cultural and class differences among African Americans in the city—and that these were reflected in how they understood the role of their congregations.

John Burgess, a future bishop in the Episcopal Church, grew up in St. Philip's Episcopal Church. He also acknowledged the cultural divide that appeared among the African American community. He recalled:

> The sterility of this superficial identification with the white community became dramatically apparent with the advent into our city of Southern Negroes after World War I. No welcome mat awaited them for either black or white groups. Shunted off into the area around the railroad tracks, they found little warmth in churches, fraternal organizations, or social groups. Parents cautioned us about "those new people"; high school students were embarrassed by the dress and the behavior of their newly-arrived companions. Unaware that the white community had, for generations, classified us as Negroes and therefore "different," we were afraid that these new people would create a "problem" and we would all be the object of the white man's displeasure. It can be said that the Negro community, though its reluctance to take leadership in helping migrants to adjust to their new surroundings, was largely responsible for the many problems that did ensue.[25]

Four years later, in 1923, the *Grand Rapids Press* commented on the education of the Negro clergyman. The newspaper contended that the three mainline Negro churches—Messiah Baptist, St. Philip's Episcopal, and First Community AME Church—were "a credit to the race and the new church buildings recently erected can compete splendidly with the white man's church." The editorial continued: "Most of the Negro preachers, especially in the northern states, are earnest and fairly intelligent men who are trying to give their people that leadership which will help the race to a respected place in the life of our nation. One of the biggest problems facing the Negro churches is that of obtaining an educated ministry. About 1,600 men are needed every year and at the present time, there are only four hundred students in Negro seminaries preparing for the ministry. The result is that many untrained men are entering the Negro ministry every year and the intelligent Negroes of our northern cities deplore this situation."[26]

The editorial went on to suggest that the solution to the lack of clergy education could be solved through correspondence courses between African American colleges and clergy. The *Press* editorial was not inaccurate:

concerns about the poor education of the clergy had been a post-Reconstruction issue articulated by many educators and leaders, ranging from Carter G. Woodson to Booker T. Washington. However, Afro-Southerners continued to support their local clergymen, whether ill-prepared or not, because they were indigenous leaders who spoke the familiar language of the South.

The churches of the migrants, such as True Light Baptist and New Hope Baptist, were driven by men and women with their own sense of respectability, which neither African American leaders nor white press editorial writers understood.[27] These men and women put a great deal of effort into building churches as extensions of themselves and their own communal values. According to one scholar, the relationships built in these churches were part of the complex balancing act that migrants had to navigate in order to rebuild their networks of family and friends from the South.[28] At the onset of the Great Depression, there were six new Negro churches in the city, the largest of which were Baptist.[29]

Scholars have pointed out the importance of religion in the great migration,[30] emphasizing its significance for migrants and for those who established black churches in the North. The culture of established Northern black churches was challenged, and churches started by the Afro-Southerners provided parishioners continuity and support to make the transition from South to North. African American Southerners took refuge in churches when they wearied of being a minority in their new white world. Through their congregations, Afro-Southerners changed the religious landscape of local black culture. The old churches either joined them in praise or faced a slow extinction.

The growth of black churches ran parallel with the employment opportunities and brewing labor tensions in the city and around the country.[31] In 1917, the American Cement and Plaster Company hired forty African Americans from East St. Louis, Illinois, as replacement workers for fifty Italian workers who went on strike.[32] The newspaper reported that the cause of the strike was not over wages or working conditions, but rather over the company's firing of the officers of a newly formed union.[33] Since there are no interviews with the Italian or the African American miners themselves, we do not know the extent of the animosity between these two ethnic communities.[34] We do know, however, that these forty African American laborers escaped the explosive race riot in East St. Louis that occurred only weeks after their arrival in Grand Rapids.[35]

In 1919, the tensions between white ethnics and blacks ran so high around the United States that Rev. Henry Beets, in an article titled "How to Solve the Negro Problem," commented that "Negro[es] of the North were engaged in largely menial work and kept out of the labor market. They were porters, chauffeurs, servant girls, etc. But the newcomers from the South are shopworkers, at least many of them."[36] The desire for well-paying industrial jobs was fervent for many in the African American community, not those just from the South. However, the manufacturing plants of World War I continued their paternalistic relationship with white ethnic workers. Only when whites refused to cooperate did companies such as the American Cement and Plaster Company hire black workers. This hiring strategy fostered animosity between various ethnic communities and allowed employers to discriminate against African Americans without just cause or punishment. The African American newcomers had to take the grimmest jobs in industrial workforce, such as those in the plaster mines. These were the most physically taxing jobs—and the most susceptible to layoffs. There was little recourse for these workers. "Labor Unions do not care to absorb these people," Beets observed. "Only here and there have they been admitted to membership. . . . Unorganized labor also looks askance at the colored worker." According to Beets, the explosions of race riots between 1911 and 1919 were a disgrace, "strain[ing] relationships nearly everywhere."[37]

Beets's observations confirmed what R. Maurice Moss found in his survey of the African American population. Moss reviewed the major manufacturing employers within the city and discovered that, in total, only sixty-three African Americans were employed by the seventy-four largest firms. For example, the largest employer in his group—the Hayes-Ionia Company, manufacturer of automobile bodies—employed no African Americans in its eighteen-hundred-member workforce.

The largest employer of African Americans was the Pere Marquette Railroad Company, which "utilized roughly one hundred and fifty men in its shops."[38] Moss interviewed the superintendent of the company, Mr. Griffith, who explained that labor troubles caused the company "to start a vigorous open shop policy in opposition to the unions."[39] As in the plaster mines, black laborers often benefited from such labor tensions, but in this case the black laborers also benefited the rail company by keeping the wages down. When there were no labor tensions in the city, however, African Americans generally remained underemployed by local industry. For instance, the city's other rail company, the Michigan Central Rail Road, employed no black workers.

"Industrially, the Negro in Grand Rapids is plainly laboring under several handicaps," Moss wrote. He noted five of them. First, the jobs that most African American workers were hired to do required "little or no preparation. As a consequence, the wages for the work which they perform [are] low." Second, the utilities and the public service sectors hired no African Americans. He wrote that there were "no colored employees on the street railway lines as motormen, conductors, etc." Third, not only were African Americans in the lowest paid jobs, but they were also "in those that are most affected by the seasons. Common labor and construction workers suffer greatly through loss of employment due to seasonal changes in the amount of work." Fourth, there was no systematic employment placement for potential African American employees, as most gained employment through word of mouth or personal relationships, "or tramp[ing] from place to place until hired." Finally, there were few employment opportunities for high school graduates. Moss warned, "If Grand Rapids fails to make provision for these young people on whose preparation the city is spending its money, they have no alternative but to seek opportunities elsewhere. The city can ill afford to have its more educated Negro youth desert it, while only those who are satisfied with the unfortunate conditions remain."[40]

The organizations that most closely resembled labor unions were the Association of Hotel Employees and the Chauffeurs Club.[41] Unfortunately, these organizations served more as social clubs than as collective bargaining agents.[42] In the domestic sector, labor negotiations were based on the paternalism of the white hotel owners. Though individual acts of kindness by owners should not be dismissed, their generosity did not compensate for the financial difficulty that many African American families faced.

The slow process of gaining industrial employment and the chronic underemployment among African Americans created a constant social welfare crisis within the community. Poor wages and economic marginalization created the need for a social welfare agency before advent of the Great Depression. The community had real needs: poverty was a constant in the lives of many people in the city, especially African Americans.

Racial tensions never reached the intensity of those found in larger, neighboring cities. Rather, the influx of new migrants created heightened anxieties for whites who feared African American social mobility, particularly with regard to housing.[43] In 1923, forty-three white citizens, led by Thane H. Ives, came before the Grand Rapids City Commission, protesting that African Americans had moved onto their block.[44] In another case, Joseph Nasser, along with thirty-two other white citizens, complained to the city commission about African Americans living on their street. As a result of such perceived threats, acts of racial intimidation occurred. True Light Baptist Church, then the fastest growing African American congregation, was attacked by an unidentified arsonist.[45]

The awareness among whites about African American migration north was heightened by the most popular radio show of the 1920s, "Amos 'n' Andy."[46] The locally owned radio station, WOOD, even started its own version of this nationally syndicated show, calling theirs "Sambo and Abie."[47] Ironically, in 1930, the Keith Theater—the theater in the Emmett Bolden case—hosted the two white radio personalities, Charles Correl and Freeman Gosden, who played Amos and Andy dressed in blackface to a sold-out, all-white audience.

The African American population grew throughout the city and the state in the 1920s. In 1926, the Reverend Robert Bagnall of Detroit described, to readers of *The Messenger*, the challenges of Michigan's newest residents. He noted that with the arrival of Afro-Southerners in Detroit, discrimination and racial violence intensified. Bagnall asserted that the "Negro is destined to play a large part in the life of Michigan. He is yet in a period of storm and stress. Just how big that part shall be, no man can say."[48]

The following year, 1927, the Bureau of Negro Welfare, a subdivision of the Michigan Department of Labor and Industry, sounded more ominous than Bagnall. A 1927 bureau press release stated: "That the Negro is the helpless victim caught in the strong grasp of the economic whirlpool, is the opinion advanced by officials of the State Bureau of Negro Welfare at Lansing. In the role as such victim he is buffeted by prejudice in industry and society in general, and by the avarice of landlords; is denied, too frequently, the hand of succor that might ordinarily be expected from welfare and public health agencies, and the protection due him from his municipal, state and national government."[49]

Throughout Michigan, the problem of welfare and migration generated even more discussion. On October 21, 1927, the State Bureau of Negro Welfare met in Detroit at its annual conference. George M. Smith, representing Grand Rapids, estimated the Negro population to be anywhere "from 3,000 to 5,000." He also noted that among Negroes, there was no "appreciable amount of employment in factories." "Negroes," he reported, "are almost entirely confined to street and hotel work." The reports from the smaller cities in Michigan echoed Smith's report.[50]

The smoldering racial tensions in other regional cities in the wake of migration caused concern in Grand Rapids and led to renewed discussions between white and black leaders over conditions within the African American community. In 1926, Charlotte Donnell, the general secretary of the Family Service Association (FSA), a Grand Rapids social welfare agency, wrote to Eugene Kinckle Jones of the National Urban League (NUL) for advice.[51] The FSA had been in contact with John Dancy of the Detroit Urban League, who encouraged them to use the expertise of the NUL. Donnell's letter to Jones explained that the FSA had become interested "in the changing conditions among the colored people," which "led to the formation of an inter-racial group which for the time being has designated itself as Community Service Committee." "The immediate objective," she wrote, "was plans for some sort of study of the colored community here and the use of such information as was gathered to study the needs of that community more satisfactorily." Donnell stated there was "no critical situation here but the community has, of course, increased greatly in size and the leaders among the colored people, as well as the social service organizations, of this city are anxious that growing needs be met in order that if possible any tenseness may be averted."[52]

In June 1927, the Community Service Committee and the Interdenominational Union, a Negro ecumenical organization, formed the Interracial Council. The Interracial Council followed the traditional pattern of social welfare organizing from the late nineteenth century and was born of black and white women's Protestant church networks. The objective of the committee was to "address the recreational needs of young colored people." The council appointed Ethel Burgess, Mrs. Thomas E. Jefferson, Vivian Gould, Daniel B. Lampkins, and C. C. Stillman as a committee to draw up a plan of action. On July 21, 1927, the committee, headed by Ethel Burgess, concluded that a survey should be carried out to "study the colored population" of Grand Rapids.[53]

Burgess then corresponded with Eugene Jones, again inquiring about a possible survey of the black community. She recollected that Mary Jackson of the national board of the YWCA had done a survey of the black community in 1918, which showed "total population 200 families, 900 individuals, resident in Grand Rapids." She stated that the "current belief at present is that the colored population is between 4,500 and 5,000, located for the most part in two sections of the city, the east and the west." Burgess explained that "five churches which have carried on most of the work done for colored young people, but is felt that possibly an interdenominational paid worker for young people should soon be sought and this is the immediate objective of the survey."[54]

Jones wrote back to Burgess saying that the NUL would be "pleased to undertake the survey of the Negro population of Grand Rapids." Jones offered the services of Charles Johnson, the director of Department of Research and Investigations (once he completed a similar study in Fort Wayne, Indiana) at the cost of four hundred dollars to Grand Rapids.[55]

A month later, Charles Stillman, the secretary of the Grand Rapids Welfare Union, an organization that distributed funds to social service agencies, wrote to Jones at the NUL headquarters. Stillman extended an invitation for Jones to come to Grand Rapids and address Negro and white leaders. In his invitation, he repeated what Donnell and Burgess had stated in their previous correspondence with Jones: "We want advice on the whole problem of organizing our forces for intelligent provision by our colored people to promote their own community interests."[56] Jones accepted the invitation and visited the city on September 22, 1927.

According to the *Grand Rapids Press*, Jones reiterated the sentiments of many in the community that African Americans needed their own social center outside the white community. "It is possible in America today for people of one race to find contentment and happiness in opportunities offered by every race for human expression and activities." Jones suggested that having "a colored social worker in Grand Rapids to assist in providing social expression for its colored people" might be helpful. He explained, "Wherever the Negro population of 1,000 or more is recorded, there is a need for a special Negro social worker."[57] Eight days after his visit, some members of the Interracial Council had taken Jones speech to heart, recommending that "a Grand Rapids branch of the National Urban League be organized for the promotion of social work among colored people, that a trained Negro social worker be employed and that the Grand Rapids Urban League, if and when organized, be made of a member of the Welfare union."[58]

The call for a Grand Rapids Urban League created a philosophical firestorm for the absolute integrationists. In a letter to Jones, Stillman wrote, "One of our negro friends, present at the meeting called for actual organization of the League, got off on the question of segregation and instituted a debate which did little to further the cause for which the meeting was called."[59] There were two different tactics at work among the black leadership in the city. Men like George Smith, Emmett Bolden, and the young lawyer, Floyd Skinner, were ardent integrationists. They believed that self-segregation was just as bad as the policies of formal and informal Jim Crow. For them, the proposed social center for blacks would serve only to revive the practice of customary Jim Crow. It was clear from the debates over the National Urban League proposal that two different philosophies had emerged. Some activists, influenced by Booker T. Washington, followed a pragmatic, self-help, work-ethic model.

Others, influenced by the civil rights protest ideas put forth by W. E. B. Du Bois, were resistant to segregation in any form.[60] On December 28, Ida W. Wilson, the chair of the Interracial Council, sought out the wisdom of W. E. B. Du Bois in the matter. In a letter, Wilson told Du Bois of the work of the Interracial Council that was "working for the betterment of the Negro population of about 5,000 and other residents of the city." She then sought Du Bois's advice on establishing an Urban League in the city. The other concern was "whether we should favor separate YMCA and YWCA buildings to meet the needs of colored people." In her letter, Wilson acknowledged that these centers were segregated and that local blacks were split regarding how best to address the needs of the community and the problem of segregation. In a postscript, Wilson invited Du Bois to the city in the spring.[61]

Du Bois willingly accepted her invitation to speak in the city and offered a short standard for judging the issue of segregation. "I would not like to express my judgment concerning a racial policy in a city that I know practically nothing about. I am opposed to racial segregation as a principle but I am compelled to recognize it continually as a fact. How, where and when principle can be successfully defended must, of course, be a matter of judgment among those who know all the circumstances."[62]

Meanwhile, correspondence with Eugene Kinckle Jones continued. Writing on behalf of the Interracial Council, Alice Yonkman, a white member of the council and the current general secretary of the Family Service Association, inquired once again about the cost of a NUL survey. Her letter, too, reflected the torn sentiments among African American civic leaders concerning the Urban League. She wrote: "There is a feeling here for and against the Urban League. We are not in the least certain that a branch of the Urban League will meet our needs but we do feel that much depends on the type of person undertaking the study. His or her personality, familiarity with the weaknesses and strength of the Urban League and other organizations, method of approach and ability to establish contact, will be a large factor in creating feeling for or against any movement or decision."[63]

Several months later, W. E. B. Du Bois traveled to Grand Rapids to address the Interracial Council regarding the history of the Negro in the United States. He told the audience at the Trinity Methodist Church that African Americans had contributed to the United States as agricultural laborers on cotton, sugar, tobacco, and rice plantations. He stated that Negroes constituted 13 percent of the Union forces in the Civil War—and that the percentage of African American men in the army was higher

than the total percentage of African Americans in the American population. He also pointed out that African Americans contributed to the
shaping of democracy and art. He concluded his speech with supportive
remarks about interracial cooperation: "It is significant that the institutions started by the Negro in this country have been maintained through
the years, and it is also interesting to note that whites and Negroes are
appearing together in several of the most popular plays now being produced in New York." Du Bois wisely avoided the squabble over which
organization best represented the interest of African Americans locally,
leaving the decision in the hands of community leaders.[64]

On May 27, 1928, Charles S. Johnson, who managed a one-day visit,
and R. Maurice Moss of the National Urban League held a mass meeting
at the First Community AME Church to begin the process of gathering
information for the survey commissioned by the Interracial Council.
Moss, under the supervision of Johnson, had been assigned the survey. He
spent approximately two weeks gathering the data in the city. Directed
by the Interracial Council and the Grand Rapids Welfare Union, he con-
ferred with a small collective of African American leaders, visited the
"leading officials" of fourteen companies, and met with twenty-seven
various social agencies—from the YMCA and the local hospitals to the
Legal Aid Bureau. He also held mass meetings in the four primary black
churches, Messiah Baptist, Community AME, St. Philip's, and True Light
Baptist.[65] Moss intended the survey to be comprehensive as possible,
given the time constraints.

Moss found that Grand Rapids was the forty-seventh largest city in
the United States. It was a city with a diversified manufacturing base.
"Unfortunately little of authoritative value can be found concerning of
the Negro in Grand Rapids. Most of [its] history must be judged from
observation and from accounts of old residents," he wrote. Moss stated
that "the major industries are those into which few Negroes have been
introduced and domestic service has not been large." He accounted for
this lack of industrial employment by noting that "Grand Rapids was *on
the road to nowhere else* and the itinerant worker was not apt to *stop off*
in the city to settle here."[66] The total growth of the African American
population bore out this comment.[67]

Moss attributed the size of the city's African American population
to the lack of employment opportunities, even in the domestic sector.
He discovered an "even" sex ratio among black men and women, 555
males to 535 females. From this ratio, he concluded, "In communities

where there is a demand for the domestic worker the percentage of Negro women is much higher than that of men. The figures would show that this field of work is not open on a large scale to Negro women in Grand Rapids." However, if black women were not employed in great numbers, neither were black men.

Moss dealt empirically with concerns about the total African American growth in the city, noting, "The size of the present Negro population of Grand Rapids is a much disputed matter locally. Conscious of new faces in the community, observing more houses held by members of their race, noting new accessions to church and lodge, and hoping for greater political influence, Negro leaders place the figures rather high." White civic leaders, he believed, were "influenced by the increasingly vocal group among their colored friends, [and this] also places the figures high." The population was estimated to be anywhere from fifteen hundred to five thousand. After checking varying local records, he concluded that "the Negro population of Grand Rapids in June 1928 was very close to 2,400." The black population had grown in size two and half times from 1920, even though it remained small.

The limited demographic questionnaire Moss used indicated that the African American population had come from a variety of places in the Great Lakes region, the Southeast, and the Deep South; however, the survey did not indicate whether they had come from cities or rural communities. When he asked why they moved to Grand Rapids, most respondents said that they were "looking for better conditions." And, in fact, the majority of the families surveyed expressed a degree of contentment with living in the city. Moss wrote that if there were more "industrial opportunities assured," more African Americans might have moved to the city.

Moss paid close attention to housing patterns in the city. He reported that there had been some effort to steer and "prevent the Negro from buying and living in certain neighborhoods." Rental housing also proved difficult to obtain in particular areas. Moss noted that restrictive covenants (property deeds that prevented sellers from selling homes to a specified ethnic or religious people) made it difficult for blacks to purchase certain homes. However, he also observed that the "Negro is fortunate in that he does not live in one well-defined segregated district which is easy to over look when streets are paved or when they are cleaned and when the garbage and trash collectors make their rounds." He indicated that there was no "black belt" and "even in the blocks most heavily populated by Negro members other races are to be found."[68]

Moss outlined three sections of the city where African Americans lived. The streets of Wealthy, Market, Cherry, and Division (including King Court) bound the first section; Franklin, Buchanan, Buckley and Jefferson, the second; Franklin, Union, Wealthy, and Fuller, the third. He estimated that 580 Negroes lived in section one, 500 in section two, and 920 in section three. Approximately 400 Negroes lived outside the areas of the embryonic ghetto. He reported that, overall housing was good, with the bulk of the African Americans living in single frame dwellings. However, the newcomers and the poorer African Americans lived on the southwest side along the railroad tracks. "This entire section has an old appearance," Moss wrote, describing this area as having the King Street railroad tracks running through the backyards of many of the homes and "within a few feet of the houses." This section of the city also had "no fence to protect the children who play in these yards, although there is a fence on the opposite side of the track to protect a coal pile." Moss noted that the area of Commerce Street from Goodrich to Bartlett contained ill-maintained buildings and the slum property owned by Globe Knitting Mills, a local manufacturer that allowed the property to deteriorate so they could tear it down and enlarge their plant. Though the property was in disrepair, the company generated rents from it. The other area with an increasing black population was the Miller-Grant-Graham district east of the railroad tracks. These streets, "together with the Commerce Street district," Moss wrote, figured "frequently in police records for gambling and other offences."[69]

Moss noted proudly that African Americans "east of Division Street in section II and the scattered Negro homes are, almost without exception, in excellent condition. . . . These Negro homes compare favorably with the best homes of the middle class and are a credit to the race and the city." Although Moss did not mention the number of African American homeowners living in this section of the city, he presumed it to be high. In the poorer sections, the percentages of people who owned their homes were small; but even in those sections, there were homeowners. He also noted that there were no "building and loan associations or other organizations for encouraging home buying among Negroes, but several individual Negroes have purchased property through five white associations in the city." In the 1920s, the housing pattern in the city was not large enough for a spatial ghetto; however, the seeds of ghettoization were sprouting.

The negative consequences of the seedling ghetto and the unsteady employment of African Americans were apparent in Moss's description of crime. He discovered that of the total arrests in 1927 "for all crimes, Negroes furnished 262, or 7.6 percent of the total arrest [sic]." He concluded that Negroes were "no more than 1.4 percent of the total population" and "figured in police records from five to six times as frequently as their percentage of the population would warrant." Additionally, he observed "Negro women in 1927 furnished 16.6 percent of the total arrests of females."[70] Gambling offences accounted for most Negro arrests. (Although the newspapers often portrayed gambling as the sole province of African Americans, it was not. Among numerous low-wage earners, gambling was a vice to be exploited. The odds of making good money through gambling were about even with making a sustainable wage.) The next most frequent offense was the violation of liquor laws.[71] To keep vice in check, the city of Grand Rapids police department hired its first African American officer, Walter Coe, in 1922. Coe's job was to patrol the African American community and keep vice limited to their sectors of the city. According to local lore, for over thirty years Coe met the arriving train downtown at Union Station and inspected new arrivals for bad elements. His work never stopped local vice; it only checked it from extending into the greater white community.

One of the chief entrepreneurs in the early ghetto was Stanley Barnett, who owned two hotels near Union Station that boarded transient laborers and new arrivals. Barnett, who had lived in the city since 1902, allowed vice to flourish in and around his establishments. The other growing business in this area was Milo Brown's mortuary. Brown's success was not immediate, but as new arrivals (who were accustomed to segregation and African American morticians) came to the city, his business began to thrive. In fact, the growth of these businesses was accompanied by the success of smaller businesses such as barbershops and beauty salons and by the increase in the number of Negro professionals in the city.

By the 1920s, the geographical contour of the ghetto had been seeded. Racist public policy and inaction by white political leadership would water its growth.[72]

The problem with the ghetto was not that African Americans were clustered together; indeed, it was wise for them to live together for safety and cultural affinity. What was unfair was their physical, social, and political marginalization based on race, which limited their economic mobility. Integration, as a positive social philosophy, was not as important to them as wages. Whether they lived around whites was not central to blacks; what was central was having the freedom to build their own communities outside of the confines and control of white domination. They simply wanted economic and social opportunities that would enable them to control their own lives in the same way that other ethnic communities did.[73]

On the other hand, established black residents of Grand Rapids had grown up in the midst of a white community. They, too, sought to break the power of white domination over their lives. Living in an overwhelmingly white community, they realized, through personal and social interactions at school and in neighborhoods, that they were just as good as their white neighbors. Constant exclusion made them ashamed and angry. With the arrival of Southerner newcomers, African American leaders were pressured to fight racial segregation even more.

In his research for the National Urban League, R. Maurice Moss also uncovered the simmering resentment that African American leaders held toward the YMCA and YWCA. Moss wrote, "Justifiably or not, this is the issue which has overshadowed every other matter before the Interracial Council; the issue on which the most intense feeling has been aroused; the issue toward whose solution the least progress has been made." For longtime residents, the racially exclusive practices of the YMCA and YWCA were insulting, primarily because both organizations were purportedly guided by Christian principles. Moss summarized the feelings of these residents, stating, "The two associations should bear in mind that they cannot escape the moral obligation which is implied in their very names."[74] Also insulting to longtime residents was the fact that both organizations received public funding for providing community swimming pools. As taxpayers and citizens of the city, African Americans were justifiably irate at their exclusion. The leaders of the YMCA and YWCA recognized the racial exclusion, even freely admitting it to Moss. But they also confided in Moss their belief that if they opened their organizations to Negroes, they would be inundated by them, and this would result in "serious defections on the part of their present white membership."[75] They believed that if African American leaders were amenable to a compromise, the problem could be solved by building a separate social center, as other cities had done.

Moss, being diplomatic, attributed the fight between African Americans and the two organizations to a "misunderstanding on both sides." He wrote, "Negroes entertain the conception of these Associations as on a par with hotels, railroads, etc—that is, public affairs which should be open to every one on an equal basis and which, if necessary, may be forced by law to make available to Negroes their facilities." Moss, however, saw the Y as a private organization that could extend its membership to whomever it desired. Unwittingly, he repeated the same line of reasoning that the legal counsel for Grand Rapids Operating Corporation had used in arguing to keep local theater seating racially exclusive. Not surprisingly, "New Negroes" such as Floyd Skinner, Emmett Bolden, William Glenn, and George Smith, who had spent so much time fighting legal racial segregation, found this logic preposterous.

In the mind of the integrationist, the full equality and access had to be protected as a first principle in alleviating the immediate need for social services within the African American community, which argued for building a separate facility for blacks. On the other hand, black community leaders were in a constant fight to resist racial exclusion at every turn, and they saw the NUL position as one that compromised the constitutional rights of African Americans. Thus, while the black leadership fought the illegality of segregation, vast social issues went unaddressed. This tactical debate drove a wedge between an already divided leadership. By end of January 1929, the Grand Rapids Welfare Union had, in principle, recommended that "a trained colored social worker be obtained in order to promote racial understanding" and social activity among Negroes of the city.[76]

In February 1929, Charles Stillman of the Grand Rapids Welfare Union wrote again to Eugene Kinckle Jones to express his concerns about the NUL survey. Stillman had no major quarrels with Moss's work; in fact, he thought it "creditably done." But Stillman did not believe the nature of race relations in the city warranted the kind of investment that Moss recommended. He offered two reasons for the Welfare Union's hesitation over hiring a social worker: lack of money and the size of the African American population. He stated, "We are in no sense opposed to the employment of a colored worker but I am frank to say that I am not quite so sure about the need of one as I was before we started the survey."[77] The Welfare Union planned instead to support African American needs through volunteer efforts and churches. Stillman and the Welfare Union, however, did not take into consideration the denominational loyalties and divisions that had previously caused a schism among activists. In the end, the survey prevented the Welfare Union from having to take direct action.[78] White civic leaders, like their neo-abolitionist predecessors, believed that life in Grand Rapids was better for African Americans than in the South. And although they were correct to an extent, the city's demographic data would only worsen, and the future would demonstrate their shortsightedness.

In the spring of 1930, the Interracial Council recommended that the Welfare Union support an organization called the Grand Rapids Negro

Welfare Guild, whose purpose was "to have supervision over the welfare and recreation activities among colored residents [between the ages of 16 and 21]."[79] The justification for the guild's activity was the racial exclusivity of organizations such as the YMCA and YWCA. The Negro Welfare Guild received an endorsement from the Civic Round Table, a council of charitable organizations and business leaders, to raise three thousand dollars for its work. It was also recommended by the Civic Round Table that "the Welfare Union should determine whether such an activity should be supported permanently and whether the Negro Welfare Guild should be included among the constituent members of the Welfare Union."[80]

The plans for the Negro Welfare Guild rekindled a fight among African American leadership over integration. A May 17, 1930, *Grand Rapids Press* editorial sided with the integrationists in condemning this approach to Negro welfare. The *Press* argued that Grand Rapids social agencies were not uniformly racist and that African Americans were not totally excluded from public facilities such as playgrounds. With respect to the Civic Round Table's action, the editorial stated: "The theory itself is wrong, in the first place. Negroes do use the city services. This is still a northern town, not a Jim Crow town. Every Negro faces certain prejudices and embarrassments daily because of color, but compared to the segregated condition of his race in the south he is infinitely happier under conditions here. It will not help to relieve prejudice if he is forced to keep by himself. As one colored man of a high type expressed himself on the matter, *the worst thing a man has to bear is to have something forced upon him merely to get rid of him.*"

The paper cited several leading churches, the NAACP, Grand Rapids Study Club, and Pierian Club of Negro Women as opposing the Negro Welfare Guild. The editorial also invoked Moss's study to support its claim that the city's small African American population did not justify separate facilities. "Finally," the editorial stated, "the plan was not new in northern cities, where the community center either had failed, as in Flint, or had led to the far more serious segregation of a separate Negro school."[81]

Ethel Burgess, secretary of the Negro Welfare Guild, responded to the newspaper's editorial with a sixteen-point rebuttal. She asserted that there were members of the NAACP who were also members of the Negro Welfare Guild. She testily charged that the propaganda of the NAACP had badly influenced local clubs idea about the Welfare Guild and said that the "*Press* editorial had dodged our issue—*the constructive character-building program we wish to offer our young people. We wish supervised* recreation for their idle time." The work of the Negro Welfare Guild was to train young leadership: "It is only in organizations of his own race that the Negro youth is trained in leadership. It is rarely encouraged in our public schools."[82] She contended that white philanthropic support was needed for the establishment of a social center in the black community. Based on the NUL's survey, Burgess pressed for a community social worker who would be housed at the AME Church facility.

The logic of her argument was that ethnic civic associations were not considered Jim Crow organizations. She contended that the YMCA and YWCA raised money from the public at large and should serve all constituents who donate, regardless of color. Her challenge was that all youth organizations should serve children irrespective of their circumstances. "Only those who have devoted some of their lives to young people's work can fully appreciate the happiness and fellowship which comes from allowing them to have something of their own." In the end, Burgess desired a place where black children could have middle-class socialization. She thought that those who attacked the work of the Negro Welfare Guild ought to be more introspective and work harder for the black youth betterment. "We who are interested in the fourfold development of our boys and girls," Burgess wrote in conclusion to her rebuttal, "are the ones who realize its need; and we are not allowing ourselves to be influenced by denominational prejudices which are only human but not Christlike or by that certain group of radicals who are ever present in any community to try to crush any effort which to them does not seem perfectly ideal."[83] Burgess was unrelenting in her drive to serve the needs of black children.[84]

African American male professional leaders resisted the plans of the Negro Welfare Guild, painting them as a justification for Jim Crow.[85] The work of the Negro Welfare Guild and the effort to fight against racial discrimination were pitted against one another, as though one or the other were enough to resolve poverty or racial discrimination. This war always had to be fought on two fronts; in their squabbles, local leaders seemed to forget that both fronts were essential to what they were trying to achieve.

The voluntarist model of social welfare set up by the Grand Rapids Welfare Union and the Negro Welfare Guild was put on hold by the Great Depression.[86] The Depression not only slowed the rate of migration into Grand Rapids; between 1930 and 1940, the African American population actually declined. The source of African American welfare during the

Depression shifted from local private charities and social agencies to the federal and state government. The economic collapse of 1929 devastated the African American community in Grand Rapids and exacerbated their already-impoverished social conditions. Unfortunately, strategic divisions among black leaders concerning the best means for countering racial and economic inequality continued during this time as well.

6 The Making of the Brough Community Association: The Limits of Class and Interracial Cooperation

In the 1930s, a small, clustered ghetto had taken root in Grand Rapids. Afro-Southerners who found their way to Grand Rapids slowly joined the established black families in settling down, raising families, and building new churches. Although racked by poverty, the city's African American community continued to share and create an expressive culture of music and dance. Louis Armstrong, Ethel Waters, Bessie Smith, Robert Johnson, Duke Ellington, and Count Basie touched the African American community through the radio and in clubs like Frank Lamar's place, the Club Indigo, and in Idlewild, a vacation and leisure resort seventy miles north of the city.[1] Grand Rapids' black community was also thrilled and enraptured by the great revival preachers who crisscrossed throughout the North and the South, visiting black congregations and giving the faithful good news in an era of hard times. The rise of the "gospel blues" came from the hands of pianist "Georgia Tom," a.k.a. Thomas Dorsey, who sold Gospel music throughout black Baptist congregations in the United States.[2] During this time, some workers in Grand Rapids made their own heaven or hell laboring as athletes, bootleggers, numbers runners, and sex workers. These were jobs that paid. The vast majority of people worked continuously as day laborers or domestics; many others had to take any legitimate work they could find.

During these years, the leadership class of the community continued to press forward with its reformist agenda of full democratization for African American citizens in the areas of employment, education, housing, and labor. Organizations such as the NAACP, which showed such promise in the 1920s, struggled throughout the 1930s to keep any dues-paying members but also to keep the branch afloat.[3] Like the masses, the small group of professionals struggled to keep their heads above water.[4] Racial segregation and the meltdown of the economy made their world as unstable as the clientele they served.[5]

The Depression allowed radicalism to thrive briefly in the city. The Communist Party preached the rights of workers and the equality African Americans and working women.[6] Party members marched in the streets of Grand Rapids and were beaten, as they had been elsewhere. While the Communist Party did not capture the imaginations of most African Americans in the city, it did exert influence over a few, offering these individuals new ways to think about the problem of class and race and providing them with a fearless way of fighting against discrimination through collective action. Further, Communism offered an alternative view of history and social change—a view that encouraged working people to fight against the debility of economic hardships.[7] In a city so dominated by churches, the communists gave a clarion call—clearer than any congregation—on issues of racial and economic justice.

The labor movement and the organizing effort of the CIO had a negligible affect on African Americans in Grand Rapids until World War II. Unlike Detroit, where the numerical size of the black community gave it more political clout within the union movement, the African American community in Grand Rapids wielded no such influence.[8] What little labor movement there was in the city reflected Grand Rapids' conservative civic culture that constrained the growth of the labor movement. Captains of industry continued to maintain a strong paternalistic relationship with white workers, excluding African Americans from most manufacturing jobs.

Overall, during the Depression, African Americans joined people around the city in focusing on economic survival. Community leaders would challenge the dominant community when they were able. The bitter economy made the alliance between black and white civic leaders a necessity, even among those who thought this to be an embarrassment.

If there was a center of African American middle-class social life in Grand Rapids in the 1930s, it was St. Philip's Episcopal Church. Organized in 1911, the congregation was led by women who desired an Anglican expression of Christian worship for their families. Mrs. Calvin Grayson and several other women petitioned the local bishop, John McCormick, to establish an Episcopal Church for Negroes. Mrs. Grayson and Ida Stevenson networked among their friends, including Ethel Burgess, and acquired nineteen names representing families who desired this type of congregation. With the Bishop's approval, these women then organized the first Women's Guild of the Church and raised $110 to purchase the lot where the church stands today.[9] The Church's founding members were the "who's who" of respected Blacks in the city. While St. Philip's was never the largest African American congregation in the city, its educated members and clergy positioned it in the community as a local institutional leader. For its members, the congregation functioned both as a spiritual communion and a social center for light-skinned blacks and the aspiring middle class.[10]

Twenty years after its establishment, the congregation remained small and struggling, its organization supported by the Diocese of Western Michigan. In the church's early days, the Bishop John McCormick provided the mission with monthly pastoral leadership. What made St. Philip's particularly successful as an institution in the city was the educational level and constancy of its members, and the ability of the diocese to attract formally trained pastoral leadership. In 1920 the congregation called its first colored priest, Rev. Ellis A. Christian. Father Christian served the congregation until 1929, followed by Rev. M. E. Spatches, who led the congregation until 1933; Rev. John M. Burgess (a deacon under Spatches) succeeded Spatches in the summer of 1933. Burgess had grown up in St. Philip's congregation, and his parents, Theodore and Ethel Burgess, were charter members of the church.[11] At the time of the church's twenty-fifth anniversary in 1936, the congregation—with the assistance of the diocese—paid off its mortgage. In 1938, Rev. Burgess resigned from the congregation.

In February 1938, St Philip's called Rev. Jesse Anderson, from New York City, to be its priest.[12] Anderson brought with him a sensibility for social ministry, which he had cultivated while serving the St. Philip's Church in Harlem, and he quickly extended the youth outreach begun by Burgess in the church's undercroft. He also used the institutional muscle of St. Philip's to push the case for a social welfare agenda even further than his predecessor had. Writing in the June 1938 church newsletter, Father Anderson informed St. Philip's parishioners that the Social Service Council of Grand Rapids had appointed a commission to study the effects of the economic depression in the city. He reported:

> We are forced to wonder whether a Negro was appointed to that Commission. Though the Negro is a small minority here, still because of his economic status he looms large when it is a question of sociological problems. A disproportionate number of relief cases, inadequate housing (slums), insufficient recreational facilities make his plight a sad one. A town can be no richer than its poorest group of people. The Negroes' case is therefore one which must be studied and remedied. No one can understand Negroes better than a Negro. No one can come as close to his individual problems and needs as can a Negro. Surely there is some one man or woman of that race capable of serving such a commission. It would help the Negro. In the end, it would help Grand Rapids for it would raise the status of its minority group.[13]

Anderson—and many of his parishioners—believed that the church had a duty to promote the community's betterment. Further, they believed that because congregation held middleclass social aspirations, they best represented the interest of the entire African American community. Anderson also believed that African Americans could best articulate their own interests. To him, and to many others, St. Philip's was the best representative model of African American leadership in the city. Lewis Bliss Whittemore, the Bishop of the Diocese of Western Michigan, observed that St. Philip's had "obtained a position of leadership in Grand Rapids which [was] of the utmost importance of the city as a whole" and had become "a gathering place for many representative people of your community."[14]

In a revealing letter written to Bishop Whittemore by Charles Hopper, we see the impression the church made on local whites. Hopper, a former resident of the city, made a donation to the St. Philip's Church organ fund after having read the Bishop's *Newsletter* while in attendance at St. Mark's Cathedral, located in downtown Grand Rapids. Hopper explained: "I might say that I have a twofold urge to get in on the fund: [first,] the old Hopper homestead in which my sisters still reside is located in the same general vicinity of St. Philip, at Pleasant and Union Street; [second,] I have ridden in Pullman sleeping cars for the past forty years with Porters who have worshipped at St. Philip, all of whom I have found to be courteous and efficient. Jim Lasch is the one I know most intimately by name."[15] For Hopper and many whites, St. Philip's were models of what local African Americans could achieve.

Because St. Philip's was seen as the city's representative congregation of African American propriety, Father Anderson nurtured the idea that it should support a community center. Unlike the situation in the early twentieth century, the realities of the Depression now demanded that African American social welfare be addressed. Anderson believed that his church could be instrumental in carrying out the social gospel.[16]

While Anderson nurtured the idea that a community center was part of the church's ministry, the ministry did not have the capacity to fund the center itself. St. Philip's, as an institution, reflected the general economic conditions of its members, who struggled to keep up with the day-to-day expenses of the church, including its portion of Father Anderson's salary. One explanation for the congregation's financial situation had to do with the fact that very few Southern migrants were Episcopalians; most Southerners who migrated to the city were Baptist, Methodist, or Pentecostal. Because Episcopalians were associated with the upper-class American life, they were a minority within the city at large—and were truly a minority within the city's African American community. The class aspirations of St. Philip's members prevented them from reaching out to African Americans who came from more revivalist traditions, which, in the minds of the St. Philip's membership, epitomized ignorance and backwardness. For many rural Southerners, the "high church" tradition of St. Philip's was simply cold and joyless.

Nevertheless, St. Phillip's denominational ties enabled it to grow into a community institution willing and able to respond to racial incivilities. In June 1940, for example, the local American Legion Council held a fundraiser for needy young people in the black community. The event, however, was a minstrel show. Father Anderson took umbrage on behalf of the congregation and the community. Henry Romyn, the commander of the American Legion Council, responded with an apology.[17]

Anderson's rebuff and Romyn's apology were atypical. Being a part of a mainline denomination gave members of St. Philip's and its clergy social standing as well as the opportunity to interact with whites as equals. Members of the congregation, therefore, were well equipped to battle offensive public behavior. Anderson sent copies of his letter to Rabbi Jerome Folkman, Bishop Lewis Bliss Whittemore, and Dr. Milton H. McGorrill, the senior minister of the Fountain Street Baptist Church. As evidenced by this incident, Anderson did not hesitate to use his connections to the white religious establishment and charitable organizations to advocate for civility and racial equality.[18] This style of advocacy and interracial cooperation made St. Philip's an institutional leader in the African American community.

In the spring of 1940, the Interracial Committee (formerly known as the Interracial Council) agreed to sponsor another Urban League survey of the African American population. The Interracial Committee was composed of a variety of community leaders, including eight leading white and black clergymen: Dr. Milton McGorrill, Fountain Street Baptist Church; Rev. Albert Keith, Messiah Baptist Church; Rev. W. H. Jones, First Community AME Church; Rev. Jesse Anderson, St. Philip's Episcopal Church; Rev. Melvin Trotter, Mel Trotter Rescue Mission; Adjutant William Jobe, Salvation Army; Maj. Belle Hubbell, American Gospel Mission; and Rev. Charles Helsley, East Congregational Church. The committee also had other representatives from other agencies in the community.[19]

The need for this survey arose out of 1939 meeting of white and black clergymen to discuss a plan for liquidating the mortgages on the city's African American churches. The discussion, however, raised the more pertinent question of the economic condition of the city's entire African American population. The Council of Social Agencies (a consortium of Grand Rapids' leading welfare agencies) appointed Rev. Milton M. McGorrill to head a research subcommittee to make recommendations concerning the church mortgages and the condition of the African American community. The committee McGorrill headed was essentially a reconstitution of the Interracial Council that had been formed in 1927. The committee recommended the National Urban League (NUL) be invited to update the 1928 survey undertaken by R. Maurice Moss. Mr. C. C. Ridge, the executive secretary of the Council of Social Agencies, corresponded with Eugene Kinckle Jones and negotiated arrangements for the survey.[20]

In April 1940, Warren Banner, director of the Department of Research for the NUL, arrived in Grand Rapids to survey the community.[21] Reverend W. H. Jones, the president of the Grand Rapids Ministerial Alliance, arranged for Banner to be accompanied in his canvass by various African American church volunteers. His canvass of the Grand Rapids community took four weeks.

Banner's survey revealed much about the African American community in Grand Rapids, including the devastating effects of continued racial discrimination and the Great Depression. Banner and his team estimated the city's African American population at 3,877, reflecting a growth of nearly 20 percent since 1930. He calculated that blacks represented less than 2 percent of the city's total population. Banner also estimated that between 1920 and 1930, the black population, outstripping the growth of the general population, had grown more than 150 percent.

Banner's survey confirmed Moss's assessment that employment opportunities drew African Americans into the city. His survey team interviewed 319 families. Of those families, "32 were native families and of the other 287 families over half (151) came [to the city] to work." The canvassers discovered that two-thirds of the families were natives of Grand Rapids or residents of the community for over fifteen years. They interviewed only two families who had arrived in the city during 1939.[22]

Although Banner did not mention it in his report, the city's demographics certainly influenced the local black culture. Most African American families in Grand Rapids were born in the region and shaped by the regional Protestant civic culture. And the type of racism they experienced was somewhat different in style, if not in substance, from the racism endured by their counterparts who arrived from the Deep South. The net result of this regional cultural variation was that regionally born African Americans were not isolated from whites. This interaction with whites, however, made local racial exclusion all the more bitter and hated.[23]

Southern African American migrants, on the other hand, were subjugated by what one scholar Aldon Morris calls "tripartite domination." Jim Crow customs and laws throughout the South dominated them personally, socially, and economically.[24] Their arrival into the Great Lakes region in the aftermath of World War I was an essential step in their journey toward civic freedom and economic opportunity. As a result of this history, Afro-Southern migrants arrived in the city with a stronger sense of cultural unity and solidarity than those blacks native to the city. Unlike the native-born blacks, Afro-Southerners were not looking to the white community's approval in terms of being educated and middle class. For them, Grand Rapids was about finding decent wages.

Although the NUL's original 1928 study indicated the poor laboring conditions of African Americans, the 1940 study documented the employment disparities in far greater statistical detail. The results were disappointing. Banner reported that over two-thirds of the black population were employed in "domestic and personal service, and in unskilled, low-paid occupations." There were no African Americans employed in unionized shops. While the Congress of Industrial Organizations (CIO) had pushed for nondiscriminatory practices throughout the 1930s, this did not mean employers such as the Hayes Corporation, Grand Rapids' largest employer, willingly accepted blacks.[25] Banner also reported that there was only one black member of the CIO and none in the American Federation of Labor (AFL). For black males in Grand Rapids, the best employer was the Pere Marquette Railroad Company. Railroad employees such as James Green, a foreman, and twenty-five other skilled workers enjoyed a modicum of mobility and job security. Even though African Americans earned a decent wage working on the Pere Marquette, they nevertheless were excluded from the railworkers union.[26]

No civic or governmental agencies hired African Americans in any representative fashion.[27] There were only ten African Americans employed by the city of Grand Rapids: two police officers, one junior clerk, five asphalt repair workers, one janitor, and one park laborer. There was only one African American employee of the Grand Rapids public schools—a janitor. And there had been no African American teacher in the school system since the early 1920s.[28]

The most stable jobs for blacks continued to be in the field of domestic and personal services, particularly in the local hotels. One former employee of the Pantlind Hotel, Lewis Smith, described his work as being on one great big plantation. "Negroes," he said, "would gamble and get arrested on Saturday night and the hotel manager would bail them out for work on Monday."[29] The hotel management had established a paternalistic relationship with its employees. In fact, workers at the hotel had an arrangement with the manager of the Pantlind to get advances or loans to keep their families afloat. The loans were rarely ever paid back. Although this was a kind gesture, it did not offset the low wages that African American domestic workers were paid.

Both males and females in the black community needed to work to earn enough money to survive financially. Banner pointed out that the average income of black families was $69 per month, or $828 per year. While Banner did not provide income comparisons for the entire population, he concluded that income was "the crux of the problem in the Negro community." The result: a disproportionate number of African Americans utilized relief services. Banner reported that the Kent County emergency relief rolls had a total of 2,055 cases, 86 of whom were African Americans. Although African Americans constituted less than 2 percent of the total population, they constituted 4.1 percent of the relief rolls. The same was true of the Work Progress Administration (WPA): the total number employed was 2,403; of those, 129 (5.3 percent) were African Americans. According to Banner, the average wage for African American WPA workers was $52.80 per month—much less than the average monthly wage for the city's African-American population.

This economic vulnerability was cancerous, affecting housing, health, crime, and, more importantly, education. Moss warned in 1928 that the inability of blacks to use their education was a great danger to the life of the city. His warning proved prophetic. Banner reported that the African American dropout rate was higher than the rate among whites in Grand

Rapids. Furthermore, the only professional schools in the city—Butterworth, Blodgett, and St. Mary's schools of nursing—excluded African American women. The technical schools could not place African Americans in apprenticeships because employers and trade unions dominated by white ethnics refused to hire them. And there were no African American schoolteachers, although there were qualified teachers available. Almost every interview Banner conducted with white school officials included the tacit assumption that schools were for whites only. Banner cited the following interview with Charlotte B. Pope, principal of Finney Street School, as indicative of the school system's attitude toward African Americans:

> The occasion was a routine interview at Finney School which has the largest percentage of Negro students in the City, although a small school. This school goes only to the fifth grade—has enrollment of 92, of which ... 74 [are Negroes]. Miss Pope has only been in the principalship for about two years. She states that when she first came there was quite a disturbance from one particular grade, which was the result of the incapability of the teacher in that particular grade. That person has since been transferred and now that problem has been adjusted. Miss Pope feels that the home life of the family, from which the child comes, is a definite hindrance to the child. She has been unable, so far, to get cooperation from the Negro parents. Only a few have been interested in the work of the school. Miss Pope feels that the problem of the area surrounding the school is definitely economic. She states that the WPA breakfast, which is now served in many schools, had its origin in her school last year. This, she says, she inaugurated because she found that so many children were coming to school without breakfast, either because of parents not being out of bed, or because they were paying little attention to their child. When the teacher, who was having disciplinary problems (mentioned above), was transferred, a man was brought in. Expressions of the community indicated that the people felt that this was an effort to strong-arm the citizens in so far as the children are concerned, instead of through the educational (psychological) approach. Feeling in the community has subsided with time.[30]

The disdain of Miss Pope for her student's parents confirmed what many African Americans had come to expect—the educational system was for whites only. Only the exceptional blacks—those who had immense talent and the psychological wherewithal to withstand the constant bigotry—excelled in the Grand Rapids Public Schools.

The 1930s saw little growth in the already small group of black professionals in the city. At the time of Banner's survey, there were three physicians: Eugene Alston, Eugene Browning, and Robert Claytor; two dentists, Cortez English and Robert Redd; one undertaker, Milo Brown; and one attorney, Floyd Skinner. Being a black professional in Grand Rapids was difficult. For instance, Banner pointed out that there had never been an African American intern in any of the city's hospitals. Of the three physicians, only one was "on the staff at two of the large hospitals." "In the case of each hospital," he wrote, "his role is insignificant and, from the present general practice of the institutions concerned, will never be other than this."[31]

The great growth in the professional class was among clergymen, whose numbers increased from six in 1928 to twelve in 1940. The majority of these men did not have formal theological training. In fact, of the twelve, only three had gone to college and seminary. Despite the informality of their education, however, these men had larger followings than any other African American activist in the community. During the 1930s, three new churches were established, two Church of God in Christ congregations and one Baptist Church—New Hope. Each of these congregations was consumed by mortgage debt. According to Banner, the ratio of churches to the populations they served was higher, he thought, in black community than in the general population of the city. He surmised that the relatively small black population in Grand Rapids could reasonably sustain no more than four congregations. While Banner's point might have been true statistically, he seems not to have appreciated the social function of these churches. In particular, he viewed Afro-Southern congregations primarily as sociological institutions, not as ethnic and religious ones. Each church, though small, was extension of a region, a family, and a network of associated individuals.

The black business enterprises in the community, according to Banner, were beauty salons and barbershops, a small grocery store, a poultry market, two hotels, and two night clubs—the Club Indigo and the Midwest Club. These entrepreneurs were sorely undercapitalized.[32] Given the African American population base and its attendant economic conditions, many of these businesspeople had to cater to whites as well as African Americans just to break even. As in the 1928 NUL study of Grand Rapids, the only entrepreneurs who made money were those who operated in the informal vice economy. The crime statistics Banner reported showed that African Americans were arrested in Grand Rapids for gambling and prostitution more than for any other offenses.

In summarizing his data, Banner offered the committee fourteen recommendations, which laid the foundation for the creation of a community center. Briefly, Banner's survey recommended the city create recreational programs that would work in conjunction with crime prevention programs, hire African American social workers, form an African American ministerial council, hire African American teachers, and end racially discriminatory practices in employment. He observed that "the greatest need of the Negro community appears to be that of obtaining jobs in order to provide necessities of life."[33]

In his closing remarks, Banner anticipated the "double victory" campaign waged by civil rights activists who, when the United States entered World War II, used the German Nazi aggression and the spread of fascism in Spain and Italy to demand that the United States government end racial discrimination at home. The goal of the campaign was to win democracy at home and abroad. Banner, concluded his study in April 1940 prophetically: "Since this study began, our country has planned to increase facilities for national defense in order to be able to adequately protect our democracy. This means that the industrial pace will be stepped-up and additional men will be employed. Many plants in Grand Rapids will, no doubt, benefit from orders distributed throughout the nation, and will find it necessary to add to their personnel. The Interracial Committee should make every effort to have industrialists realize that, in accord with the tenets of democracy, Negroes should be given a fair share of the job openings."[34]

In the spring of 1940, Father Jesse Anderson created a large-scale summer outreach program designed to offer young people healthy recreational activities away from street life. Bishop Lewis Whittemore gave his full support to the program. The bishop's support was supplemented by financial gifts from Maud Brough, a former Grand Rapids resident who had retired to Pasadena, California. Brough, a devout Episcopalian, and Whittemore held strong religious convictions in line with city's neo-abolitionist tradition. With Brough's support, Whittemore's steadfast leadership, and Anderson's determination, the establishment of a Negro youth center became a reality.

During summers of 1940, 1941, and 1942, St. Philip's was running a full-scale youth recreational program. By 1941, the program had become a nonsectarian operation. By the late winter of 1942, Anderson and interested parties had visited community centers in Kalamazoo and Indianapolis, laying the groundwork for full-fledged black community center in Grand Rapids. In 1943, with other generous gifts from Brough, the city's African American churches allied to form a community association.

The community association came with its share of difficulties. In 1942, Father Anderson, who had been instrumental in developing the program, began contemplating calls from larger congregations looking for a new pastor.[35] As well, some members of St. Philip's were distressed because the programs were being housed inside their small church facility. Even neighbors complained about the damage that the unruly youth caused to property.[36] Another concern of the St. Phillip's parishioners was helping their own children before they put out money and time to help the neighborhood children. Jealousy had also arisen among members at the First Community AME Church, which had a better facility to accommodate the youth programming but did not have the white denominational ties to support it (even though local white philanthropists aided the building of First Community AME in the 1920s to house a youth center).

The political implications of having a separate facility for black youth also plagued the youth programming. In a letter from Bishop Whittemore to Miss Brough regarding a larger gift, Whittemore described the problem from his perspective. He explained to Brough that he was in favor of erecting a parish house for St. Philip's, which would ideally be used for black youth recreational programs as well as for the congregation's needs. However, he thought that a community board made up of African Americans plus two leading white members might not be able to build a consensus to get the project started. He hoped that he could avoid the complaints about segregation from the NAACP that had stymied earlier efforts to begin a community center. Whittemore informed Brough that if the youth center were connected to St. Philip's, "we would avoid the segregation issue and it would be a great deal simpler."[37] The church coalition, led by the bishop, walked a fine line between meeting the African American community's expressed desire for a community center and reinforcing Northern Jim Crow. However, the terrible social indices of African Americans and the onset of World War II held local activists—those most determined to dismantle the local practices of segregation—at bay.

Through the political leadership of Whittemore, African American churches finally agreed to the plans for a community center. In the spring of 1942, the committee began looking for a building to house the program that had begun in the undercroft of St. Philip's. That summer, Rev. Anderson received and accepted another call from a congregation in Wilmington, Delaware. With the project under way, the diocese purchased three properties adjacent to St. Philip's.[38] The congregation, on the other hand, struggled financially, and the bishop searched for a new energetic pastor to replace Anderson.

For the balance of 1942, Bishop Whittemore juggled the interest of the congregation and the development of the community center. In

December, Whittemore wrote John Burgess concerning his quandary and acknowledged that Burgess's leadership would certainly be helpful. He explained that he had to avoid the jealousy of other congregations toward St. Philip's. The moment was ripe to build a community center, Whittemore thought.[39]

Later that month, Bishop Whittemore wrote Miss Brough, telling her of the Council of Social Agencies' approval for the community association: "I believe that in this movement we have the germ of the biggest thing which has ever happened for the colored residents of Grand Rapids. With ten white people on the board meeting monthly with the group of colored leaders, we have the finest possible example of race cooperation and it is hard to calculate the extent of the benefit."[40]

By January 1943, many of the problems that Whittemore foresaw were in the process of being resolved. First, he had been in correspondence with Wendell Pasco, a graduating seminarian from the Episcopal Theological Seminary in Cambridge, Massachusetts, about accepting the call to St. Philip's.[41] Second, he worked out cooperative relations with the police youth center by having one of its members appointed to the board of the community center.[42] With these details in place, the most pressing problem for the community association's board was finding a trained social worker to run the organization, the idea for which had been recommended by Eugene Kinckle Jones, the executive director of the NUL in 1927.[43] At that time, however, the Interracial Council and the Community Chest were reluctant to help generate the revenue to support a social worker for the African American community. This time around, the Community Chest stipulated that having a trained social worker was a requirement if it were to financially support the community center. Bishop Whittemore corresponded with E. T. Attwell, the National Recreation Association's director of Colored Works, Warren Banner of the NUL, and John Burgess in his search to find the best director for the new community association. He explained to each of them that the director of the new community association needed links to the churches in order to be successful.

Meanwhile, the Community Association voted to name the organization after Miss Brough. In January, Whittemore telegraphed Brough informing her that the board of directors for the Center wanted to "be called the Brough Community Association." Whittemore emphasized that the "proposal was made by negro members of board."[44] Initially, Brough rejected the idea. She thought the association rightfully deserved to be named after Father Anderson. She wrote, "I am deeply appreciative of the feeling which prompted the negro members of the Board to propose calling the center The Brough Community Association but I cannot help feeling that the Jesse Anderson Community Association is more appropriate, and would show honor where honor is due." The same day, Bishop Whittemore telegraphed Brough, stating that it was "impossible to name the center after Anderson or any other of the Negro clergy here without exciting jealousy from other congregations. All are absolutely agreed that your name should be used." The following day, Brough telegraphed her reply to Whittemore: "I withdraw objections and humbly accept honor extended to me."[45] The naming of the community association after Brough prevented the African American church leaders from being embroiled in yet another controversy in their competition for white philanthropic support.

The new Brough Community Association (BCA) elected officers and crafted bylaws. Bishop Whittemore was elected president, Rev. Albert Keith of Messiah Baptist Church was secretary, and Rev. W. H. Jones of the First Community AME Church, Rev. H. C. Toliver of True Light Baptist Church, and Mr. Edward Shields Sr., a St. Philip's layman, were elected to the committee. The BCA stated that its purpose was: "To promote good citizenship, progress and happiness among it members and throughout the community in general, through a program of wholesome activities, neighborliness and self-development, without pecuniary gain or profit to its members; to do intercultural and interracial work in the community; and in accomplishing these objects, to seek the cooperation of the city government, social agencies and all organizations fostering plans for community welfare."[46]

The committee also resolved that the board of directors be "composed of fifteen colored and ten white people of the community" and that "a male social worker, who meets all the standards of the American Association of Social Workers, be secured" as director of the association.[47]

The search for an executive director did not take long. In March 1943, Edward P. Simms of Boston, Massachusetts, contacted Bishop Whittemore. Simms served the Robert Gould Shaw House as its assistant director. Simms's résumé was impressive: he had been educated at Boston University, earning a bachelor's degree in education and two master's degrees, one in history and the other in social service; he had also served on the faculty of two historically black colleges, Virginia Union University and Tuskegee Institute. In September 1943, Simms was hired as the first director of the BCA.

In a span of just a few months, the BCA was incorporated, moved into its first building, developed a cooperative relationship with three African American churches, was approved by the Community Chest as an official social agency, and became an affiliate organization of the National Urban League. When the Association opened its doors on June 4, 1943, it was the culmination of nearly forty years' struggle and debate about African American welfare.

In the foreword of the BCA's first annual report, Bishop Whittemore wrote that the Association was "typically and fundamentally American, . . . dedicated to belief in the dignity and the possibilities of every citizen whatever his race or creed. More than this, it holds that America will never rise to its inherent greatness until every group, whether majority or minority, makes it full contribution. All are needed. As Americans work and plan and play together in the spirit of mutual confidence, respect, and friendship, obstacles will be overcome, difficulties removed, injustices righted. It was in this spirit that 'Brough' was born and is making its contribution today."[48]

Edward Simms's introduction to the annual report stated the goals of the organization. "The Association," he wrote, was "a character building agency," which did not "seek to reform; rather, it seeks to guide vocationally, socially and civically, creating at all times an atmosphere in which 'It is popular to be good.'"[49] Whittemore and Simms were both optimistic about the prospect that racial inequity could be overcome through interracial cooperation and social outreach.

What neither Whittemore nor Simms foresaw was that this approach alone was not sufficient to tackle the embryonic ghetto. Banner's 1940 study intimated that middle-class reforms were not sufficient to change the inertia created by ghettoization, and community civil rights activists were suspicious of an approach that dealt with the needs of African Americans without confronting the *de facto* segregation that created poverty in the first place. Another issue that the founders of the BCA overlooked was the financial ability of African Americans to sustain the association; St. Phillip's, for example, continued to be a struggling mission church.

In July 1943, Bishop Whittemore asked Bravid W. Harris, the Episcopal Church's secretary for Negro Work, to conduct an evaluation of St. Phillip's. Harris spent two days doing so. Much as the Banner report had revealed, Harris's report noted the limited employment opportunities of blacks in Grand Rapids. His assessment of the housing conditions and general welfare was as Banner described. "The new community center," he observed, "is rendering a limited service to a limited number for the present." Harris also noted that "a group of Negro citizens under the leadership of the NAACP is in opposition" to the community center. Harris then went on to assess the church situation in Grand Rapids. He believed the city had only three outstanding churches within the black community. The other churches he saw as having "indifferent leadership, poor buildings and equipment, and making a doubtful contribution to the general religious life." He spoke positively of St. Phillip's but noted the congregation's rapid turnover of clergy. Also, much of the congregation's offering at St. Phillip's was generated through entertainment, and they were supported as well by contribution from the diocese. Harris noted that the "congregation is made up of some of the best citizens of the community"; however, he wrote that the "general attitude" was "one of indifference. The congregation as a whole is indifferent, satisfied simply to attend the services. A few active members work for and support the church, but do not appear to be interested in the people of the community as a whole."

Harris recommended that St. Philip's do more evangelism, develop more church organizations, offer religious education, and canvass every member regarding giving.[50] What Harris did not seem to understand was that the people of St. Philip's were not totally indifferent to the community activism; many of the members of the church were, in fact, community activists. The members of St. Philip's were simply conflicted: on the one hand, they wanted the church to be engaged in outreach and the struggle for civic equality. On the other hand, the church functioned as a middle-class social club, given the city's limited social environment for the African American middle class. In addition, some members simply wanted a religious institution that met their religious needs without the constant reminder of the "Negro Problem"—for them the Church was a transcendent institution.

If the church that was seemingly the most representative of middle-class status among blacks in the city was institutionally fragile, this meant that the BCA itself was built on quicksand. Financially, none of the other black churches was in any better shape. Without the expected financial backing from the black churches, the BCA soon shed its religious and indigenous community ties and became more dependent on the largesse of the Community Chest.[51] To survive, the association became more responsive to the needs of its financial supporters than the needs of those whom it was created to serve.

The other unforeseen problem in the creation of the BCA surrounded the implicit cultural biases evident in the bylaws and in reports written about Afro-Southern migrants. The founders of BCA clearly believed that Afro-Southern behavior was improvident and needed correcting, which may have been true to an extent. However, the way the reports read in retrospect says more about the attitude of the writers than the people they served. The fact that the BCA was created to reinforce middle-class norms of behavior fostered old-fashioned class resentments. Rural Afro-Southerners had a long history of their ministers moralizing about their group's personal behavior; however, when the formally educated middle class moralized about the behaviors of new arrivals, it was deeply injurious.[52] This was especially true in a small community where gossip circulated about the sins of the middle class as well as the poor.

The BCA represented the aspirations of middle-class African Americans, not the needs of poor—although this was not intentional. It occurred because middle-class and new urban migrants had different interests and needs. It was already clear by the 1920s that the growth in the African American middle class had been sizable enough to create a growing gulf between the attitudes and interests of the middle class and those of the working poor in the city.

In 1944, journalist and historian Roger Wilkins arrived in Grand Rapids from New York City at age twelve to live with his mother, Helen Wilkins Claytor, and his stepfather, Dr. Robert Claytor. Wilkins remembered his life in Grand Rapids as being one where his family's middle class status and their race stood in conflict. "It was not that we in my family were direct victims of racism," he wrote. "On the contrary, my stepfather clearly had a higher income than most of the parents of students in my high school. Unlike those of my contemporaries, black and white, my parents had college degrees. Within Grand Rapids' tiny Negro community they were among the elite. The others were the lawyer, the dentist, the undertaker and the other doctor." Being part of the local elite caused Wilkins considerable unease about his "blackness." He observed, "I knew that other blacks were targets of harsh job and housing discrimination; but, though being Negro did pose some inconvenience for us, those major life-numbing blockbusters were not present in our daily lives. I did have a sense that it was unfair for poor Negroes to be relegated to bad jobs—if they had jobs at all—and to bad or miserable housing but I didn't feel any great sense of identity with them." Wilkins's remarks about the dilemma of race and class captures not only his adolescent sentiments but also the feelings of the local middle class like his parents. Reflecting further, Wilkins wrote, "In high school, I thought I was doing my bit for the race when I served as student council president. By being a model student and leader, I thought I was demonstrating how well Negroes could perform if only the handicaps were removed and they were given a chance. But deep down I guess I was also trying to demonstrate that I was not like those other people; that I was different. My message was quite clear: I was not *nigger. But the world didn't seem quite ready to make such fine distinctions, and it was precisely that fact—though at the time I could scarcely even have admitted it to myself—that was the nub of the race issue for me.*"[53] Racial segregation affected middle-class and working-poor African Americans alike.

The creation of the BCA was an attempt to develop young African Americans into model citizens like the young Wilkins, black people whose example would serve to convince the white community of the impoliteness of its racism. In their frustration, the small African American middle class secretly loathed the black poor for improvident behavior, and the poor loathed those who pretended to be middle class while working mainly as porters and maids.

The BCA evolved over a thirty-year period. The evolution of this community institution created an interracial organization dedicated to carrying out social work, recreation, and community uplift. The work done by the BCA fulfilled the earlier hopes of women leaders such as Mabel Groggins and Ethel Burgess. They had seen the need for a positive outlet for African American children and families; indeed, they saw it as a civil rights issue. These women and the civic organizations they influenced shared the belief that the African American community could flourish positively if families were nurtured. The faith and work of these individuals had come to some fruition in the founding of the BCA. Although the work of the Community Association was laudable, it did not change the daily pains of racial and economic discrimination in the lives of ordinary African Americans. The unpleasant fact was that racial discrimination was deeply embedded in the culture of the city. The 1942 Detroit race riot in the Sojourner Truth Housing project a year before the incorporation of the BCA was a clear reminder of the constancy of racial discrimination.[54] In the mind of many African American activists in Grand Rapids, the best course for attaining respectability in all of its dimensions continued to be agitation and protest.

7 *"Today's Negro and Tomorrow's World": African American Protest and the Politics of Leadership*

"We are living at the turning point of civilization; at the cross roads," Rev. Adam Clayton Powell Jr., the pastor of the Abyssinian Baptist Church—the largest Negro Church in the country—and a New York City councilman, told the gathering of the Grand Rapids branch of the NAACP at its 1943 annual membership kick-off drive. "Regardless of what the people of the post-war world will be, the world as we knew it and our forefathers knew it is never going to be the same again in all its viciousness. The date of domination of the world by any group or individual is passing. The next will be a society lived in by every creature on the basis of their individual contribution and it will not matter whether we are black, brown, or otherwise. We will be judged individually. None will be able to live in that world because of contributions of his forefathers." He continued, "We have a new Negro now, a man who has made up his mind that he is not going to take the injustice any longer. He is neither young nor old. He is just new. He doesn't follow any program of violence, but made up his mind to use every legal means of direct social action to obtain in this day and hour, everything that the Constitution promises him."[1]

Powell's assessment reflected the sea change in world politics, especially the transformation among African Americans. The conclusion of World War II afforded African American communities new opportunities to forge political coalitions and to break the bars of legal segregation. As a result of President Franklin Roosevelt's Executive Order 8802, which prohibited racial discrimination in companies that held military contracts, African Americans were given the opportunity to join the industrial workforce. Following much of the national pattern, local leaders of civil rights coalitions fought to open the local civic and economic institutions to all citizens. Not only did they fight for access, they also continued to fight each other politically regarding strategies for full integration of African Americans into the urban middle class.

The fractionalized civil rights coalition sought legal redress, access to electoral politics, school integration, the hiring of African American teachers, open housing, and fair employment practices in industry. The issues surrounding race and economic class stratification became even more pronounced as the numbers of African Americans increased in the city. The civil rights leaders who came of age politically in the late 1920s were now tight-knit, seasoned veterans at organizing the community against Jim Crow practices. Throughout the 1940s and into the early 1950s, they banded together around the NAACP, the Urban League, the Communist Party, and church-related committees, with each organization offering its own strategy to achieve African American inclusion into the mainstream of American society.

The city's various civil rights organizations were energized by the mass influx of Southern migrants after the war. By 1950, the Grand Rapids NAACP branch was the second largest in Michigan. The challenge for the Urban League was finding jobs for the recent arrivals, which justified its existence and allowed for its organizational growth. Although fractured at times with internal dissent regarding leadership tactics, cultural style, and personal recriminations, this coalition kept political and moral pressure on the local corporate and governmental institutions. And they reminded their own politicians and community of the grievous injustices that were occurring to African Americans locally and throughout the country.

In 1944, Daniel Lampkins (see chapter 4),[2] a long-time citizen of the city, articulated the civil religion that served the middle class leadership of the black community while running for the state legislature. Announcing his candidacy, he stated, "Faith is a great agency in the molding of well-ordered opinion. I have the faith that we will not be weighed in the balance and found wanting in this movement for a bigger spirit of oneness among all people regardless of race, stature or creed."[3] Moved by faith, this coalition fought to change the social status of the African American community.

Floyd Skinner was the lone African American attorney in Grand Rapids in 1940. Born in 1900 in Benzie County, Michigan, where his father had worked as a lumberman, Skinner moved in 1914 to Grand Rapids where he attended school, worked in the rail yards of the Pere Marquette, and played baseball with a semi-pro baseball team, the Grand Rapids Colored Athletics. In 1919, the smart and determined Skinner entered the University of Michigan, where he earned degrees from both the college and the law school.

Somewhere between high school and college, Skinner embraced the work of the NAACP. From the late 1920s until his death in 1962, Skinner was Grand Rapids' staunchest leader of the NAACP. Between 1927 and 1962, he served five separate terms as its president and was a committee member for both the local and state chapters. Skinner held an unswerving belief that African Americans must resist Jim Crow in all its dimensions. In 1926, Skinner supported Oliver Green, his senior peer at the University of Michigan Law School, as a researcher in the legal case *Bolden v. Grand Rapids Operating Corporation*. As a young professional he embroiled himself in the running feud over a separate recreation center and social welfare center for African Americans. He opposed the creation of such an organization, fearing that self-segregation might justify Jim Crow customs and laws. Skinner thought that winning on the legal argument was one of the primary ways to achieve full equality. The Bolden case bolstered the confidence in the small NAACP branch and gave Skinner confidence that the law was the chief instrument for achieving social equality.

Two years after the Bolden victory in the Michigan State Supreme Court, Skinner represented Herbert Pratt, who the *Grand Rapids Press* reported was a thirty-four-year-old mulatto married to a white woman. Skinner took Pratt's case after a white attorney withdrew from the case shortly before trial. The paper stated that Pratt held a series of jobs from musician and window washer to baseball player. Skinner outlined the case in an unsigned, handwritten note to the Twentieth Annual Conference of the NAACP as well as in a letter to Robert Bagnall, the director of NAACP branches. Skinner reported that Pratt was originally arrested on the charge of assault with the attempt to rape. The prosecution subsequently changed the charge to armed robbery of two girls for the sum of eight dollars. Pratt's defense was that he was not at the scene of the crime. The prosecution presented three witnesses who reported seeing Pratt at the scene of the crime. The defense, led by Skinner, had three witnesses who contradicted the prosecution's witnesses and corroborated Pratt's alibi that he was home in bed at the time of the crime. The jury found Pratt guilty. He received a sentenced of life imprisonment at the state penitentiary in Jackson. The judge in the case, Leonard D. Verdier, uttered biased and racially insensitive remarks in his sentencing of Pratt. In his talk before the Annual Conference and in his written letter to Bagnall, Skinner tried to convince the national organization of the NAACP to assist the local branch in raising one thousand dollars to set an appeal. In his letter, Skinner pointed out that "[t]his case has enhanced local interest in the NAACP as we have already added about 125 new members and prospects are good for several hundred more."[4] The Pratt case had done something the Bolden Case had not: it gained the interest of the working class, and Skinner was eager to build on the momentum. Unfortunately, the appeal for funds did not meet its goal, and Pratt stayed in prison. With the onset of the Great Depression, there were few local cases to unite the Negroes around the work of the NAACP.

In the early 1930s, Skinner went to work for the State of Michigan in the tax division of the attorney general's office. He spent much of his free time trying to organize the Progressive Voter's League, an organization dedicated to brokering the African American vote for tangible gains in city hall. Skinner encouraged African American voters to use their electoral power to get the attention of local government. The gains were few, however.[5] George Smith ran for city commission and Daniel Boone Lampkin ran once again for a seat in the state legislature. Although neither man won, their efforts reminded those in city government that African Americans in the city desired their share of the civic pie.[6]

Throughout the 1930s, the NAACP branch activity remained confined to fighting local governmental policies deemed to be Jim Crow in nature. For example, in January 1935, the branch confronted the Kent County Relief Commission for attempting to organize a separate center for "indigent colored men." Later in the year, the branch took on Harry C. White, a candidate for the city commission. Several years earlier, White, who firmly believed that racial segregation was justifiable, had led the opposition to blacks living in certain city neighborhoods. The branch went on record as opposing White's candidacy and organized Negro voters in the third ward to get out the vote.[7]

As Skinner and some NAACP members such as William Glenn and George Smith had done in the late 1920s and the early 1930s, they continued a protracted battle against the idea of a separate black social center. Ironically, in 1940 the local chapter of the NAACP elected as their president Rev. Jesse Anderson, the rector of St. Philip's Episcopal Church and one of the main forces behind the eventual creation of the Brough Community Association (BCA) in 1943. Bishop Whittemore and other white supporters of the BCA hoped that the election of Anderson would assuage the branch's strict integrationists in the NAACP's membership. As soon as the BCA was chartered, Skinner led the attack, in a resolution to the members of the branch. His resolution stated that the BCA was a "Jim Crow project" that would "increase segregation and Jim-Crowism." The Skinner resolution called for an investigation into the BCA's alleged segregationist practices. The investigating committee was made up of Skinner's allies: Stanley L. Barnett, local hotel owner; William Glenn, employee of the Hayes Corporation; and William Gilbert. They concluded that they were "of the opinion this center is a stepping stone to further Jim Crowism. Therefore, we recommend the NAACP go on record as opposing the Brough Community Center."[8]

The attack on the BCA sent the NAACP organization into a tailspin. Members were divided over the actions that Skinner and the investigating committee had taken. Carl A. Thomasson, a local janitor and the president of the branch in 1943, overturned the committee's report. In a letter to Ella J. Baker, the director of branches for the national NAACP, Thomasson explained the situation: "The National office should also have known of the controversy over the Brough Community Center, especially since I felt it necessary to countermand a decision of the body and set forth a Presidential Policy regarding the Center, which was the exact opposite of the vote taken at the previous meeting. The body later upheld my action but the meeting was too stormy for a formal adoption of the Presidential Policy, though the majority of the membership is in accord with it. Thus, it was better to let the matter rest."[9]

Thomasson's overturning of the Skinner resolution and the special investigatory committee report on the BCA represented the internal split in the NAACP over the strategy that had appeared as early as 1919. Interestingly enough, Thomasson's wife, Mary, was Skinner's secretary. Thomasson saw the advocacy of the NAACP and the social welfare approach of the BCA as complementary. Skinner saw the NAACP as a vehicle for demanding civic equality. In his view, the BCA set a dangerous precedent by accommodating segregated social practices.

In addition to internal disagreements, the NAACP took on other external challenges as well. During one of Skinner's presidencies, the local NAACP branch joined the statewide fight for the enactment of a Fair Employment Practice law in the Michigan legislature. The branch also confronted the Grand Rapids Public Schools to prevent them from segregating children in all–African American schools. In addition, the branch fought to meet the needs of the increasingly visible African American population in the city, which had grown significantly with the influx of Southern migrants after the war. The NAACP believed that one way to meet these needs was for the city to hire African American teachers— individuals who could teach throughout the school system and serve as role models to African American and white students alike. The branch waged a vigorous battle to force the Grand Rapids Public Schools to recruit and hire African American teachers.

In every venue, Skinner, as leader in the NAACP, led the charge against segregated practices during the 1940s and 1950s. He was one of the few African American professionals to be widely connected to various groups, people, and organizations among African Americans and the established white community. As one *Grand Rapids Press* article stated, Skinner was "the man who could talk to the man."[10]

In 1947, Paul I. Phillips became the executive director of the BCA, replacing Edward Simms.[11] Upon his arrival, the BCA's board of directors moved to strengthen its affiliation with the National Urban League. They believed that the connection with the NUL would enhance the BCA's programmatic efforts. After the affiliation, the BCA was charged with job training, industrial employment, and youth work. As the new director, the thirty-three-year-old Phillips walked into the middle of the ongoing controversy among local leaders over the existence of the center. Instead of entering the debate, he followed social work policies of the Urban League.

During the summer of 1947, Phillips organized a study of the influx of Afro-Southerners into the city. Along with 169 volunteers he surveyed 436 blocks. In the survey area, Phillips and the volunteers found that there were approximately 2,845 families, of whom 1,656 families, or 58.1 percent, were interviewed. The survey revealed that 52 percent of the families were white and 44 percent were Negroes. The balance of the population remained racially or ethnically unidentified. Phillips reported that the African American population had increased from 1.8 percent of the population in 1940 to 3.8 percent in 1947. Only 8 percent of the African American families were born in Grand Rapids or in Michigan; 66 percent were born in Southern states. The largest group of Afro-Southerners in Phillips's research migrated from Mississippi.[12] Their motivation for migrating, Phillips observed, was to decrease racial oppression and improve economic opportunities. In the South, life was unbearable for many African American males after they returned from

World War II. Additionally, the higher wages in the Northern industrial economy and the rise of mechanized cotton picking gave many African Americans enough incentive to leave the rural South for the city.

"Before the war," Phillips wrote, "[the] number of industries that employed Negro Americans in their plants were conspicuously few, but today the converse is true." The biggest problem for African Americans was housing. The study concluded that high rents, overcrowding, and lack of residential mobility—e.g., restrictive covenants and other discriminatory actions in the local real estate market—kept African American families trapped in neighborhoods with the "potential threat of slum development."[13] In both housing and employment, Phillips recommended that the Michigan Equal Rights Law be strengthened and restrictive covenants be outlawed. Phillips mentioned nothing about the Fair Employment Practice legislation that was then being fought over in the Michigan legislature. He urged employers to "adopt a specific uniform policy with reference to hiring, based on the qualifications and ability to perform, and without regard to race, color, creed, or national origin."[14]

The study—and the publicity Phillips received from it—was a persuasive argument to the white civic and business community that African Americans deserved access to fair employment opportunities. As he later recalled, "There were no civil rights laws then. All we had to work with was our persuasive powers; it was simply a matter of going to the factories, the banks, the Employer Association, the Chamber of Commerce, the hospitals, the Board of Education, to all the individual employers. We appealed to their pocketbooks, talking about what a good worker could do for them regardless of his color, and to their decency and morality."[15] The moderate leadership Phillips demonstrated, like Booker T. Washington before him, was non-confrontational. Phillips's tenure at the Urban League allowed white leaders to see the organization as constructive and as offering the best solution for integrating African Americans into the life of the city. Consequently, Phillips was able to generate a great deal of sympathetic coverage in the local newspapers for his work, and he quickly became the best-known African American leader in the city.

Phillips's 1947 study indicated a cultural transformation of African Americans within Grand Rapids: it had documented the Southernization of Grand Rapids' African American community. In 1940, when Warren Banner of the National Urban League studied the African American population, it was a community populated by African Americans born in the Great Lakes region. Seven years later, Afro-Southerners numerically controlled the community. This shift significantly changed the dynamics between whites and blacks along class and social continuums.

Afro-Southerners, especially rural Mississippians, arrived with a clear view on race relations, black and white. The supremacy that whites exercised in the South over blacks skewed aspects of black perception about white life.[16] Though class status mediated race to some extent, among black Mississippians, whites were categorically lumped together as "white folks."[17] As a result, African American migrants did not initially perceive whites as having distinct ethnic identities. The distinction that Afro-Southerners made among whites was that there were some "good white folks" and some "bad white folks." What was clear to Afro-Southerners was that being white trumped all other classifications.

Mississippi scholars described aspects of African American life in the state as being a living hell.[18] Living under tight social conditions of Jim Crow customs and laws made these Afro-Southerners suspicious of whites and interdependent. They arrived in Grand Rapids with a stronger sense of identity and communal mores than Negroes who were native to the area. They came to the city with a strong Southern sense of family and extended kin networks that provided them with support. Respectability for these Afro-Southerners meant controlling one's own life outside the overarching purview of a white community. And while interracial relationships had been a fact of life in Grand Rapids throughout its history, Afro-Southerners—particularly those from Mississippi—were reluctant to interact socially with whites and did so in only the most cursory manner. The most important institutions to black Mississippians were the ones they controlled. Historian James Grossman recognized that the history of Southern race relations, especially those in Mississippi, profoundly influenced Afro-Southern racial attitudes.[19] Phillips saw these tensions: "Not only did we have to try to open doors to equal employment," he wrote, "we also had to encourage the nonwhites to walk through those doors once they had been opened, and prepare themselves for the time when doors previously closed would be open."[20] Afro-Southerners wanted job opportunities, but they wanted little else to do with white folk.

The change in demographics was striking not only in terms of attitudes but also in terms of class dynamics with the African American community.[21] These new dynamics transformed local institutions such as Messiah Baptist and First Community AME; their respective worship communities became more Southern in style and expression. This wave of migration created the basis of new community leaders outside of formal civic roles. Frankie LaMar, the owner of the HorseShoe Bar, was one. LaMar was involved in local baseball, gambling, and prostitution.

At his bar, such diverse musicians as Louis Jordan, Billie Holiday, Charlie Parker, Big Mabel, Ray Charles, and Muddy Waters bellowed from his juke boxes in the late 1940s and throughout the 1950s. LaMar's place and a few others became cultural centers for the working-class Negroes. LaMar proved to be a good citizen, promoting the work of the NAACP and arranging personal loans to those in need. LaMar also worked with the both the NAACP and the local politicians to get out the vote.

LaMar, however, was more than simply a good citizen. He was the most well-known bar owner in the black community. The HorseShoe Bar sat in the center of the growing migrant community west of Division Street and was one of the community's entertainment centers as well as a place to find personal assistance that neither the NAACP nor the Urban League provided. Those organizations represented the formal interest of the African Americans in the courts, within city government, and with employers; informally, however, the local bar owner and petty racketeers held influence over and the respect of Afro-Southerners. They understood and appreciated the culture and class of their constituents in an intimate way; they identified with their struggles personally and in ordinary social interaction.

These new migrants also gave a wider base of support to African American clergy. New churches rapidly sprang up in storefronts and in homes all round the city.[22] In the 1950s, young clergymen such as John Vanion Williams at New Hope Baptist, Willie Patterson at True Light Baptist, and Horace Young at Bethel Pentecostal took the stage, ably serving as leaders in their congregations and in the most enduring institutions within the African American community.

The steady influx of Afro-Southerners strengthened civil rights activism. In 1946, the Grand Rapids branch of the NAACP took on the case of Bonnie Morrow, who had been extradited to Mississippi. According to one newspaper account, Morrow claimed that on his way to church, a local police officer in Monroe County, Mississippi, charged him with drunkenness. He denied the charge and the officer then proceeded to draw his gun and slap him. Morrow wrestled the gun from the officer and held him at gunpoint. The officer then promised to forget the incident if Morrow returned his weapon to him. Morrow claimed that he returned the gun to the officer and they parted. Morrow stated that later that same evening, his home was attacked by a white mob that was going to lynch him. He fled his home, eluding the mob and making his way (through kin networks) to Grand Rapids. In the summer of 1944, he was arrested as a fugitive and held in the Kent County jail for eight months before being extradited to Mississippi. In February 1945, according to Morrow, while in the Mississippi jail awaiting trial, he was beaten three times with bullwhips. The beatings were so severe that Morrow "recalled his shoes being filled with blood." The severity of the beatings left him with a twisted spine and paralysis from the hips down. The newspaper account noted that Morrow "came to Grand Rapids a strong healthy farmer and . . . came back two years later, a wasted, crippled—paralyzed—man." The NAACP joined with other civil rights groups asking Governor Harry Kelly not to release him to Mississippi authorities.[23] The local branch pursued a letter-writing campaign to dissuade the governor from extraditing Morrow for a second time.

The work of the Grand Rapids chapter of the NAACP was not always as dramatic as its role in the Morrow case. The battles they fought, though important, focused on issues of education and fair employment. The branch was not alone in this fight, either, being part of a statewide network of NAACP branches and the Michigan Congress for Civil Rights (MCCR) that pressured the state legislature to pass fair employment legislation. Throughout Michigan a political battle ensued as presidential Executive Order 8802, given in June 1941 and banning racial discrimination in all war plants, was allowed to expire throughout the country. The expiration of this order and lack of any replacement legislation forced a statewide political battle. In Michigan, the battle for fair employment was a partisan one—supported by Democrats but criticized by Republicans, who consistently defeated the legislation each time it came up in the state's house of representatives. However, Gov. G. Mennen Williams, a Democrat elected in 1949, was able to join with a coalition of moderate Republicans, led by Louis Cramton of Lapeer, Michigan, to finally enact fair employment legislation in 1955—ending a fourteen-year struggle.[24]

This battle was important for Grand Rapids because the expiration of Executive Order 8802 in 1945 allowed industrial employers to lay off African American workers without penalty. Throughout 1944 and 1945, the NAACP frequently invited speakers to address the subject of fair employment legislation, and it encouraged its membership to petition their representatives and ask them to vote for the passage of the legislation.[25]

Presidential Executive Order 8802 had opened industrial employment opportunities to African Americans throughout the country. The Hayes Manufacturing Company, the largest employer in Grand Rapids in the 1920s and 1930s, hired no African Americans workers in their plants in 1940. Two years prior, Hayes diversified its operations to munitions manufacturing for the Navy. On the eve of the United States' entrance into World War II, the Hayes Corporation manufactured everything from auto bodies to aerial bombs.[26] With the Executive Order 8802 in place, African Americans secured local plant jobs and joined the United Auto Workers Union (UAW). Hayes Manufacturing Company was the first of the large local manufacturers to have their doors forcibly pushed open. Their African American employees joined Local 801 and slowly moved into the other plants as they got the opportunity. Upon the expiration of Executive Order 8802, it was doubtful whether these newly industrialized workers would keep the jobs they had earned.

For African Americans, maintaining employment was also hindered by an ambivalent relationship they had with their employers and the UAW locals. The NAACP branch joined with the CIO to work against job discrimination; however, the unions could not always assure local management would be fair on issues of race. In 1951, Herbert Hill, assistant field secretary for the NAACP national office, spent seven days in Grand Rapids assessing racial discrimination. During that time, he visited several factories, including two divisions of General Motors (GM)—the Fisher Body Plant and the GM Motor Diesel Plant. At the GM plants, Hill observed management's refusal to give African American trainees a fair opportunity for apprenticeship training programs. He noted that local union officials had no history of "vigorously enforcing contractual provisions and securing equal job opportunities for the Negro workers, . . . in violation of the official UAW anti-discrimination policy." Second, he confirmed what Phillips also had seen: African Americans did not use the full apparatus of the UAW to pursue discriminatory claims. In a private meeting with African Americans, Hill criticized them for "their withdrawal from active union participation and their history of not filing grievances for admitting discriminatory practices." Workers complained to Hill that their inactivity was "due to a feeling of resentment and futility with the union and its leadership." He explained to them that the NAACP would "attempt to counteract" the union lapses in hearing claims of racial discrimination.[27]

Hill also visited the Doegler-Jarvis plant during his stay. In his report, Hill noted that in addition to the usual on-the-job discrimination against African Americans, the management of this plant attempted "to divest itself of its Negro employees wherever possible and [was] replacing them with white workers." Working in conversation with Leonard Woodcock, the UAW 1D regional director, Hill drove home the point that the UAW should be an advocate for its African American members.[28]

Hill also assisted the local branch in reorganizing its labor committee. The new seven-member committee developed a three-pronged strategy for fighting discriminatory practices in the automobile industry. As with everything the NAACP pursued, this strategy was designed to open doors. When individuals applied for jobs, they were to appear at the factory in person, accompanied by a local union representative and an NAACP representative. African American union members were to actively pursue the "highest possible classifications through open bidding" and file grievances where they were warranted. In addition, union members were also encouraged to educate themselves and fully participate in all union activities. Their participation, the NAACP believed, would ensure the election of African Americans to union councils and committees.[29] Union participation alone did not guarantee job security, however. The NAACP had to remain vigilant about documenting and contesting racial discrimination in the workplace—a task at times too great for a volunteer civic organization to manage.

The NAACP waged another battle throughout 1940s as well—against racial discrimination in public schools. As the numbers of Southern migrants increased, the racial composition of neighborhood schools changed, and according to the NAACP, there were two forces at work in this shift. The first had to do with housing. Phillips observed that "99.8 percent of the blacks lived in tightly restricted segregated area[s] bounded by Eastern, Grandville, Wealthy, and Franklin Streets, an area [of] about 30 blocks." This embryonic ghetto, which R. Maurice Moss observed in 1928 and Warren Banner saw in 1940, had become a reality by 1947. The NAACP feared that this increasing ghettoization in schools had created *de facto* segregation. They believed that services and effective teaching would be limited by having African American children in all-black schools. Tied to the question of all-black schools was also the professional issue of employment for African American educators. The Grand Rapids Board of Education had not hired an African American teacher since 1920.[30] It was quite apparent to the NAACP that the Grand Rapids Board of Education had intentionally excluded the hiring of African American teachers. The *en masse* arrival of Afro-Southerners, however, enabled the NAACP to address the exclusionary practices of the board of education.

Carl Thomasson, the local NAACP president in 1945, addressed these issues in a letter to the superintendent of public schools, Lee Hutchins. Thomasson wrote, "During the past year I have listened to the complaints of Mrs. Silverstine, who is baffled by the behavior of students recently from the south. Three white parents have complained to me that teachers at Franklin School were partial to Negro students. Twice as many Negro parents have complained of discrimination against Negro students." Assessing the conditions at the school, Thomasson wrote, "[I]t is my firm belief that the situation existing at Franklin School, with its 50% Negro attendance, is crying for a good, impartial disciplinarian of Negro ancestry." Thomasson did not want to appear as though he simply desired an African American teacher solely based on race. Qualifying his comments, he explained, "There is no question of being able to find a good Negro teacher. Nor is there any reason to suppose that *none* of the Grand Rapids women of Negro ancestry, who have qualified themselves, would not have proven to be good teachers in Grand Rapids since some of them are teaching elsewhere." He further refined his opinion, stating that "even the situation at Franklin does not call for hiring a Negro teacher simply because of race, but it is a crying need for at least one teacher who understands the emotional effect of the burden that Grand Rapids and America forces upon every Negro child from the first glimpse he has of his second rate status in Grand Rapids and in America." Offering names of potential teachers, Thomasson drew upon democratic patriotism to drive home his point. "The glory of one excellent Negro teacher has long dimmed with time," he wrote. "We hope the day will soon come when neither the Board of Education nor the people of Grand Rapids will be concerned about the racial identity of any its employees." He concluded, "The blood of the Grand Rapids veterans, white and black, deserves further effort to achieve the ideal in action."[31]

NAACP leaders hoped that employing African American teachers throughout the school district and ensuring the full participation of African American children throughout the school district would help to overcome the community's racialized fears and practices. Thomasson's interwoven argument on behalf of African American children and teachers was used in the educational policy debate from the 1940s into the next two decades.[32]

The civil rights coalition in Grand Rapids was an assortment of religious, political, and labor activists. Local activists often affiliated themselves with a number of different civil rights and labor organizations—using the various platforms of the Urban League, the NAACP, the UAW, and religious communities when needed—to effect social change. Two visible personalities within this coalition—besides Floyd Skinner and Paul I. Phillips—were William Glenn, a Communist Party member, and Hillary Bissell, the NAACP's most visible active white member.

Glenn was a lifelong resident of Grand Rapids who had been a member of the NAACP since the 1920s. He came from a rich family history of activism in the pursuit of freedom and racial justice. Glenn's grandfather, Matthew, had been a mulatto runaway slave from Riley, South Carolina, who had not only run away from slavery, he had also run off with his slaveholder's daughter, heading to Ontario, Canada, before the Civil War. The Glenn family left Ontario in late 1886, moving to Manton, Michigan, and then settling in Grand Rapids in 1893. Emma Cole, Glenn's mother, also came to Grand Rapids in the 1890s. She traced her lineage to the freed slaves of Edward Cole, who later became governor of Illinois in the 1830s. Emma Cole became an active member in such civic and political organizations as the Frederick Douglass Club, which pursued racial equality in the late nineteenth century. Matthew Glenn Jr., William's father, met and married Emma Cole, Glenn's mother, around 1900. William, who was born in 1903, was their only child.

Like many individuals of mixed race, Glenn was always acutely conscious of race in his life. He reflected in his later years about the irony of his own racial identity. Reminiscing about his years in Grand Rapids, he recounted that at "the time of my birth, the city was 88,952 white and 604 Negro people. The event of my birth should have brought the Negro population to 606; however, apparently it didn't—my birth certificate states both parents were white." Sardonically he asked, "Could it be I've been passing for a Negro for 64 years, when I'm white? Well, what difference does it make? I've found out in life it makes a hell of a big difference."[33]

Glenn's mixed racial ancestry was a source of both pride and conflict for him. He described his mother, Emma, as being "a beautiful woman with a fair skin, in whom no one could detect Negro ancestry." He observed that "she could have passed for a Caucasian woman like millions of other women in our country are doing, either consciously or unconsciously." Glenn portrayed his father in similar terms, noting that his father's ancestors were "Indian, African, French and Irish." Glenn observed that "[l]ooking at father always convinced me purity is an undesirable quality; it is like the musician trying to compose music using only the whole tones of the scale, or the pianist playing the piano using only the white keys on the piano."[34]

Mixed ancestry was also the source of Glenn's pain. The city where he was born was neither tolerant nor interested in his mixed ancestry; he was black, no matter how subtle his skin color happened to be. Glenn wrote that he became conscious of race in kindergarten. He recalled, "Shortly after I was enrolled in kindergarten the teacher was teaching us a game where we started out by forming a circle and holding hands; the little girl next to me wouldn't hold my hand; the teacher had to insist; then she reluctantly held it as if it wasn't as clean as hers. We all knew why she didn't want to hold it, even though no one mentioned the reason."[35]

Another formative memory for Glenn was his father's inability to gain a job as an auto mechanic—although he was formally trained as one—"because he was colored." Instead, Glenn's father worked as a chauffeur to a wealthy banker. Thinking back over his early years Glenn wrote, "[A]s I grew up I began to learn that the wage slavery my father was subjected to did not differ greatly from the chattel slavery that my grandfather was subjected to. The change in the type of slavery was due to the production change of the country. Chattel slavery was no longer profitable in a country that was becoming industrialized, but wage slavery was."[36]

Glenn also recollected the value of his civics lessons. It is revealing that he kept his fifth grade journal, with numerous quotes from great American historical figures about democracy and equality. One of the entries that stands out is "Civic Creed," by Mary McDowell.

> God hath made of one blood all nations of men and we are his children, brothers and sisters all.
>
> We are citizens of these United States, and we believe that our flag stands for self-sacrifice for the good of all people.
>
> We want therefore to be true citizens of our city and will show our love for her by our works.
>
> Grand Rapids does not ask us to die for her welfare, she asks us to live for her; and so to live, and so to act, that her government may be pure, her officers honest, and every corner of her territory shall be a place fit to grow the best men and women, who shall rule over her.[37]

As a young man, Glenn sought to make this civic creed a reality by joining the NAACP. Glenn and Roger Grant filed the initial lawsuit against the Keith Theater, laying the groundwork for Emmett Bolden's case in 1927. Glenn always took great pride in being part of the initiative that brought down Jim Crow in public accommodations in Grand Rapids.[38] Sometime in the 1930s, Glenn had an ideological conversion to radical politics and became persuaded to the virtues of the Communist Party. The local party, though small, pursued racial equality vigorously, opening their bookstore to African Americans and registering volunteers to fight on behalf of Ethiopia against the fascist Italian invasion. For Glenn, the Communist Party offered a more complete answer about the seemingly endemic nature of racism than his parents or schools had offered.

While still employed at the Pantlind Hotel as a doorman, Glenn became involved in the Michigan Farmers Union. The Farmers Union, a communist Popular Front group, organized statewide in Michigan with the hope of linking farmers with industrial labor unions throughout each county.[39] Glenn believed the labor conditions of African Americans necessitated collective action. He noticed that "discrimination in the employment of colored people [was] rigidly adhered to. They [were] never employed in any capacity other than waiter, bellhop, doorman or porter, even though they [had] college degrees. After being employed inside for twelve year[s] as a bellhop, I was advanced outside to doorman, if that can be called advancement."[40] Glenn worked for the Pantlind Hotel for nineteen years, leaving in 1941 to work for the Hayes Manufacturing Corporation as its fourth African American employee. As he related the story, it was only divine intervention that he got his job at Hayes. "In the summer of 1939, the beginning of World War II," Glenn recalled, "a brusque, arrogant, middle-aged man drove his car up to the hotel entrance and parked it in the middle of the entrance way. I told him he wouldn't be permitted to leave his car parked there, but he said he intended to leave it there. I blew my whistle for the police officer on the corner and he came and made the gentleman move his car. I had made an enemy, the man I later learned was the new president of the Hayes Manufacturing Corporation that was going to produce wings for the Bruster dive bomber the navy was going to use in the war." This incident notwithstanding, Glenn was hired by Hayes in 1941. His employment there, he felt, was due in part to the advocacy efforts of the NAACP. And he also knew that fortune had fallen his way when Hayes hired him. Somehow, he was able to avoid the president of the company until his probationary period was complete—and after he joined the UAW. When the president found out that he had been employed, "he was so angered he spat on the floor and dashed off to the employment office to have me fired, but he was a little late."[41]

Glenn thrived in his job at Hayes and in his UAW Local. In 1944, he became the chairman of the bargaining committee of Local 801. He was also elected steward in his department, then chairman of the stewards. He later became a member of the plant committee and eventually its chairman. Glenn used his positions to advocate racial justice. As a member of the Kent County Industrial Union Council, he was chosen to represent labor on the Family Service Agency of the Community Chest (today the United Way): he was the agency's first African American member. Glenn used his membership on the Union Council to pursue the enforcement of the Fair Employment Practice Commission (FEPC) mandates in industrial employment.[42]

Glenn's work in the union and the NAACP also was a service to the Communist Party. Using his offices in the NAACP, he began a Russian War Relief Committee and affiliated the NAACP with the International Workers Order (IWO). His efforts were perfect for the Popular Front work of the Communist Party, supporting initiatives to build political coalitions with progressive organizations throughout United States in the 1940s—labor unions and civil rights organizations—to legitimatize party activities. Glenn, as a lifelong resident of Grand Rapids, an active member in the NAACP, and a laborer, seemed ideal to build such coalitions.[43]

In 1944, Glenn was elected NAACP branch president. Among other civil rights activists, Glenn's politics were suspect. The Grand Rapids NAACP members were distrustful of the intentions of the Communist Party as being anti-democratic. Historian Wilson Record documented the battle that ensued between the Communist Party and the NAACP from the 1920s until mid-1950s. Wilson explains that most members of the NAACP were political reformers and not radicals. They followed a course of traditional middle-class and legal political protest through the courts, whereas the Communist Party exploited existing class tensions among African Americans using rent strikes, labor protests, and civil discord to bring African Americans into the party.[44] The local NAACP consistently inquired of the national office about the links between the IWO and the Communist Party. The reason local activists were suspicious of Glenn's affiliation was their belief that it caused the NAACP trouble in the broader white community and unnecessary investigation into their organizations by local, state, and national law enforcement. They feared a backlash that would taint the goals of the NAACP as being subversive. Some NAACP members also objected to the philosophical principles of the Communist Party; they thought the dictatorship of the proletariat was simply a ruse—for political dictatorship. In the spring of 1944, the FBI began surveillance of Glenn using local informants, and perhaps other members in the NAACP.[45]

In 1945, Glenn formed an organization known as the Civic League for Democracy. According to FBI files, the League met every other Sunday evening at the CIO hall. In an interview with the FBI, Glenn said that the organization was designed to introduce the "major political and economic problems of the nation and the world before the working man, particularly the Negro, so that they would have a better understanding of the problems that are facing this country and the world and the problems of the Negro." He also admitted his interest in the Communist Party. He also stated that "as far as he knew, there was no discrimination against the Negro person by the Communists."[46]

To local NAACP loyalists, Glenn's activities were troublesome to the broader goals of civil rights. They felt that his kind of activism drew attention away from achieving basic citizenship rights. Glenn was viewed with even greater suspicion when he and his wife, Virginia, became involved in progressive politics; in fact, the Glenns both ran for state office on the progressive Henry Wallace ticket in 1948. Although Glenn claimed that he had abandoned the Communist Party in the early 1950s, he continued to show interest in the Soviet Union and Eastern Europe. Glenn's political involvement drew the attention of the Michigan Red Squad, a unit of the Michigan State Police that kept track of people thought to be political subversives. As the 1940s came to an end, Glenn's political activism conflicted with his fellow activists and friends.[47] He saw his himself connected with a worldwide struggle for racial and economic justice. In 1950, Glenn published his progressive points of views in his own monthly newsletter entitled *The Civic Reminder.* The newsletter criticized unfair government action with regard to labor and the unfair racial injustice occurring throughout the American South. In an editorial, Glenn wrote, "Jim Crowism must be licked before America can be called a democracy." "Jim Crow," he contended, "is the cancerous growth in America that is eating away the vitals of the country—destroying its democratic institutions and affecting every aspect of our lives."[48]

In 1951, Glenn's radical activity became the pretext for his unlawful removal from his job. During the late spring of 1951, Glenn took a month's vacation to travel to Paris to attend a labor conference sponsored by the American Committee to Survey Labor Conditions.[49] On this trip, Glenn visited France, Italy, Czechoslovakia, Poland, and the Soviet Union. Upon his return, the U.S. State Department confiscated his passport in New York City.[50] The State Department then informed the Hayes Manufacturing Corporation of Glenn's trip, and the company fired him for allegedly failing to report that he was visiting the Soviet Union on his leave. Hayes also stated that because "it worked on Navy contracts making torpedoes, a man like Glenn was not trustworthy to work in this sensitive area." Glenn and his Local 801 fought the charges brought against him. The union collected enough information against the corporation to have the state arbitrator reinstate him. However, the publicity created such uproar inside the plant that Glenn's fellow workers protested his return to work.[51]

The local branch of the NAACP also distanced itself from Glenn, although he had been active in the branch for more than twenty years.

Three years later, in 1954, the U.S. House Un-American Activities Committee subpoenaed Glenn to testify. At the hearing, Glenn claimed his Fifth Amendment privilege against self-incrimination and refused to answer any questions. He did, however, criticize the House subcommittee for failing to investigate the lynching of African Americans in the South. Although others later testified to Glenn's involvement in the Communist Party, Glenn never revealed his own political membership.[52]

Radicalism as an alternative political strategy was effectively silenced with the ouster of Glenn from his job. The African American community lost an effective advocate within the labor movement with his departure to the margins of local politics. If Glenn had anything to offer, it was insight into the structural dimensions of class inequality. Although, Glenn continued to work on issues of equality, his influence within the established civil rights coalition had been broken. Without his presence, the NAACP lacked a critical voice—someone who was able to see the connections between racial inequality and economic disparity. The social recognition Glenn sought through a worldwide workers movement receded into the larger background of the Cold War. After Glenn's removal, reformist middle-class politics as articulated in one form or another by the traditional civil rights activist held sway. Working-class Afro-Southern migrants crowding into Grand Rapids, therefore, needed to look to the clergy for political leadership.

The Grand Rapids NAACP was interracial to a limited extent. One of the chief advocates within the branch was Hillary Bissell, an upper-middle-class white woman who worked tirelessly for civil rights. Bissell was born in Greenville, Michigan, a small city northeast of Grand Rapids, in 1913.[53] After high school, she attended the University of Michigan, graduating in 1934 with a degree in sociology. She subsequently married Wadsworth Bissell, heir to the Bissell Carpet Sweeper Company of Grand Rapids. Hillary Bissell's work can be traced back to the Depression, when the Kent County Emergency Relief employed her as a caseworker.[54] This work brought her in contact with the county's poorest individuals, many of whom were African Americans. Bissell extended her involvement in civil rights in 1943, becoming a member of the NAACP in Sioux City, Iowa, where she and her husband then resided. There, she worked to integrate public pools.[55] Through her activism in Sioux City, Bissell met Thurgood Marshall, the chief counsel of the NAACP Legal Defense Fund. She and Marshall soon became regular correspondents.

In 1949, the Bissells returned to Grand Rapids. Immediately, Mrs.

Bissell wrote to Marshall, telling him that she and her husband had "joined the Grand Rapids chapter" of the NAACP. She complained that the branch was "having a heck of a problem with the Communists." She believed that Skinner thought she and her husband were "being '*do-gooders.*'" She wryly remarked, "I wish I could find some symbol to wear so that we wouldn't spend the first six months, of each new job assignment, proving that we have *joined the human* race and aren't the Lord and Lady Bountiful gesture makers."[56] Not to be deterred, Bissell asked Marshall about the work of the branch and inquired into the opinions of Lester Granger, the executive secretary of the National Urban League. Granger had recently given a speech in Grand Rapids that, in Bissell's mind, compromised FEPC legislation in the state legislature. She felt that the "passage of FEPC" was "the best educational device we have, because it creates a pattern that is *education* in the best since [sic]." Later in the same letter, Bissell explained to Marshall why she was involved in the NAACP. "No one in his right mind would ever voluntarily choose this work. Of course, you don't choose, the bug bites you and you are a goner. You fight the reactionaries and the communists. You fight the timid Negroes as well as the whites. Sometimes you wonder if the human race is worth saving—but it is a lot of fun, even if it is a damnable breed."[57]

Being one of the few white members of the NAACP was not easy. She complained to Marshall about the lack of "*white* support": "We have members but not active participants—or even people who attend except the *party liners.*" Although white members of the Communist Party were steadfast, the members of the established white community were not. Bissell maintained that the Urban League had tremendous white support, but not the NAACP. She stated that she had been invited to join the interracial committee of social service agencies and the Michigan Civil Rights Committee but none of the white people in these groups came to the NAACP meetings. She noted that these people were "not even thinking of [the] NAACP as an effective organization." Bissell committed herself to changing the lack of white support for the NAACP: "That is one thing I am going to change before I leave or raise the devil trying at least," she wrote. She concluded her observations on white involvement by stating, "I think it is fine that these groups exist; they perform functions; they can enlist certain support that we couldn't get in NAACP, but to our way of thinking there isn't any substitute for NAACP."[58]

Politically, Bissell fell to the left of most white civic leaders in the city. The established white community was far more at ease in supporting the social work efforts of the Urban League than endorsing the advocacy efforts of the NAACP. Paul Phillips, president of the Grand Rapids Urban League, had won over the white leadership with his gentlemanly and pragmatic approach to gaining jobs, education, and social service for African Americans. In the eyes of the city's white community, the NAACP was seen as the "bad cop," while the Urban League was viewed as the "good cop." The tactics of both were symbiotic; however, the mutual benefit between the two organizations was often torn down by the public recriminations lodged against the Urban League by NAACP. *The Pittsburgh Courier,* a paper sympathetic to the NAACP, stated in its Detroit edition that the local Urban League affiliate was a Jim Crow organization because of its unwillingness to challenge the city's public schools on the issue of neighborhood boundaries.[59] These attacks by the leadership of the NAACP in the newspapers and in public caused some sympathetic whites to shun the NAACP in favor of the more moderate Urban League.

Bissell made only minimal gains in getting whites to join the NAACP, however. Writing the report for the Branch News section of the *Crisis Magazine,* she quoted Floyd Skinner at the close of the 1951 membership drive:

> Although Grand Rapids is an integrated branch, the non-Negro members constitute considerably less than 1% of the total membership. This relatively small Negro-American community of approximately 6500 individuals, including children as well as adults, has given astounding evidence of its faith in the NAACP program and has vigorously expressed its determination to get rid of the specter of jim crowism and move into the realm of first class citizenship for all. We are serving notice that this branch will wage an uncompromising attack on the *Uncle Toms* and *appeasers* as well as the jim crow elements in the community. We will justify the faith of those who have so generously sacrificed their time for the NAACP cause.[60]

In a letter to Gloster Current, the director of branches for the national office, Bissell thoroughly discussed the problem of white membership in the branch. She wrote Current to correct the misperceptions of Clarence Mitchell, the chief Washington lobbyist of the national NAACP, who, after visiting the Grand Rapids branch, believed that the white members played a great role in branch activities. Bissell explained to Current that "the role of white members in our Grand Rapids NAACP" was "one of the trickiest and most dangerous questions that can be discussed." She stated that the "active white participation in Grand Rapids [was] quite small. We have 4 white board members out of 25, three of these are very active. We have no white officers." Her assessment was that there were "perhaps half a dozen white members who on occasion can be called upon to contribute real effort in the organization. I doubt whether we have more than 75 white members and most of these are *token.*" Bissell did mention that when notable speakers like Walter White, the executive director of the National NAACP, came to speak for the membership drive, the branch attracted whites to the audience to listen, but rarely to participate in its organizational work. The activism of the branch, Bissell asserted, was "due to our size, the quality of our Negro leadership, our program of activity, and should not be attributed to the role of our white members." She reiterated that the Grand Rapids branch was a "completely *grass roots* organization and its success depends not on the whites but upon the support of the Negro community. We don't even get the complete support from the *Gold Coast* Negro community because this type of Negro tends to give support to the Urban League, which carries a sure social status, which we neither seek nor desire in NAACP. We are truly a little man's mass movement here."[61]

Bissell continued, noting that Floyd Skinner's leadership skills made the NAACP a positive force in Grand Rapids. "He really is a positive genius at seeing to that all areas and all economic and social groups feel that they are being given representation and recognition in the organization." "[O]veremphasizing white participation," she wrote, did not give an accurate portrayal of the branch and created a "very deep and justified resentment." Finally, she felt that it was not helpful to solicit white members indiscriminately in the work of the NAACP unless they were committed. "It is true that many whites do not know that NAACP is interracial," she wrote, "and there is some excellent white talent that could be brought in, but before they are approached a branch ought to be awfully sure they are real integrationists and not *do-gooders* who want to make half way gestures." Bissell assured Current that "the role of our branch here is a rugged one and we are a long way from total community acceptance. The gains we make here, we make because we fight for them and we have a strong organization to back us up as well as allies in labor and other liberal and minority groups." And the gains of which Bissell spoke were accomplished through advocacy appeasement. Her assessment was that the NAACP was "not considered one of the nice *do-gooders* groups that it is safe to join. The people who work with us are the ones who are willing to go all out on the entire NAACP policy and program."[62]

Throughout the early 1950s, tension remained between the Urban League and the NAACP. In a letter to Roy Wilkins, the deputy director of the NAACP, Bissell noted that there were "under-currents here which are perhaps more dangerous to our objective (integration) than on the points on which I have touched." However, the differences between the League and the NAACP were important to Bissell, and she pointed out that "the Urban League Pilot Placement program [was] being used as a tool to justify opposition to FEPC." She feared that remarks made by NUL officials while visiting the city "were used by the Opponents of FEPC as ammunition for their position." Bissell wrote that the "[business] men sitting on the Urban League board [had] personally refused to hire Negroes in their plants. At the present time, the husband of the president also fits this category, altho [sic] it might be said that it is unfair to judge a partner to marriage by the actions of the spouse." What concerned her most about the actions of the Urban League was its accommodation toward discriminatory practices. "As you well know," she told Wilkins, "segregation in a northern community doesn't usually arrive full blown, it [is a] creeping paralysis, which often appears in the guise of special favors to the Negro community. Schools represent the final and crystallized fact of it[s] being."[63]

In Bissell's estimation the Urban League was the "*safe organization* and officials and community leaders tend to turn to that group for information and confirmation rather than to [a] militant group like the NAACP." The Urban League, she noted, had "only 150 members here and I would judge that over 50% are white. In contrast we have 1,711 and reach a complete cross-section of the community." The most bothersome aspect for Bissell about the Urban League in Grand Rapids was its role as "the agency for consultation on school boundaries." Bissell thoughtfully reflected the growing fear about ghettoization. "In view of their past activities, we have no reason to place confidence in their ability to judge what constitutes segregation. We fear that through their agency we will find ourselves in the position of being further frozen into the ghetto and that officials will justify their activities by having consulted with Urban League leaders."[64]

Bissell continued to provide to the national NAACP office with her opinion regarding the errors of the local Urban League and its leader Paul Phillips. Initially, Bissell viewed Phillips as a good leader, but after working with him on different matters, she viewed him as an easy compromiser. Phillip was elected to the City Charter Commission as the city's first black elected official in 1952—a feat that had not been accomplished in and around Grand Rapids area since William Hardy was elected to the Kent County commission in 1872. Bissell charged that once Phillips was elected to the Charter Commission, he let down his constituency by voting for a new city charter that supported having city commissioners elected at large rather than by wards. Bissell believed that this move would dilute African American political strength and representation. She informed Roy Wilkins that Phillips "was Exhibit A of the forces supporting at-large elections up until now, because he sat as a Negro elected at large *representing the Negro community.* Now since he voted against the Negro community, he is only *incidentally a Negro* and the Negro community has no right to criticize him because he is simply *a citizen.*" Bissell alleged that Phillips had contradicted himself because he ran for office so "that a *Negro American could serve upon that distinguished body.*" Cynically, she remarked, "One wonders whether the Negro American was to be there simply for decorative purposes or to represent the needs and desires of the Negro community, which Mr. Phillips has not done."[65]

The NAACP charges against the Urban League grew acrimonious. Neither Phillips nor the Urban League's board responded to NAACP's allegation as represented by Bissell. The NAACP attack on the Urban League created controversy within in its own ranks. In 1952, Patricia Verdier wrote the national office of the NAACP—not the local branch—to request a membership form. Verdier cited her objection to the local branch because of the controversy between two organizations. She wrote: "The local controversy is not between those who favor and those who opposed the advancement of colored people, but rather between two local factions, one of which, it appears to me, is trying to use the NAACP for its own purposes. One proof of this is that there are colored and white people on both sides of this controversy. Another is that the local N.A.A.C.P. on a very flimsy pretext accused the local Urban League of promoting segregation, which is certainly not the case, and in other ways they have tried to embarrass the Urban League."[66] Although Verdier saw the issue as a power struggle by some members of the NAACP, there were some genuine political choices that faced African American leaders at the time. One of these choices concerned public education.

Bissell served on the NAACP education committee and a board of education subcommittee that studied school boundaries and sites. In 1952, she wrote to Gloster Current: "We are fighting the location of a school in the heart of the Negro community, which would inevitably be all Negro. Through a study on projected enrollments in the area which I did, we were able to dispose of that school but now we are going further to attempt to bring about redistricting for better integration and because of the distribution of our Negro population this is entirely feasible, although at present we have one school 88% Negro, one 75%, and one 52%." Bissell informed Current that the NAACP study "will show the effects of segregation on both whites and Negro children and will attempt to develop techniques by which schools may lessen tensions."[67] She requested more information from him on psychological testimony that showed the effects of racial segregation on whites and blacks. She also wanted more information on school redistricting for the purposes of integration. The education subcommittee threw itself behind the use of the psychological analysis of race relations that the national NAACP legal defense used to support its various civil rights lawsuits. The fight to keep public schools integrated in Grand Rapids hinged on the ideas of psychologist Kenneth Clark, who believed that segregation gave Negro children inferiority complexes and white children superiority complexes.[68] The fight to educate black children was tantamount to creating an integrated city, and Hillary Bissell was a ubiquitous personality in this cause of fairness and decency.

One of the more important African American women activists in the civil rights leadership cadre was Helen Jackson Claytor, a native Midwesterner born and the second child of Amy Wood Jackson and Madison Jackson. The Jacksons had three daughters and pushed them to excel. Claytor and her sisters would each graduate from the University of Minnesota; Claytor earned a Phi Beta Kappa key for academic distinction by the end of her junior year of college. In every sense of the word, the Jacksons were what W. E. B. Du Bois called the talented tenth.

In January 1941, Helen Claytor's first husband, Earl Wilkins, died of tuberculosis. Shortly thereafter, Claytor took a job with the national YWCA in New York City. She traveled around the country promoting racial equality in YWCA branches. In 1943, her work brought her to Grand Rapids to foster a resolution between local black leaders and the YWCA. While in the city, she met Dr. Robert Claytor, whom she married in October of that year.[69]

Claytor's move to Grand Rapids brought the civil rights coalition a wealth of experience locally and contacts on the national front (as well, her ex-brother-in-law Roy Wilkins, was executive director of the national NAACP). According to Claytor, when she arrived in Grand Rapids, she was the only African American woman in the city with a college education.[70] Claytor, with her vast leadership skills, was almost immediately able to resolve the controversy between the YMCA, YWCA, and the African American community. She became the first African American woman elected to the board of directors of the Grand Rapids YWCA; she subsequently became its first African American president. Her passion was her work with the YWCA, and her goal in the Y was to serve as president of the World Council of the International YWCA. As soon as Claytor settled in, she joined her husband in membership at St. Philip's Episcopal Church, the Urban League, and the NAACP. Her driving ambition, to paraphrase her son's description of her, was to blast open any doors that whites closed to her.[71]

Unlike Floyd Skinner or Paul Phillips, Helen Claytor worked quietly and steadfastly behind the scenes to broker changes in the Grand Rapids community. Claytor never viewed herself as an "activist"; rather, she saw her activities as simply bettering her community. She strongly believed that she was enlightening people through her intellect and Christian principles. Like Hilary Bissell, Claytor also threw herself into working on the issues of education and advocacy for African American teachers. Her most important contribution during this era was behind-the-scenes work in the creation of the Grand Rapids Human Relations Commission.

The flow of Southern migrants into Grand Rapids created urgency among those advocating for civil rights who greatly feared permanent ghettoization. African American leaders and their allies had seen what racially ghettoized communities looked like in Chicago and Detroit. With alacrity, therefore, they pushed the city government to adopt the idea of a human relations commission, believing that such a body would be able to investigate claims of discrimination and foster an equitable relationship between all the city's residents. The city commissioners were reluctant to create a new commission, but in a compromise with the civil rights advocates they nevertheless appointed seven members to a study committee to address whether such a commission was needed in the city. Claytor was the only African American appointed to the study committee.

The study committee conducted thirty-five meetings in which it solicited a wide range of testimony from area residents. Responses indicated that discrimination against African Americans in Grand Rapids fell into six main categories: "employment, housing, education, heath and welfare services, recreation, and civil protection."[72] This was not new information; previous studies had cited the same issues. The recent increase in the city's African American population, however, did exacerbate existing patterns set in motion after World War I. The hope among the advocates of the human relations commission was that it would be given enforcement powers to penalize businesses and agencies for racial discrimination. Advocates of the proposed commission wanted to bring a cross section of people together from religion, labor, ethnic communities, government agencies, schools, police, and businesses to address discrimination in city life. The commission's task, as they saw it, was to hear complaints and make the city commissioners aware of problems they could legally correct.

On July 31, 1954, after extensive hearings, the study committee recommended to the city commission the establishment of a human relations commission. On August 5, 1954, the study committee met with the mayor and the city commission. At that meeting, however, the city commission attempted to avoid discussion of the committee's work. Regarding the meeting, Harry J. Kelly, a committee member and treasurer of the American Seating Company, wrote to George Schermer, the consultant hired to assist the study committee, that it "also seemed that the City officials wanted to talk about most everything except the matter at hand."[73] The work of the study committee could not be avoided for long, however. The civil rights coalition persisted, and in April 1955, the city commission established a human relations committee.

These were heady days for civil rights in Grand Rapids. In 1947, President Truman integrated the U.S. Armed Forces. In 1948, his administration sent to the U.S. Congress the first comprehensive civil rights legislation since Reconstruction. By 1950, the Grand Rapids Branch of the NAACP had pressured the local National Guard to integrate its unit. In the spring of 1954, the U.S. Supreme Court ruled in *Brown v. the Board of Education of Topeka* that segregation in public schools was not the law of the land. It had finally overturned its 1896 ruling, declaring separate but equal facilities to be unconstitutional. The coalition of labor, religion, and radicals had accomplished tangible changes in the life of the state and the city. The city's human relations committee, although not an enforcement agency, became a strong advisory board in local governmental affairs. Fair employment law became binding in the state of Michigan. Together, these set new precedents in the areas of civil rights and labor law in the city and the state.

The internecine battles of civil rights coalitions won victories despite themselves. In Grand Rapids, the coalition's division always centered on tactics, never on goals. All parties in the leadership cadre believed that integration was the only way to successfully combat Jim Crow and provide the African American community with access to opportunities; they differed, however, about the means to achieve these ends. The struggle over how integration was to be achieved was ultimately indicative of the black community's differing ideas about how social recognition was to be attained. In spite of their division, the civil rights leadership managed to accomplish genuine change in the laws, if not in the attitudes, of people in the city.

The first ten years after World War II were exciting times for the civil rights efforts in Grand Rapids. Afro-Southerners joined forces with the established middle class to crack the walls of racial exclusion. The rhetoric of democracy and the Cold War now forced whites to acknowledge that African Americans were entitled to just treatment under the law. The Grand Rapids civil rights coalition was at its zenith, joining forces with labor and religious communities to effect just social changes throughout the State.

Yet, the civil rights cadre failed in understanding the vital questions of ethnicity and culture that shaped so many Afro-Southerners. Because the appeals of the civil rights coalition were often made to white lawmakers and the business community, black leaders missed an opportunity to establish an ethnic power block that would appeal to Afro-Southern traditions of self-help and self-reliance; advocacy alone did not establish ethnic empowerment.

By 1955, the nation's focus turned south. The death of Emmett Till in Money, Mississippi, the Montgomery Bus Boycott in Alabama, and the integration of schools in Little Rock, Arkansas, received far more media coverage than local racial struggles in medium-sized cities like Grand Rapids. Though underexposed, African Americans in cities like Grand Rapids saw their efforts as a part of the general liberation of African Americans throughout the country.

Despite the fervent work done by the civil rights coalition in Grand Rapids, they also failed to halt the racial and economic ghettoization they feared. The G.I. Bill, the post–World War II housing boom, and the growing automobile market allowed whites in Grand Rapids to move to the fringes of the city and into its growing new suburbs, leaving the old core city to the newly amassing Afro-Southerners and other new migrants.[74] This shifting population took resources away from the neighborhoods and areas where African Americans were the primary occupants. This further exacerbated the racial divide and economic class divisions that had grown in the city. By the mid-1950s, Grand Rapids was a far less integrated city than it had been in its earlier history, when the small size of the African American population made it appear as though they were included in all aspects of the city's life. By 1954, the black population had grown to roughly 5 percent of the city's total population and continued to grow. The ghettoization of the African Americans had become a reality in the 1950s, just as it had in most American cities.[75] The inability of civil rights activists to prevent ghettoization took a psychological toll on the community's efforts to secure middle-class social reforms. The harsh realities of racial discrimination and economic exclusion in the city slowly began to convince the African American working class and the poor that the normal avenues to social upward mobility were closed. The rhetoric and the politics of respectability lost its currency.

The hardening boundaries of the ghetto and the death of ideological radicalism were, for a time, replaced by the youthfully reinvigorated rhetoric and ideology of black separatism. The old idea of assimilationist Black Nationalism had given way to Black Power. It was the dawning of tomorrow's world and a new chapter in the fight for freedoms for blacks in a highly urbanized and socially stratified world.

Conclusion: "Outstretched Hand into a Clenched Fist"

As one local historian observed in a study of the history of the Grand Rapids human relations commission that the city was a microcosm of the transformation of urban and race relations throughout the United States.[1] He was correct in his assessment. The historical shape of the African American community in Grand Rapids reflects all the pertinent issues that arose throughout the history of the Great Lakes region.

The Grand Rapids story also gives us another perspective on the topic of African American community formation. African Americans shaped their ethnic community alongside and in interaction with their white neighbors, sharing with them a common civil society and the cultural ethos of a conservative city. Any measurement of the politics of respectability within an African American community has to be considered as they occurred in the context of and alongside other ethnic communities. As African Americans attempted to define their own self-respect as an ethnic community, they did so in a Janus-like manner; they viewed their challenges with one face on their own surrounding community and the other face on neighboring black communities in larger cities. African Americans—especially local leaders—desired the social life of the larger black middle-class communities in neighboring cities. They hoped to avoid the pitfalls of ghettoization. Their pursuit of integration was an attempt to stem the social dynamics that ghettoization and impoverishment fostered. Neighboring bigger cities provided a dire warning of the consequences of racial exclusion.

Following the story of African Americans in Grand Rapids also suggests to us how the politics of respectability among African Americans
themselves was entangled and confused around the issues of ethnicity,
social status, and racial exclusion. The struggle for social recognition
cannot be delineated from the internal fight to define acceptable black
behavior in an urban people. For African Americans, being respectable
meant achieving respect collectively as an ethnic community. The driving force behind the community's efforts to build civic associations,
churches, and civil rights organizations was to bring to an end to racial
stigma and gain political power. From the 1850s into the 1950s, this
was the defining paradigm as African Americans urbanized. However,
in the 1960s, an attitudinal shift took place as a new generation resisted
social conformity to behave like white Protestants. African American
self-definition and ideas about respectability shifted from an assimilationist paradigm to a cultural nationalist one. This attitudinal shift occurred
simultaneous to the rise of the civil rights movement throughout the
South and as black Southern migrants moved north in the last decade of
the Great Migration.

In 1958, the president of the Grand Rapids NAACP, William Wilberforce Plummer, continued the longstanding local debate with the
Urban League. Plummer wrote, "I believe that the NAACP must have
an aggressive and active program. We must be a social action group; we
have neither the funds nor the trained personnel to be a social work group.
We must take the lead in the community in protesting and denouncing
all forms of racial segregation and discrimination." He continued: "I
firmly believe that the Bus Protest Movement of Montgomery, Alabama,
demonstrates the power of protest. I do mean that the NAACP should
work with constructive social-work programs, but we must never allow
these organizations to modify our program as we see it. If we allow ourselves to be put in a position in which we cannot speak freely for fear of
offending our so-called 'friends' or if we hesitate to speak, lest we suffer
political, social or financial set-backs, then the effectiveness of our unit
is severely damaged." The civil rights activism after the *Brown* decision
of 1954 galvanized many in the African American community. Plummer
poignantly observed:

> We can believe in a gradual program, providing the delay is necessary to
> plan a constructive program working toward the end of segregation and
> discrimination within a reasonable length of time. We do not believe
> in gradualism if it represents the stealing and the denial of Civil Rights
> because of the violence directed toward Negro-Americans by those that
> believe in racial superiority. We believe that education will aid solving

our problems, but we do not believe that Civil Rights should be denied any citizen while another is being educated. We believe that America cannot afford any more "Little Rocks" for the Inter-national stakes are too high for the Land of Freedom to become known as the Land of Race Hatred.[2]

This wave of activism also accompanied changes in the city's physical and demographic landscape. Urban renewal and suburbanization by late 1950s was gnawing away at the city's core. The intense growth of the black population in Grand Rapids between 1950 and 1970, linked to customary racial exclusion throughout the city, kept most blacks locked out of jobs and newer housing. By 1962, sociologist Rodger Rice had documented the full-blown inner city black belt.[3]

Additionally, the post–World War II boom created deeper social-class strains among African Americans. By the late 1940s local black professionals were moving into newer housing away from the old clustered ghetto that existed from the 1920s through the 1940s. For example, in the 1950s, attorney Floyd Skinner, the leading activist in the community, had moved into the inner-ring suburb of East Grand Rapids from his old home on Antoine Street. Other professionals had established their own development, Auburn Sweet, on the northeast side of the city early 1960s.[4] These changes in Grand Rapids and in the African American communities began the formation of what the historian Arnold Hirsch has termed the second ghetto.[5]

In the second ghetto, Afro-Southerners arriving in the city came with a deeper distrust of whites as a whole because they were firsthand witnesses to Southern brutality. They also learned through kinship networks and the news media about the daily struggle of civil rights protesters in the South. From these experiences they grew wearier of the white South and whites in general. The North of the 1950s was no longer the "Promised Land," but a place to get a job and not be bothered with "white folk." The assimilationist Black Nationalism that had guided African Americans' struggle for nearly seventy years, with its emphasis on Protestant culture and behavioral social conformity, faced competition with a youthfully invigorated separatist Black Nationalism in the city's changing landscape.

The separatist version of Black Nationalism re-emerged in the 1950s, as it had in the World War I era under Black Nationalist advocate Marcus Garvey. In the 1950s, its roots were found in Michigan. Former Michigan resident Malcolm (Little) X personified the new rhetoric of urban blackness in his reinterpretation of Garvey. X reshaped assimilationist Black Nationalist notions of respectability with renewed emphasis on black pride. He defined this pride as the love of an African cultural heritage, and black political and economic solidarity. X turned the old language of assimilationist Black Nationalism on its head and gave it an urban, street-savvy voice through Moslem street revivalism. Of interest to this study is that X came of age in Lansing, Michigan (some 65 miles east of Grand Rapids)—a city that shared a regional and religious ethos similar to that of Grand Rapids.[6] It was in Lansing where X's formative racial resentments were fueled. Like the black people in Grand Rapids, X lived side by side with his white neighbors and saw assimilationist Black Nationalism as articulated by the local black middle class as neither aggressive enough nor helpful to blacks' desire for political and social recognition. His resentments found an outlet in the teachings of the Nation of Islam. X, as exemplified in his autobiography, made this teaching appealing to the impoverished urban masses and the college-age black middle class by his seemingly uncompromising image. He expressed his views in the angry and often chauvinistic language of a separatist religious rhetoric. X said things that most black people dared not say in public for fear of retribution. The Lansing resident promoted the ideals of blackness as being beautiful.[7] Living in this region put X in close proximity to whites, which made him feel all the more frustrated and hostile. According to his account, the close interaction with the white community showed him the hypocrisy of racial exclusion. From X's vantage point, this racial exclusion made his criticism of American apartheid and its religious base in Protestantism all the more sharp and pointed. His need for positive recognition after living in Lansing and then in Boston was similar to that of people in Grand Rapids who in the 1920s clamored about their exclusion from the local YMCA and YWCA. Malcolm X's rhetoric, though couched in the language of separatist religious Black Nationalism, was nevertheless the same demand for honor that had been pursued in black communities like Grand Rapids and throughout the United States since the Civil War.

As African Americans made the cities their home throughout the 1960s, "Blackness" became the new cultural symbol of urban respectability.[8] The new rhetoric of blackness in the mid-1960s expressed a positive self-awareness within black urban communities as well as a growing resentment for white middle-class norms of behavior. Increasingly, the rhetoric of blackness was used against the black middle class, who had reportedly "sold out." For many who were caught in a continual spiral of socioeconomic divestment in America's cities, blackness served as the rhetoric for age-old class resentments that had festered among African Americans themselves. These social conditions and black people's attitudinal change fueled urban turmoil from 1965 to 1968. In 1967, following the Detroit riots, the black community in the Grand Rapids exploded in a two-day riot.[9] The politics of blackness unhinged the quest for respectability from its basis in Protestant morality. It was now about ethnic power.

Paul Philips, the executive of the Grand Rapids Urban League, reflected on the changing sentiment within the Grand Rapids black community in 1973: "Attitudes of the blacks have also changed; before the 50s the black man's hand was open, but the white man wouldn't grasp it. In the 1960s, the outstretched hand changed to the clenched fist."[10] Philips believed he was watching a sea change in attitudes in race relations. To an extent, he was right. The riot of 1967 and the 1968 assassination of Martin Luther King Jr. left the black community wary of whites, and whites wary of the black community.

Of the many positives in the Black Consciousness movement, as it evolved in Grand Rapids, was in the arts. For instance, a young man by the name Cedric Ward, who was caught in the struggle for racial justice and also had ambitions to be an actor, formed within the black community a theater group called the Robeson Players, in honor of Paul Robeson, the renowned singer and actor of the 1930s and 1940s. This theater group raised the level of consciousness of the community and gave outlet to aspiring young actors, directors, and singers—black and white—to do interesting, funny, and provocative works by significant American playwrights for nearly thirty years.[11] In addition, the movement pushed a local sign painter, Paul Collins, to become a nationally recognized artist.[12]

Black consciousness notwithstanding, some things remained the same. The local NAACP continued the fight for access to the established system of public education by fighting for school integration through lawsuits, court-ordered busing, and increasing the number of black teachers hired by the school board. In 1971, Lyman Parks, pastor of the First Community AME Church, was appointed and then elected as the city's first and only black mayor.[13] Local congregations between blacks and whites continued to serve as forums for discussions of local race relations. Finally, black civic associations and political groups continued to search for ways the Grand Rapids black community might control its own political and economic destinies. Although the population had grown within the city proper in the 1950s, blacks were still only 8 percent of the total population in the metropolitan area by 1975. The community continued to compete with larger white and ethnic communities in the economic and political arena, where whiteness was a social advantage. Yet many black middle-class leaders, following the legacy of George

Smith and Floyd Skinner, kept faith and continued the legal fight for full integration in all civic and economic institutions. Others continued the legacy of Ethel Burgess and Paul Philips, gently persuading the white corporate leaders and social agencies to offer training and open doors to black people. By the 1980s, African American middle-class leadership was expressing the old ideas of assimilationist Black Nationalism in the corporate managerial culture that dominated the city and the country in the era of Ronald Reagan. No longer was assimilationist Black Nationalism an effort at civic equality: it was now defined in terms of black capitalist prowess.

The thirty-year decline in the American labor movement from the 1950s to 1980s in Grand Rapids as elsewhere denied black working-class people a voice and training ground for political activism. Without labor organizing, the average black working-class person was left without a key resource in building progressive and inclusive political coalitions. Instead, the working class was left with the bitter vituperations of a hollow chauvinistic Black Nationalism or the poetic cultural anger found in the embryonic hip-hop culture of 1980s and the valiant but ultimately unsuccessful politics of rainbow coalitions. The labor movement begun in the 1930s, which had served as a vehicle of upward mobility and a source of education, along with churches, in the lives of working-class black women and men, died in the inner city of Grand Rapids as it had throughout the Great Lakes industrial corridor. With the demise of labor organizing within black communities, no alternative organizing strategy was left in the wake of the civil rights victories to aid the interest of black laborers.

The growing black middle class, though desirous of political change, lacked the organization to build an effective political coalition in order to pursue social policies that would alleviate the difficulties faced by the black working class and poor. They raged at corporate glass ceilings and black poverty without a plan of political action to empower black citizens. They held onto a shallow ideology of blackness that could not sustain their fight against racism or build effective institutions to address the declining state of the black poor.

Outside the arena of formal politics, black people in Grand Rapids continuously found joy in their churches, civic associations, and in the embrace of family and friends. They learned to live within a white conservative community and welcome new immigrants. They continued to defy convention and marry interracially, blurring the bounds of race and class distinctions. They continued, despite meager resources, to urge their children to get working-class jobs or a formal education and to take care of one another in community. They unrelentingly struggled with the impoverishment and the harshness of life as the working class and poor. They persisted in doing battle with the wiles and romance of the streets. Remarkably, despite all these things, many in the African American community of Grand Rapids kept faith and hope in some unseen providential goodness that would ultimately vindicate their struggle and see them honored as a powerful American people.

NOTES

Abbreviations

BC	Bentley Historical Collection
CCH	Calvin College History Seminar
CA	Grand Rapids City Archives
DAT	*Detroit Advertiser & Tribune*
DFP	*Detroit Free Press*
E&H	*Enquirer & Herald*
GRHT	*Grand Haven Daily Tribune*
GRD	*Grand Rapids Democrat*
GRDT	*Grand Rapids Daily Times*
GRE	*Grand Rapids Eagle*
GREH	*Grand Rapids Enquirer & Evening Herald*
GRH	*Grand Rapids Herald*
GREL	*Grand Rapids Evening Leader*
GRPO	*Grand Rapids Post*
GRP	*Grand Rapids Press*
GRWE	*Grand Rapids Weekly Enquirer*
GRPL	Grand Rapids Public Library
GRTH	*Grand Rapids Telegram-Herald*
KCA	Kalamazoo College Archives, Kalamazoo, Michigan
LC	Library of Congress
MHC	Michigan Historical Collections, Bentley Historical Library, University of Michigan, Ann Arbor
MSN	Michigan State News, Grand Rapids, Michigan
SA	State of Michigan Archives
WMRA	Western Michigan University Regional Archives

Preface

1. Z. Z. Lydens, *Story of Grand Rapids*, 2–16.

2. See, for example, the home furnishing design in Carron, *Grand Rapids Furniture*.

3. Olson, *Grand Rapids Sampler*, 86–89.

4. The history of African American life in the Great Lakes region is rich with monographs, beginning with Katzman's *Before the Ghetto* and Kusmer's *Ghetto*

Takes Shape. See also Trotter, *Black Milwaukee*; Thomas, *Life for Us*; Williams, *Strangers.*

5. Kusmer, *Ghetto Takes Shape*, chap. 1.

6. For a wonderful and picturesque overview of churches in Grand Rapids, see Bratt and Meehan, *Gathered at the River.*

7. Burgess, "This I Believe," 333.

8. Ibid, 334.

9. Levine, *Black Culture*; Mays, *Negro's God*, chap. 8; Wilmore, *Black Religion*; Sernett, *Promised Land*, 3.

10. Weber, *Protestant Ethic*, chap. 5. A helpful interpretation of Weber's work can be found in Giddens, *Capitalism*, 119–32.

11. Hobsbawm, *Age of Capital*, 263–64. See also Blumin, *Middle Class*; Gay, *Bourgeois Experience*; Himmelfarb, *Poverty and Compassion.*

12. Higginbotham, *Righteous Discontent*, chap. 7.

13. Boxill, "Self Respect," 58–69.

14. Grossman, *Land of Hope*; Phillips, *Alabama North.*

15. Huggins, *Harlem Renaissance*, 142.

16. See Gaines, *Uplifting the Race.* Gaines's wonderful book falls short of the mark in recognizing the roots of uplift in Protestant social theology.

17. For my understanding of social recognition, I am heavily indebted to Thomas Hobbes (*Leviathan*, 74) via a reading of Orlando Patterson's *Slavery and Social Death* (see especially pp. 78–79). The present study builds upon their theories. As Hobbes stated, in analyzing the human motivation for and the use of power, that which is "[h]onourable is whatsoever possession, action, or quality is an argument and sign of power. And therefore to be honoured, loved, or feared of many is honourable, as arguments of power. To be honoured of few or none, dishonourable. Dominion, and victory is honourable, because acquired by power; and servitude, for need or fear, is dishonourable." Hobbes addressed his concerns primarily to the individual and the warring state of mid-seventeenth-century England and Europe. However, following the Hobbesian philosophical impulse, Patterson (*Slavery and Social Death*) explains that honor, and conversely dishonor, are crucial elements in understanding slave societies and the collective experiences of those peoples with slavery as their past. Slaves, Patterson states, have a "sense of debasement inherent in having no being except as an expression of another's being." He further explains that those who can compete for honor are those who belong to the social order. He says, "To belong to a community is to have a sense of one's position among one's fellow members, to feel the need to assert and defend that position, and to feel satisfaction if that claimed position is accepted by others and a sense of shame if it is rejected. It is also that one has a right to take pride in its past and current successes of the group, and to feel shame and dishonor in its past and present failures." Following the leads of Hobbes and Patterson, this study argues that fundamental to the struggle for bourgeois respectability and democratic freedoms were the centrality of honor and dishonor. I call Patterson's concept of honor "social recognition" in this study.

18. Rancière, *Nights of Labor*, x.

19. Katzman, *Before the Ghetto*, 211.

Chapter 1: "The Negro, North and South"

1. *GRE*, April 2, 1872, 1.

2. Holt's *Black Over White* is one of the definitive monographs on this subject in the South. Little has been written on the few African American politicians elected in the North post-emancipation.

3. Tocqueville, *Democracy in America*, 341. His entire argument reads, "In antiquity, the most difficult thing was to change the law; in the modern world, the hard thing is to alter mores, and our difficulty begins where theirs ended. This is because in the modern world the insubstantial and the ephemeral fact of servitude is most fatally combined with the physical and permanent fact of difference in race. Memories of slavery disgrace the race and race perpetuates memories of slavery. . . . The Negro transmits to his descendants at birth the external mark of his ignominy. The law can abolish servitude, but only God can obliterate its traces."

4. Tocqueville, *Democracy in America*, 343.

5. Ibid., 344.

6. Ibid., 384–85.

7. *GREH*, June 24, 1858, 2.

8. The idea of racial stigmatization is indebted to earlier historical discussions of racial castes in the nineteenth century. See Berreman, "Concept of Caste," 333–34; Ogbu, *Minority Education*. For criticism of this concept see Cox, *Caste, Class, and Race*. Katzman (*Before the Ghetto*, 223–24) used caste as the defining feature of his work. The concept of caste continues to be very instructive for understanding the depth of American social inequality in the mid-nineteenth century. Although this literature is helpful in understanding the shape of racial inequality, it shares a common problem—that is, inequality as previously argued was discussed as though it were a static social phenomenon, which allowed little room for social class status, change over time, and human social agency. Although the term caste is misleading, its relevancy as an analytical tool is helpful in understanding the depth of racial stigma that was constructed sociologically to limit African American economic and social mobility.

9. A broad spectrum of American historians has noted the caste-like conditions of Northern Afro-American communities in the antebellum era. They have observed that Afro-Americans were economically immobile and castigated by Northern whites. They have also commented extensively that free people of color both in the North and the South at times exceeded or defied the socially proscribed limits and exercised a considerable amount of social agency. Within these Northern communities institutions were forged: Afro-American newspapers, the Independent Black Church Movement, the National Negro Convention Movement, the Prince Hall Masons, and other benevolent groups. See Berlin, *Slaves without Masters*; Curry, *Free Black*; Horton, *Free People*; Horton and Horton, *In Hope*; Litwack, *North of Slavery*; Nash, *Forging Freedom*.

10. Chapman, *History of Kent County*, 732; Death Certificate Index, GRPL.

11. Katzman, *Before the Ghetto*, 8.

12. U.S. Census, 1840, Michigan C120, "Wm. Hardy Washtenaw County."

13. U.S. Census 1850, 127, James Watts; see also Kent County Death Records on Eliza Watts as well as U.S. Census records of 1860, 1870, and 1880.

14. State Land Patents, Kent County, Michigan; compiled by the Western Michigan Genealogical Society.

15. U.S. Census, 1850.

16. Lydens, *Story of Grand Rapids*, 19

17. Chapman, *History of Kent County*, 733.

18. Turner, *Ritual Process*, 95.

19. See Piersen, *Black Yankees*. This seminal work addresses Afro-American culture from a regional perspective.

20. Berlin, *Slaves Without Masters*, chap. 3.

21. Anderson, *Imagined Communities*. See chap. 10, "Census, Map, Museum," for a discussion of census categorization.

22. Porter, "Fur Trade," 426.

23. Gordon, "Michigan Journal, 1836," 433; Baxter, *History of Grand Rapids*, 29 and 731; Chapman, *History of Kent County*, 796; Lowell, *100 Years*, 21.

24. "Idea of Ship Canal for Grand Rapids Dates Back 100 Years to First River Channel," *GRP*, January 1, 1936, 16; GRPL Local History Collection, Afro-Americans.

25. "Underground Railroad," *GRE*, July 3, 1857, 2; "Came to Grand Haven by Famous Underground," *GRHT*, July 8, 1919, 1.

26. Michigan Department of State, *Pathway*, 11.

27. See Formisano, "Edge of Caste."

28. Katzman, *Before the Ghetto*, 6.

29. *GRE*, March 28, 1851, 2.

30. *GRE*, September 3, 1851.

31. V. Jacques Voegli, *Free But Not Equal*. Also see Yzenbaard, "Crosswhite Case," 131–43. Yzenbaard explains the trial of Adam Crosswhite, a mixed-race African American born into slavery in Kentucky who fled to Michgan. The case revolves around the Fugitive Slave Act of 1850. Crosswhite prevailed in his case and was not returned to Kentucky. Yzenbaard concludes, "Although the people of Michigan were zealous in their concern for the runaway, their solicitude did not extend to the civil rights of the free Negro residents of the state."

32. Pieterse, *White on Black*, 132–36.

33. See, for example, *GREH*, September 19, 1856, 2.

34. Katzman, "Black Slavery in Michigan," 55–66.

35. "Rebecca Richmond's Diaries," Richmond Family Papers, Box 6, Folder 1, GRPL.

36. Lott, *Love and Theft*, 63; further support of Lott's thesis can be seen in the *GRE*, December 5, 1864, 1. "Uncle Tom's Cabin To-Night—Tonight the great moral drama entitled 'Uncle Tom's Cabin, or Life Among the Lowly' will be played at Opera Hall. Mr. R. E. Porter of this city will personate "Uncle Tom," Mr. A. O. Miller, "Legree," Yankee Miller, "Gumptious Cute," Miss Fanny Porter, "Eva," Mrs. A. O. Miller, "Topsy", and Miss Nellie Palmer, "Aunt Ophelia." The play is an excellent one—dramatized from Mrs. Harriet Beecher Stowe's great story bearing that title, and which most everybody read with thrilling interest—The piece contains six acts and twelve tableux, and will be presented for the first and last time by this troupe, tonight."

37. *GREH*, March 22, 1859, 3.

38. "Bloody Fight," *GRWE*, July 10, 1861, 3. The report read:

> J. Thomas and J. Highwarder, a couple of colored barbers, in this city, got into a fracas on Sunday evening last, in which Highwarder received several stabs with a dirk, which though severe are not likely to prove fatal, we learn. The difficulty originated in such matters as an illicit love affair. The darkie Thomas has got tired of his wife and wished to elope with another woman, and take his children with him. This, the wife, nor the children, seemed to fancy, and had gone to the Highwarder's, as a place of greater security for the children. Thomas followed them up and endeavored to get the children one 9, the other 11 years of age but they refused to go. He then left in a rage, and soon came back onto the street with a loaded double barrel gun, which was taken from him by an officer. A few hours after he returned, and promising to behave himself, was admitted to where his wife and children were, where he remained in conversation but a few minutes before he attempted to take his children by force, and upon the mother attempting to assist the children, drew a large dirk, upon which Highwarder who was armed with a heavy cane, interfered, which Thomas flew at him and stabbed him twice, when they clinched, struggled and fell to the floor. At this juncture Mrs. H. seized the cane, knocked the dirk out of the assailant's hand and beat a retreat on his thick pate with the cane. Constable Shields and others came to the rescue and marched the darkie Thomas off to jail.

39. See, for example, Roediger, *Wages of Whiteness.*

40. *GREH*, November 29, 1859, 2.

41. *GRE*, February 4, 1868, 1. The *Eagle* reported Douglass as saying:

> Self-made men are not to be confounded with great men generally. They are men who have, without the aid of favoring circumstances, risen from destitution, to wealth, usefulness and distinction in society. Men who owe nothing to friends, schools, or universities. Men who, if they had traveled, would have made the road over which they traveled. Men who have risen against the bitter prejudices of society, whether of Anglo-Saxon or Anglo-African origin. There are three heads to be considered under this division: first, possession of superior mental endowments; second, chance and good luck; third, energy, industry, application, patience and perseverance. . . . One little word explains all work. The true definition of self-made men is work. . . . The institutions of the country have a great deal of influence upon self-made men. In America such is the case. In no other country on the globe is labor so respectable as in America. What America is dying for is equality. All that he asked for [the] colored race in this country was that they be given the same means of self-protection that the whites have. If they cannot stand with that, let them fall.

42. For a discussion of Douglass's view of self-reliance, see Martin, *Mind of Frederick Douglass.*

43. *GRD*, January 27, 1866, 1.

44. "Another Raid," *GRE*, April 16, 1870, 1; "Discharged," *GRE*, August 21, 1870, 1; "Skeddaled," *GRE*, May 18, 1870, 1.

45. "War In Africa," *GRE*, May 26, 1870, 1. "Miss Harriet a gentle daughter of African descent, was up before Justice Sinclair, this morning, 26th, charged with committing a vigorous assault and battery upon the probicis [*sic*] of a gentle

162   *Notes to Pages 9–11*

sister. 'Revenge was sweet,' and she into her affections to such an extent that nothing short of $5 greenback would heal the wounds. She came down with the stamps and left the courtroom utterly disgusted with the 'white trash' method of dispensing justice."

46. White, *Arn't I a Woman*, 30–32.

47. "Serious Affray Man Stabbed," *GRE*, July 12, 1860, 1.

48. *GREH*, July 21, 1860, 3.

49. Concerning the life of one African American on the railroad, see "The Pioneering Moores: From Kokomo Roots to RR Ties," *Wonderland Magazine*, *GRP*, July 24, 1977, 28–29.

50. *GRE*, 1866, 1.

51. "Grand Haven Items," *GRE*, 1867, 2.

52. *GRE*, August 9, 1872, 1.

53. John Wesley Lowes to Sarah Benson Lowes, June 1872, Local History Collection, GRPL.

54. Cohen, *At Freedom's Edge*, 79.

55. "A Wing," *GRE*, May 10, 1873, 1; Harms, "Comstock's Row," 43.

56. "The War Carried into Africa," *GRE*, April 18, 1873, 1; "Quarreled," *GRE*, November 8, 1873, 1.

57. I am indebted to Liah Greenfeld's notion of ressintment (*Nationalism*, 15–16); Greenfeld, building on the work of the philosophy of Friedrich Nietzsche and Max Scheler, argues that ressintment derives from a dislocation with traditional identity. In this case she is referring to growing dissatisfaction among elites in modern France, Germany, Russia, Britain, and the United States to change the identity of their respective countries in an effort to modernize structurally and culturally. This changing identity is accompanied by the importation of foreign ideas, which causes an internal reaction to the modernizing host country.

> Ressintment refers to a psychological state resulting from suppressed feelings of envy and hatred (existential envy) and the impossibility of satisfying these feelings. The sociological basis for ressintment—or the structural conditions that are necessary for the development of this psychological state—is twofold. The first condition (the structural basis of envy itself) is the fundamental comparability between the subject and the object of envy, or rather the belief on the part of the subject and the object of envy, or rather the belief on the part of the subject in the fundamental equality between them, which makes them in principle interchangeable. The second condition, inequality (perceived as not fundamental), [is] of such dimensions that it rules out practical achievement of the theoretically existing equality. The presence of these conditions renders a situation ressintment-prone irrespective of the temperaments and psychological makeup of the individuals who compose the relevant population. . . . In all cases the creative impulse comes from the psychologically unbearable inconsistency between several aspects of reality.

The problem is that Greenfeld makes no distinction when ressintment is justifiable and when it is not. I am equally indebted to the work of the theologian Howard Thurman who also uses the concept of ressintment (*Jesus and the Disinherited*, 79). Thurman explains that "hatred, in the mind and spirit of the disinherited, is born out of great bitterness—a bitterness that is made possible by essence of vitality, giving to the individuals in whom this is happening a radical and fundamental basis for self-realization." Greenfeld misses the ressintment of African Americans in her important work.

58. Owens and Jackson, "Report on Negroes," 326–27; Rev. S. Henri Browne, "The Negro of Grand Rapids," Local History Collection, GRPL, 1.

59. Freedmen's Progress Commission, *Michigan Manual*, 35.

60. See Dunbar and Shade, "Vote."

61. Katzman, *Before the Ghetto*, 35.

62. Fennimore "Austin Blair," 212.

63. Philips, "Negro in Grand Rapids," 2.

64. "The Policy of a Negro Army for the North," *DAT*, January 6, 1863, 1; "Black Men in the Rifle Pits at Vicksburg," *GRE*, July 13, 1863, 2; "Negro Skill and Courage," *GRE*, April 28, 1864, 1; "Negro Heroes," *DFP*, June 29, 1864, 2; "How the Soldiers Regard the 'Democracy' of Kent County—Its Organ Repudiated by One of His Own Correspondents," *GRE*, August 29, 1864, 2; "Disbanding Negro Troops," *GRE*, October 11, 1865, 1. Although the *GRE* reported regularly on the goings-on of Afro-American troops, the author has found no reports on the 102nd U.S. Colored Troops in the newspaper.

65. Smith, " Black Regiment," 41.

66. Formisano, "Edge of Caste," 20.

67. Ben Morgan, "A Local Perspective of Black Suffrage and Civil Rights during Reconstruction Period," May 5, 1993, 20, CCH.

68. "State Items," *DAT*, February 24, 1863, 4.

69. *GRE*, August 3, 1865.

70. *GRE*, January 6, 1868, 2.

71. "Ku Klux Klan of Grand Rapids," *GRE*, September 9, 1868, 1; "Negro Supremacy," *GRE*, September 19, 1868, 1; "Down on the 'Nigger'," *GRE*, November 19, 1868, 1; "Slaves and Free Labor," *GRE*, March 30, 1869, 2; "The Southern Blacks," *GRE*, April 9, 1869, 2.

72. Dunbar and Shade, "Vote"; Morgan, "A Local Perspective of Black Suffrage and Civil Rights During Reconstruction Period," CCH.

73. "Fifteenth Amendment," *GRE*, March 30, 1870, 1; "The Registry of Colored Voters," *GRE*, April 1, 1870, 1; "The Fifteenth Amendment," *GRD*, April 2, 1870, 2; "Negro Equality," *GRD*, April 5, 1870, 2; "Colored Troops," *GRD*, April 7, 1870, 1.

74. "A Word to the Colored Men of Grand Rapids," *GRE*, November 7, 1870, 1.

75. *GRD*, June 18, 1870, 4; *GRE*, April 2, 1872; *GRE*, January 4, 1879, 1.

76. For another anomaly of racial stigma in the Northeast, see Jelks, "Spiritual Watchman," 126–33.

77. Everett, *Grand River Valley*, 28; "Another Pioneer Gone," *GRE*, June 6, 1888, 4; "No Negro Pioneer Heirs," *GRP*, May 22, 1955, 5.

78. Wood, *Black Majority*, chap. 4.

79. Chapman, *History of Kent County*, 732.

80. Everett, *Grand River Valley*, 29.

81. Ibid., 204.

82. "That's What's the Matter," *GRD*, April 16, 1873, 4.

83. "The Gaines Supervisorship—Card from Mr. Hardy," *GRE*, April 18, 1873, 1.

84. *GRD*, April 5, 1870, 2.

85. Foner, *Free Labor, Free Soil*

86. Du Bois, *Souls of Black Folk*, 5.

87. See Nash, *Forging Freedom;* Horton and Horton, *In Hope.*

88. See, for example, Richardson, *Death of Reconstruction.*

89. Woodward, *Strange Career*, chap. 1.

90. Douglas, *Purity and Danger.* Douglas looks at the notions of purity and danger from a religious perspective. However, the ritualized stigmatization of blackness in a democratic culture must be explored as well. The repetition of black as evil and evil as black certainly functions in the same way Douglas describes. "Reflection on dirt involves reflection on the relation of order to disorder, being to non-being, form to formlessness, life to death." See also Patterson, *Slavery and Social Death*, 261.

91. "Nigger! Nigger! Nigger!" *GRE*, November 21, 1867, 1.

92. "No Negro Pioneer Heirs," *GRP*, May 22, 1956, 5.

93. For a further discussion see Stokes, "Tocqueville."

Chapter 2: "In Colored Circles"

1. "In Colored Circles," *GRTH*, June 18, 1890, 1; "Unhappiness in Comstock's Row," *GRE*, June 17, 1895, 5.

2. "Both Women Fined," *GRE*, June 2, 1889, 1; "'Black Joe' At Home," *GREL*, April 11, 1890, 4; "In Police Court", *GREL*, December 1, 1891, 1; "Josephine Gets Two Years," *GREL*, June 23, 1892, 4.

3. Elsthain, *Democracy on Trial*, 5–6.

4. Fabre, "Commemorative Celebrations," 85; White "Proud Day," 13–50.

5. Katzman, *Before the Ghetto*, 25.

6. McKivigan and Silverman, "Monarchial Liberty," 7. McKivigan and Silverman observe, in discussing Afro-Americans holidays in western Canada (Ontario) and upstate New York, that these annual events were celebrations that defined freedom in the first half of the nineteenth century.

7. "A Sable Gathering—Grand Festivities," *GRE*, February 23, 1867, 1; *GRE*, August 1, 1878, 4; *GRE*, August 2, 1886; *GRE*, July 30, 1887, 7; *Grand Rapids Evening Press*, July 6, 1895; *GRTH*, July 31, 1888, 2; "Emancipation Day," *GRTH*, August 2, 1888, 1.

8. Fabre, "Commemorative Celebrations," 85. Fabre notes that Emancipation Day celebrations required extensive planning because these "occasions included fairs, parades, picnics, banquets, and dances; and thus blended the traditional religious elements with the secular and the military."

9. The various Grand Rapids newspapers frequently reported stories about former slaves in the area. "Once Were Slaves," *GRP*, October 20, 1900, 8; "Was Born a Slave," *GRP*, March 25, 1901, 5; *GRE*, May 3, 1884, 2; *GRE*, May 22, 1884, 8; *GRE*, March 14, 1884, 4; *GRE*, January 13, 1885, 2; *GRE*, September 2, 1885; "Born in Slavery and Was with Union Army," *GRH*, October 16, 1910, 11; "A Quaint Figure," *GRP*, November 11, 1905, 8; "Happy Old Darkey," *GRP*, October 2, 1909, 10; "Ex-Slave Pays 'Debt' to City, Deeds Home," July 17, 1927, *GRH*, magazine,

5; "Grandma Tabitha, 107, Celebrates Birthday," *GRH*, October 9, 1927, 3; "Sees Good in Slavery Days of Old," *GRH*, October 23, 1927, magazine, 4; "Old Tom Corbin," *GRP*, August 7, 1947, 19.

10. "Slavery Days," *GRD*, December 6, 1885, 9; "Died in the County House" *GRD*, July 31, 1894, 5.

11. *Grand Rapids Evening Press*, December 3, 1902, 9; J. C. Craig Collection, Box 1, Folder 1 GRPL.

12. "'Senator' Ford, Former Slave and State Employee, Is Dead," *GRP*, January 18, 1939, 2; "'Senator' Ford Born in Slavery Days Dies at 87 Years," *GRH*, January 19, 1939, 3.

13. "Colored Citizens Celebrate," *GRE*, August 2, 1883, 2.

14. "Colored Residents Honor Memory of Hon. Charles Sumner," *GRDT*, March 18, 1874, 1; "On Tuesday Night: Local Colored Citizens Will Honor John Brown's Memory," *GRP*, August 18, 1900, 2.

15. Owens and Jackson, "Report on Negroes," 325.

16. Gates, "Trope," 137.

17. Moses, *Wings of Ethiopia*, 95.

18. Meier, *Negro Thought*, 53. Meier wrote that at "times the emphasis on race pride and solidarity approached a kind of nationalism." He further argued that Afro-Americans, when they referred to themselves as a nation, used the term rather loosely and did not imply the building of a nation-state. Rather, he said, Afro-Americans were referring to themselves as a "group or a nationality because they were set apart by other Americans, though they themselves actually wished to be accepted into American society." Meier thought that there exists an "essential ambivalence of Negroes in their identification with both race and nation."

19. Maffly-Kipp, "Mapping the World," 626.

20. For another read on religion and cultural nationalism, see Hill, *English Bible*.

21. "A New Club," *GRE*, March 15, 1882, 4; "United Sons of Ham," *GRE*, November 1, 1882, 4; "Campaigners," *GRE*, October 8, 1884, 7.

22. "All Their Own Way," *GRD*, February 14, 1894, 5.

23. "The Colored Men," *Evening Press*, March 14, 1894, 1; "Colored Republicans" *GRTH*, October 3, 1888, 1;"The Colored Democrats" *GRTH*, August 14, 1888, 3.

24. "Colored Voters Are Interested," *GRPO*, March 29, 1904, 3; "Colored Voters Are Interested," *GRPO*, March 30, 1904, 2.

25. Tocqueville, *Democracy in America*, 513. Tocqueville explains:

> Americans of all ages, all stations in life, and all types of dispositions are forever forming associations. There are not only commercial and industrial associations in which all take part, but others of a thousand different types— religious, moral, serious, futile, very general and very limited, immensely large and very minute. Americans combine to give fetes, found seminaries, build churches, distribute books, and send missionaries to the antipodes. Hospitals, prisons, and schools take shape in that way. Finally, if they want to proclaim a great truth or propagate some feeling by the encouragement of a great example, they form an association. In every case, at the head of any new undertaking, where in France you would find the government or

in England some territorial magnate, in the United States you are sure to find an association.

26. "Death of James Towwe," *GRP*, July 21, 1898, 1.

27. For more on this line of reasoning, see Thomas, "Historical Roots."

28. J. C. Craig Collection, GRPL, Box 1, Scrapbook.

29. *GRDT*, January 22, 1876, 1.

30. "Many Handsome Knights," *GRE*, August 15, 1893, 1; "Colored Masons," *GRE*, January 24, 1894, 4; "Colored Masons' Election," *GRD*, January 29, 1898, 2; "Colored Masons Held State Convention" *GRH*, January 31, 1908, 8.

31. For more on women's organizations in Grand Rapids, see Edmond, *We Honor Them*, vol. 1.

32. "Colored Female Mason," *GRE*, September 13, 1886, 1.

33. Hine, *Michigan Experience*; Giddings, *When and Where*; Neverdon-Morton, *Afro-American Women*.

34. Hine, *Michigan Experience*, 1.

35. Moses, *Golden Age*, 129.

36. "Colored Women Protest," *GRH*, November 14, 1898, 2; "North Unfair to Negro Says Woman," *GRH*, May 27, 1907.

37. "To Give Concert: Nineteenth-Century Club Has High Ambitions," *GRP*, December 1, 1906.

38. Mary Ruth Elder, "Rowing, Not Drifting: The Grand Rapids Study Club, 1904–1964" CCH.

39. "Annuals of the Grand Rapids Study Club," Collection 82, Box 5, GRPL.

40. "Colored Women's Convention Opens: State Association of Afro-American Women Convenes In This City," *GRH*, July 24, 1907, 3; "Club Women Elect," *GRH*, July 25, 1907, 3.

41. *GRE*, October 31, 1879, 4; "A Colored Band," *GRE*, March 19, 1880, 4.

42. Richard H. Harms, " Mr. Baseball," 10–11; On boxing, see "Stewart and Regan," *GRD*, February 25, 1897, 4.

43. Mays and Nicholson, *Negro's Church*, 286.

44. Higginbotham, *Righteous Discontent*, 7–13.

45. Hatch, *Democratization*, 4.

46. Ibid, chap. 4.

47. "Saint Luke," GRPL.

48. Baxter, *History of Grand Rapids*, 317; Works Project Administration, *Church Archives*, 11; "Souvenir Program Community A.M.E."

49. "Fountain Street Baptist Church," BC; Box 7, Folder Baptist City Mission Society; Kalamazoo College, "Twenty-Fifth Anniversary of the Fountain Street Baptist Church," 53; "Minutes of the Fifty-Second Anniversary of the Grand Rapids Baptist Association, October 1 and 2, 1895," KCA, 14.

50."Open New Mission," *GRP*, August 8, 1907, 12.

51. St. Philip's Episcopal Church, Fortieth Anniversary; Bragg, *Episcopal Church*, 239–40.

52. "African Methodist Congregations," *GRE*, April 14, 1886, 7; "Negro Churches Are Split By Factions," *GRP*, August 31, 1915, 9.

53. "Excursion to Lake Odessa: Colored People's Camp Meeting," *GRD*, July 27, 1895, 3.

54. Greenwood, *Bittersweet Legacy*, 6. Greenwood has perceptively observed that the trajectory of social class formation and identification among Afro-Americans in late-nineteenth-century Charlotte, N.C., came through churches. Her argument is confirmed in the author's own research.

55. "African M.E. Church" *GRDT*, March 29, 1878, 1.

56. "A Neat New Church: Arnett Chapel Will Be Dedicated in July" *GRH*, June 22, 1899.

57. On the AME Church, see Campbell, *Songs of Zion*.

58. Wills, "Womanhood," 140–43.

59. For a discussion of Methodism as a work discipline, see Thompson, *English Working Class*, chap. 11.

60. "Of Race Problem," *GRP*, June 10, 1902, 5.

61. Meier, *Negro Thought*, 35. Meier contended that African Americans in this period turned their attention away from partisan politics toward issues of economic development.

62. Allen, *Life Experience.*

63. "Two Diverging Views of the Modern Cake Walk," *GRP*, March 11, 1899, 3.

64. Higginbotham, *Righteous Discontent*, chap. 7.

65. See chap. 1 on the stigmatized role of African American women in the nineteenth century.

66. "Johnson Fired Out," *GRD*, December 13, 1890, 5.

67. "A Nasty Black Niggah," *GREL*, February 21, 1891, 1; "That Colored Church Fracas," *GRE*, February 21, 1891, 3.

68. *GRE*, September 12, 1973, 1.

69. See, for example, Campbell, *Song of Zion*, chap 2.

70. "AME Conference Will Open Tuesday: Bishop MacNeal Turner of Chicago Will Preside at the Sessions," *GRP*, May 31, 1913, 10; "Conference Does Not Get a Bishop," *GRP*, June 3, 1913, 13.

71. DeVries, *Race and Kinship*, 14.

72. References to networks of black civic life can found throughout the *Detroit Plaindealer* between 1885 and 1890 (microfilm, Detroit Public Library); *Michigan State News*, April 26, 1920, GRPL; "Johnson's Own Story," *GRTH*, December 11, 1890, 7; "Divorce and Damages," *GRTH*, August 26, 1891, 1.

73. "If Your Honah Please," *GREL*, September 4, 1891, 1; "Dusky Prisoners: Alexander Hamilton, the Colored Lawyer, Arrested on a Body Execution," *GREL*, February 15, 1892, 4; National Archives, RG 94, Complied Service Records, U.S. Regular Army Vol. 69, entry 822, 69.

74. "Fish Market," *GREL*, October 1, 1885, 4; "Joe Ford," *GREL*, June 25, 1885, 4; "Joseph Ford," *GRD*, January 1, 1893, 5; "Major Domo at Mich. Headquarters," *GRH*, June 21, 1912; "Introducing Idlewild's New Mayor, Just Elected after Exciting Race," *GRH*, October 22, 1916, 4; *GRH Sunday Magazine*, November 11, 1923, 1; "Simplicity, Courtesy, Mark Big Men, Says 'Senator' Joe," *GRH Sunday Magazine*, February 10, 1924, 5; "'Senator' Ford of Michigan, Golden Wedding Day Nigh, Is in Limelight Once More," *GRH*, April 25, 1931.

75. "Ways of Waiters," *GRE*, November 19, 1886, 8; "All to Be Colored: Revolution in Ottawa Beach Hotel Waiters is Planned," *GRP*, March 23, 1901, 6; "Taft Breakfast at Country Club," *Grand Rapids News*, September 21, 1911, 3.

76. Craig Collection, GRPL; "J. C. Craig Dies," *GRP*, December 3, 1902, 9; "John J. Johnson Is Pneumonia Victim," *GRP*, March 22, 1915, 14.

77. "Came from South: Story of Enoch Pettiford of This City: Free Born Negro," *GRP*, August 1, 1903, 9.

78. "Local Negro on High Plane," *GRP*, March 3, 1910.

79. "In House of Much Trouble," *GRH*, October 19, 1910, 2; "One Man Was Gashed," *GRP*, March 23, 1911, 11.

80. "Murder: John Henderson Shot and Almost Instantly Killed by Wm. A. Clark," *GRE*, March 27, 1882, 4; "Found in the Alley," *GRE*, October 25, 1888, 1; *GRE*, May 13, 1889, 5; "Climb a Fire Escape," *GRP*, January 10, 1910, 7.

81. Greenwood, *Bittersweet Legacy*, chap. 3.

82. Marx, "German Ideology," 163.

83. See Jaynes, *Branches*; Mandle, *Not Slave, Not Free*.

84. Osofsky, "Enduring Ghetto," 243.

Chapter 3: "Thirteen Races and Nationalities"

1. Abe E. Gelhof, "Teach Young Ideas of Many Nations," *GRH*, December 20, 1908, editorial section, 3.

2. Gordon Olson, *Grand Rapids Sampler*, 96–97.

3. The city's greatest labor controversy was the furniture strike of 1911. Yet even in an angry strike, religious institutions moderated the influence of some striking workers (Kleiman, "Great Strike"). The leading furniture manufacturers were disposed, by the influence of their churches, to an anti-union paternalism toward workers. Their clergy preached a type of social gospel that encouraged industry leaders to have a paternalistic relationship with their workers, especially Dutch Protestant workers. On the other hand, the Protestant Christian beliefs of the Dutch workers helped the strike take on a more conservative character, causing a split between the Dutch and Polish workers over how far labor grievances could be taken in their mutual effort to win just working conditions. The Dutch workers chose to walk off the picket lines, listening to their clergy when violence erupted. Their abandonment of the strike forced the Polish workers to settle with the local captains of industry. Historian Jeffrey Kleiman suggests that religion, particularly Protestantism, factored heavily in creating a more compliant workforce. The furniture strike left the labor movement within the furniture industry without much momentum.

The Labor agreements reached in the strike were simultaneous with reforms in the city government. The city's charter was changed from a political structure with a strong mayor and city council to a city government controlled and operated by a city manager with a weak mayor and city commission. This change from ward politics gave the city's business elite a stronger hand in governing city politics. After the furniture strike, city control rested in the hands of the local, Northeastern-born Protestant elite—the Yankee establishment. Their hegemony would remain unchallenged until the post–World War II generation.

4. See chapter 4.

5. "No Intermarriage," *GRP*, May 1, 1908, 9; "Negro Cannot Wed White Woman Here," *GRP*, January 22, 1913, 1; "Objects to Drawing the Color Line in the Mat-

ter of Marriage," January 29, 1913, 6. "Bullet In Brain: Death of George Williams, Negro, Ends Desperate Fight; Woman at Bottom," *GRP,* June 6, 1917, 2.

6. On the Yankee influence in the western half of Michigan, see Gray, *Yankee West.*

7. Baxter, *History of Grand Rapids* ; Quist, " Great Majority," 325–58.

8. "An Abolition Church," *E&H,* September 7, 1858, 3.

9. Park Congregational Church, *James Ballard,* 28–31; VanVulpen, *Faith Journey,* 4–7.

10. "Letter From Mr. Ballard," *GRE,* December 24, 1870, 2; "Letter from Mr. Ballard," *GRE,* November 29, 1871, 1.

11. "Speech by Harry Lincoln Creswell, February 5, 1931, at the St. Luke AME Zion Church," Thomas Creswell Papers, Box 1, Folder 1, MHC; *GRE,* October 17, 1865, 1.

12. Kinsey and Baldwin, *Park Congregational Church,* 95–96.

13. Brawley, *History of Morehouse College,* 52–56.

14. Fountain Street Baptist Church Papers, Box 2, Folders 1–2, MHC; "An Excellent Sum," *GRE,* September 14, 1886, 6; "Concerning the Negro," *GRE,* April 10, 1892, 5; "The American Negro: The Late Dr. Graves Paper Read to the Ministers' Conference" *GRD,* February 5, 1895, 5.

15. MacPherson, *Abolitionist Legacy,* 4–6.

16. "Help the Colored Folks," *GRDT,* May 8, 1874, 1; "Lifting the Debt," *GREL,* October 17, 1883; "A Generous Proposition," *GRD,* October 28, 1885, 5; "Spring Street Methodist Episcopal Church," *GRE,* January 3, 1887; "Liberating the AME Church," *GRTH,* January 9, 1887; "Delos A. Blodgett Died Sunday Afternoon," *GRH,* November 2, 1908; Baxter, *History of Grand Rapids,* 317–18.

17. Mulhern, " Twenty-Fifth," 53–54; "Minutes of the Fifty-Second Anniversary of the Grand Rapids Baptist Association Held with the Baptist Church of Middleville on Tuesday and Wednesday, Oct. 1 and 2, 1895," KCA; "For the Colored Brethern," *GREL,* June 31, 1891, 1; "To Build a Church," *GRH,* May 20, 1897, 5; Baxter, *History of Grand Rapids,* 284–85; "Minutes of the Baptist City Society, 1914–1922," Fountain Street Church Papers, MHC.

18. "Slavery Days," *GRD,* December 6, 1885; Alexander Hamilton appointment to the Bar, J.C. Craig Scrapbook, GRPL; "Town Topics," *GRH,* December 14, 1889, 7; "Alex Is Dead," July 31, 1894, 2.

19. "Frederick Douglass," *GRE,* March 28, 1867, 1; "Frederick Douglass' Lecture Last Night," *GRE,* Feburary 4, 1868, 1; "Reminiscences: What Fred. Douglass Remembers about the Anti-Slavery Struggle," *GRE,* January 31, 1873, 1; "A Splendid Ovation: Tendered the Colored Orator, Frederick Douglass," *GRE,* September 9, 1888, 2.

20. "Coming," *GRE,* June 5, 1874, 1.

21. See Du Bois, *Black Reconstruction;* Foner, *Reconstruction;* Logan, *Betrayal; Reunion and Reaction.*

22. "The Negro Question: Rights of the Colored Voters in the South," *GRE,* December 30, 1888, 2; "Our Colored Folks," *GRD,* October 21,1890, 3; "Pensions for Slaves," *GRD,* July 24, 1890, 1; "Our Duty Toward the Negro," *GRE,* June 5, 1890, 4; "A Supposition," *GRE,* July 1,1890, 4; "The Only Solution: Education for Colored People," *GRD,* March 11, 1894, 1.

23. "Fred Douglass Dead," *GRD,* February, 21, 1895, 1; "Fred Douglass Dead,"

GRP, February 21, 1895, 3; *GRP,* February 22, 1895, 2; "In Douglass' Memory" *GRH,* February 18, 1896, 4.

24. Harlan, *Booker T. Washington,* 227–28.

25. "Fred Douglass," *GRD,* February 21, 1895, 4.

26. "Rise of the Negro: Booker T. Washington's Eloquent Address Last Night," *GRD,* January 24, 1896, 2.

27. Harlan, *Booker T. Washington,* chap. 12.

28. Olson, *Grand Rapids Sampler,* 86–88.

29. "Why Negroes Are Patient," *GRD,* January 30, 1896, 5.

30. Baxter, *History of Grand Rapids,* chap. 19.

31. MacPherson, *Abolitionist Legacy,* 354.

32. "They Want Leaders," *GRH,* January 27, 1896, 3. In his first local press interview, Washington characterized himself as a leader of the African American cause ready to exercise his leadership prudently.

33. "For Colored Race: Booker T. Washington Speaks of Conditions in South," *GRH,* December 27, 1901.

34. "Of Race Problem," *GRP,* June 10, 1902, 5.

35. "Working out the Race Problem," *GRP,* April 2, 1903, 2.

36. Park Congregational Church, *One Hundred Years,* 41–46.

37. Ibid., 44.

38. McLaughlin, "Negro Problem," manuscript, February 28, 1904, Local History Collection, GRPL.

39. Ibid., 12–18.

40. Ibid., 19–20.

41. "Should Help the Negro," *GRH,* October 26, 1904, 5; "Aid Negro Schools," *GRH,* October 26, 1904, 5.

42. Beets, "Negro Education Injustice," 716–17.

43. Beets, "Tuskegee," 76–77; Beets, "Negro in the South," 256; "Local Church to Run New School: Christian Reformed Church Takes Over Negro Institution," *Grand Rapids News,* October 5, 1918, 5.

44. Luker, *Social Gospel;* Higginbotham, *Righteous Discontent.*

45. "Negroes of South: Superintendent Elson Visited Their Race Schools," *GRP,* February 29, 1904, 7. Elson also reported that he met "Professor W. E. B. DuBoise [*sic*], the author of 'The Soul of the Black Folk'" at Alabama University. Noting Du Bois's education and book, Elson made no mention of Du Bois's stinging critique of Washington in *The Souls of Black Folk.*

46. Sawyer, "Surviving Freedom"; "Run the Township: Community of Negroes in Cass County," *GRP,* February 10, 1903, 6; see also Cox, " Pocket of Freedom."

47. Freedmen's Progress Commission, *Michigan Manual,* 278.

48. "William Alden Smith: Portrait & Biography File," GRPL; "William Alden Smith: His Life, Struggles, and Successes," October 1894, Scrapbooks of William Alden Smith, vol. I, GRPL; Goss, *Industries,* vol. 2, 801–803.

49. "Democracy and Colored Men," *GRH,* July 5, 1908, 4; "The Government of Nations Tends to Democracy and Negro Rights," *GRH,* July 10, 1908, 4.

50. Robert Pelham and his brother Ben were owners of the late-nineteenth-century newspaper *The Plaindealer* in Detroit. The paper failed, and Robert moved the newspaper and his family to Washington-on-Pelham, D.C.; see Freedmen's Prog-

ress Commission, *Michigan Manual*; Katzman, *Before the Ghetto*; and McCain, Mallas, and Hedden, *40 Years.*

51. *GRH*, April 23, 1909; "Senator In Court," *GRH*, April 24, 1909, 4.

52. "Saves Position for Old Negro," *GRH*, July 14, 1911, 2.

53. Frank Sparks to Booker T. Washington, January 12, 1912, Booker T. Washington Papers (hereinafter Washington Papers), Box 872, Lecture Files, LC.

54. "Lincoln Day Banquet with Much Oratory," *GRH*, February 12, 1912, 1, 4.

55. "Came From South: Story of Enoch Pettiford of This City," *GRP*, August 1, 1903, 9; "Local Negro on High Social Plane," *GRP*, March 10, 1906, 9.

56. "Living Lesson of the Great Work of Lincoln for Freedom," *GRH*, February 13, 1912, 3.

57. Washington Papers, Box 872, Lecture Files 1912.

58. "Colored People Hear Washington" *GRH*, February 13, 1912, 11.

59. The novelist Dorothy West vividly captured what life was like for men like Ford. "In this heyday of the railroad's prosperity, with motorcars and airplanes scarcely dreamed of, the parlor cars were the mobile drawing rooms of the rich, and the black men who served them as waiters or porters or red caps received extravagant tips for their coldly calculated servilities. All of their bowing and scraping was directed toward an end that justified the means. They saved their tips, and sent their sons to high school; they saved their tips and started little businesses. Though the generation to come might gloss over these beginnings, this was the beginning of the colored middle-class. . . . If he could stomach the servility, a man could ensure his future." *Wedding*, 148–49.

60. "Introducing Idlewild's New Mayor, Just Elected after Exciting Race," *GRH*, October 22, 1916, 4. On Idlewild, see Walker and Wilson, *Black Eden.*

61. "Senator Joe Raps Mr. Bogert," *GRP*, October 10, 1902, 2.

62. "Josesph C. Ford Comments on the Negro and Restaurateur," *GRH*, July 4, 1908, 4.

63. "North Unfair to Negro Says Woman," *GRH*, May 27, 1907, 5.

64. See Baker, *Color Line*, for a reading of this in the progressive era.

65. "S. Henri Browne to Accept Call to Ohio," *GRP*, May 13, 1915, 8.

66. A random check of the religion section of the *GRP* provides the titles of Rev. Browne's sermons for his tenure in Grand Rapids. *GRP*, March 20, 1908, 14; *GRP*, March 27, 1909, 12; *GRP*, October 14, 1911, 12.

67. Browne, "Negro in Grand Rapids." Manuscript, GRPL, April 6, 1913.

68. Ibid., 2.

69. "Miss Beverly's Ambition," January 22, 1899, *GRH*, 4; "Color Line Drawn," *GRH*, January 20, 1899, 3.

70. Browne, "Negro in Grand Rapids," 3.

71. Ibid., 4.

72. Ibid., 5.

73. Browne, "Negro in Grand Rapids," 6–7.

74. Zunz, *Changing Face*, 47.

75. Vanderstel, "Dutch, 1850–1970"; Vanderstel, "Dutch, 1848–1900." Vanderstel has shown that the Dutch immigrants migrated in waves, with the largest group arriving between 1880 and 1917.

76. For the intellectual and religious view of the Dutch community, see Bratt, *Dutch Calvinism.*

77. *U.S. Census Bureau Decennial Population Statistics, Michigan Schedule, 1850–1900.* Washington, D.C.: U.S. Government Printing Office.

78. "They'll Fight First," *GRD*, January 28, 1890, 5; for another reading on African American nativism see Hellwig, "Strangers."

79. Zunz, *Changing Face.* Zunz has shown, in his study of Detroit, that the growing manufacturing corridor in the Great Lakes region from Cleveland to Chicago in the 1890s changed ethnic, class, and race relationships.

80. "Sank in the Water Did Not Rise Again," *GRH*, July 5, 1908, 5; "Draws Color Line: Colored Woman Objected to Having 'White Trash' in Her House," *GRP*, February 4, 1905, 7.

81. Logan, *Betrayal*, 166–68. Logan has argued that blacks were not the only people to be depicted stereotypically. This was a common feature of newspapers owned by native-born whites. He goes on to argue that, in the case of blacks, these stereotypes had a much more deleterious effect (given blacks' social status) than it had on other ethnic communities.

82. "Old Time Negroes," *GRE*, October 13, 1888, 8; "He Had Sublime Faith," *GRTH*, June 10, 1890, 8; "Passing of the 'Black Mammy,'" *GRH*, (editorial) June 6, 1909, 4.

83. "In Merry Berlin," *GRP*, September 20, 1906; "Cole and Johnson," *GRP*, Februrary 27, 1908, 6; "Shoo-Fly Regiment," *Rapids Herald*, March 6, 1908, 4.

84. "Negro Pug Drew Like Mustard Pad," February 17, 1910, 8.

85. "Booker T. Washington Is Coming Here October 16," *GRP*, October 12, 1912.

86. "Washington Glad He Belongs to Black Race," *GRP*, October 15, 1912, 14; "Would Not Trade Skin With Whitest," October 17, 1912, 4; "Not Big Words But Work Negro's Aim," *GRP*, October 17, 1912, 14.

87. "Plan No Entertainment for Booker Washington," *GRP*, October 15, 1912, 15.

88. Harlan, *Booker T. Washington*, 359.

89. "Another Washington," *GRH*, November 16, 1915, 2.

90. Beets, "Dutch People," 40–41. Although historian James Bratt does not take up the issue of race relations in his book, he does note that Beets sought to give Dutch immigrants a positive attitude about becoming fully identified as American. In my opinion, nothing could be more fully American than taking up American race relations. Beets sought to cast the Dutch as a benevolent middle class in American society. Unfortunately, Beets omitted the long history of the transatlantic slave trade that Dutch sailing companies, which served as transporters throughout the Americas, engaged in. He never mentioned that the Dutch conquered St. Jorge da Elmina (the slave castle off the coast of Ghana), taking it from the Portuguese in the seventeenth century and trading in slaves until the earliest years of the nineteenth century. See Bratt, *Dutch Calvinism*, 56; Kamper "Christian Reformed Church."

91. See, for example, Bratt and Meehan, *Gathered at the River.*

92. Wright, *Life Behind a Veil*, 4.

93. Jones, *American Work*, chap. 10.

Chapter 4: Making Opportunity

Parts of chapter 4 appeared as the author's "'Making Opportunity': The Struggle against Jim Crow in Grand Rapids, Michigan, 1890–1927." *Michigan Historical Review* 19, no. 2 (Fall 1993): 23–48.

1. "Colored Organization Hears Woman Lecturer," *GRH*, December 18, 1925, 3.

2. Meijer, *Negro Thought,* 165–66.

3. For discussions of Southern racial discrimination, see Woodward, *Strange Career,* and Murray, *States' Laws.*

4. State of Michigan Legislature. *Public Acts, 1885,* 131–32. State of Michigan Legislature. *Public Acts, 1919.* Fort Wayne, Ind.: Fort Wayne Printing Company, 1919, 657.

5. Strum, "School Segregation"; "Negro Church Man Ordered Out of Cafe," *GRP,* October 27, 1919, 1.

6. "Grand Rapids Theaters." GRPL, Vertical File.

7. *Emmett N. Bolden v. Grand Rapids Operating Corporation,* Grand Rapids Superior Court, Case No. 3043, 1925, WMRA.

8. On New Negroes, particularly those in the professions, see Hine, *Black Women in White;* Gamble, *Making a Place;* Goggins, *Woodson;* Reed, *Chicago NAACP;* Walters, *New Negro.*

9. "Cannot Buy Shoes," *GRP,* May 5, 1913, 5.

10. "Colored Men Will Demand Their Rights," *GRP,* July 11, 1904, 7.

11. "The Colored Independents," *GREL,* October 31, 1890, 1; "The Colored Men," *GRP,* March 14, 1894, 1; "They Feel Sore," *GRP,* January 26, 1898; "Race Riot," *GRP,* July 8, 1912, 7.

12. "Negroes Win Out," *GRP,* November 17, 1908.

13. "Draw the Color Line," *GRP,* November 21, 1908; "Students Are Back," *GRP,* November 25, 1908.

14. *Booker v. Grand Rapids,* 95–101.

15. Ibid., 99; "Was No Agreement," *GRP,* October 20, 1908.

16. *Booker v. Grand Rapids,* 100; "Barred from College," *GRP,* March 30, 1909.

17. "*Meisner v. Detroit Belle Isle and Windsor Ferry Company,*" *Northwestern Reporter* vol. 118 (1909): 14–15.

18. "Negro Educator to Give Address Here," *GRH,* April 29, 1917, 3; NAACP Minutes of the Meeting May 14, 1917, NAACP Papers, Michigan State University Library, Reel 2, 2.

19. "Sharing the White Man's Burden," *GRP,* May 4, 1917, 6.

20. "Patriotic Tumult Reigns at Armory Jammed to Walls," *GRH,* April 17, 1917, 1; "Seven Polish Boys Are Navy Recruits; Negro Youths Join," *GRH,* April 17, 1917, 5; "Ordered to Enroll Colored Men for Officers' Training," *GRH,* May 28, 1917, 2; "Justice to Dusky Heroes," *GRH,* June 24, 1918, 6; "Seventeen Slain," *GRH,* August 27, 1917, 4; "Negro Boys Leave for Custer Amid Cheers of Crowd," *GRH,* September 2, 1918, 3; "3 G.R. Boys Who Helped Whip Kaiser," *GRH,* November 24, 1918, 8; "15–Year-Old Bluffs Way in Army; Home," *GRH,* June 5, 1919, 12.

21. "Young Republicans Greet Colored Club" *GRH,* October 31, 1916, 3; "'I'm

[a] Colored Porter In Downtown Barber Shop,' Is Way Daniel Lampkins Introduces Himself and Tells Inspiring Story of Life," *GRH*, February 23, 1918, 1; "Lampkins' Aspirations," *GRH*, letter to the editor from H. Tyron Johnson, February 27, 1918, 6.

22. Kellogg, *NAACP: A History*, 202; Bagnall, "Recruiting in the Mid-West", 139–41.

23. "Grand Rapids, Michigan 1913–1926," NAACP Collection: Group I, Series G, Container 99, LC.

24. Kellogg, *NAACP: A History*, 134–35.

25. George M. Smith to John R. Shillady, 24 February 1919, NAACP Collection: Group I, Series G, Container 99, LC.

26. "Pioneer in Black Struggle, George M. Smith, 86, Dies," *GRP*, November 7, 1970.

27. Gerould, *American Newspapers*, 312; Gerould lists the *Michigan State News* as having been in business 1920–1925.

28. "Walter White Holds Big Meetings," *MSN*, vol. 1, no. 3, April 26, 1920.

29. Tuttle, *Red Summer*, chap. 1.

30. "Walter White Holds Big Meetings," *MSN*, April 26, 1920, 1.

31. See, for example, autobiography of Walter White, *Man Called White*.

32. "Walter White Holds Big Meetings," *MSN*, April 26, 1920, 1.

33. "Deplores Lynching of Negroes and Wonders Whether Mob Rule Will Reign Supreme: The Public Pulse," *GRP*, July 10, 1920, 4.

34. Ibid.

35. Van Deburg, *Slavery & Race*, 123; Franklin, "'Birth of a Nation,'" 417–34.

36. "The South High Annual, 1919," GRPL, 103–104.

37. "Walton Seeks Funds to Carry on Klan Fight," *GRH*, September 21, 1923, 1; "Grand Haven," September 27, 1923, 10.

38. "Ku Klux History," *GRH*, October 1, 1923, 4.

39. For examples of the expansion of the African American middle class see Reed, *Chicago NAACP*, chap. 4; Spear, *Black Chicago*; Trotter, *Black Milwaukee*.

40. "Local Negro Athlete to Open Dental Office," *GRP*, August 18, 1923, 19.

41. "Floyd Skinner, Member of Omega Psi Phi," University of Michigan Yearbooks, 1923, 1924, and 1926, GRPL; "Death Takes Attorney, 62," *GRP*, August 8, 1962, 1; Tom LaBelle, "The Man Who Could Talk to the Man," *GRP Sunday Magazine*, November 1, 1970, 3. Floyd Skinner was believed to have been the attorney of record in the Bolden case, as LaBelle's article shows. Even though Skinner was a fine attorney, a tremendous civil rights activist, former president of the Grand Rapids NAACP, and deserving of the numerous posthumous accolades he has received in the city, the record should be corrected: Oliver Green was the attorney of record in the Bolden case.

42. "Omega Psi Phi & MA Philosophy," University of Michigan Yearbook, 1923, GRPL; "Baptist Pastor Emeritus," *GRP*, March 10, 1978, C-9; Keith served as the pastor of the Messiah Baptist Church from 1932 until 1968.

43. "Omega Psi Phi Photograph," University of Michigan Yearbook, 1923, GRPL.

44. "Eugene Ellis Allston; A.B. Lincoln University 1920; M.D. University of

Michigan," University of Michigan Development Office Alumni Records; "Death Takes Doctor Here," *GRP,* February 25, 1950; "GR Doctor 22 Years Dies," *GRH,* February 25, 1950; "Medical Graduates and Omega Psi Phi Photograph," University of Michigan Yearbook 1923, GRPL. Alston was born to John and Sarah Alston of Winston-Salem, N.C., in 1899. His father was a physician. He graduated magna cum laude from Lincoln on June 8, 1920 (Lincoln University archivist Khali Mahmud, letter to Randal Jelks, July 14, 1992). Alston's obituary observed that he continued to be an outstanding student while in the University of Michigan Medical College. Alston is the only person mentioned in court records in the Bolden case as having accompanied Emmett Bolden to the Keith Theater. Sadly, he died in a sanitarium in Grand Rapids of tuberculosis and alcoholism. Names or pictures of Skinner, Keith, English, and several other figures who would achieve some prominence within the Grand Rapids African American community are in the Omega Psi Phi photographs of 1923. For a small population of Negroes to achieve proportionately the number of professionals in this period is no small achievement.

45. Oliver M. Green graduated from Ithaca High School in 1913, attended Cornell University for two years as a special student, and served as Musician 3rd class in WWI. Eventually, Green graduated from Michigan State College (University) in 1920 and University of Michigan Law School in 1924. He died in an automobile accident at age thirty-six on March 20, 1932, in Pontiac, Mich. For biographical information on Green, see Oliver Green File, University of Michigan Alumni Relations Office; "Oliver Meakins Green, Law Graduate and Member of Alpha Phi Alpha Fraternity," *University of Michigan Annual,* 1923 (Ann Arbor: University of Michigan), 134; *The Crisis* 26:3 (July23): 110; *Michigan State College Alumni Catalogue, Class of 1920,* 83; Michigan State College, *The Wolverine,* 1920, 76; *Annual Class Book of the Ithaca High School, 1913,* Ithaca, N.Y., Tompkins County Public Library; *Military Records of Cornell University in The World War* (Ithaca, N.Y., Cornell University, 1930), 300; University of Michigan Office of Development, Alumni Records Office; *Kent County Clerk, Roll of Attorneys,* September 30, 1924, 15 (other African American attorneys registered in this same book: Floyd H. Skinner, September 21, 1926, 134; John G. Shackelford, October 7, 1931, 540; all three of these attorneys were graduates of the Michigan Law School).

For additional information on African American attorneys in Grand Rapids, see Grand Rapids District Court Judge Benjamin Logan's "Historical Memorandum Written for the Dedication of the Floyd Skinner Bar Association," used with the author's permission.

Additional information on African American attorneys in Michigan can be found in Edward J. Littlejohn and Donald L. Hobson's *Black Lawyers, Law Practice, and Bar Association—1844 to 1970: A Michigan History* (Detroit: The Wolverine Bar Association, 1972), a good overall history of African American attorneys on the eastern side of the state, particularly in Wayne county. It covers very little of the legal practices in the western half of the state, including Grand Rapids.

46. "Minutes of the Grand Rapids Bar Association, February 19, 1925," courtesy of the Grand Rapids Bar Association.

47. Kluger, *Simple Justice,* 115; McNeil, 131–32.

48. "Julius H. Amberg Portrait & Biography File," GRPL; "J. H. Amberg Gained

Fame Serving City, State, Nation," *GRP,* January 24, 1951; "Julius H. Amberg, Michigan Lawyer," *GRH,* January 25, 1951.

49. More on Glenn's life is found in chapter 7.

50. Grand Rapids Superior Court, *Grant v. The Grand Rapids Operating Corporation,* Case No. 2987, WMRA; *Glenn v. The Grand Rapids Operating Corporation,* Case No. 2986, WMRA.

51. Ibid., Grant stipulation of transference to Superior Court.

52. *GRP,* July 23, 1923.

53. "Autobiography of William M. Glenn," William Glenn Papers, Collection no. 49, Box 1, Folder 14, 3, GRPL.

54. *Grant v. The Grand Rapids Operating Corporation,* Case No. 29282. Circuit Court for Kent County, Plaintiff's Declaration, April 10, 1925, WMRA; Grant and Glenn complaints written by Green are verbatim transcripts, except for the names.

55. *Glenn v. Grand Rapids Operating Corporation,* Case No. 2986, Defendant Plea, May 5, 1925, WMRA.

56. A larger biographical portrait of Emmett Bolden can be found in *Mildred Bolden v. Emmett Bolden,* Circuit Court of Kent County, Case No. 26115, June 12, 1924, Kent County Clerk's Office, Hall of Justice, Grand Rapids, Mich.; "Election at a Glance," *GRH,* April 6, 1926, 1. In addition, Bolden gained attention by running as a candidate for the Grand Rapids School Board. The outcome of his candidacy was a foregone conclusion: he came in last. Surprisingly, though, he garnered 1,165 votes. In the briefs Green wrote on behalf of Bolden, he used Bolden's school board candidacy to enhance his client's credibility in the eyes of the court.

57. "Order to Discontinue, Oliver Green, August 27, 1926," *Bolden v. Grand Rapids Operating Corporation,* WMRA.

58. *Oliver M. Green v. Harvey Van Kaughnet,* Superior Court Grand Rapids, Cal. 3, Case No. 3081, October 8, 1926, WMRA.

59. Undated and unsigned letter from Grand Rapids NAACP, in NAACP Collection, LC; "Leonard Verdier Portrait and Biographical File," Collection of Local History and Personalities, GRPL; "Negro Sent to Prison for Assault; Rum Law Violators Sentenced," *GRH,* July 31, 1924; "Ruffian Gets Term of Life," *GRP,* May 20, 1929.

60. See chapter 7 on Floyd Skinner.

61. "State of Michigan, The Superior Court of Grand Rapids, Leonard D. Verdier's Opinion, *Bolden v. Grand Rapids Operating Corporation,*" LC.

62. "Oliver M. Green Killed in Crash," *Pontiac Daily Press,* March 21, 1932.

63. "Oliver M. Green to W. E. B. Du Bois, September 14, 1926," NAACP Collection, LC.

64. For details of African American wage-earners, see Charles S. Johnson and R. Maurice Moss, *The Negro Population of Grand Rapids, MI, 1928,* chapter 5, National Urban League Collection, LC.

65. Ibid.; Johnson and Moss, *Divisions in the African-American Community,* NAACP Collection, LC.

66. "Dentist Takes Jim Crow Fight to Supreme Court," *Chicago Defender,* Chicago, IL, October 2, 1926, LC.

67. "Walter White to Moses J. Walker, October 4, 1926," NAACP Collection,

LC; "Walter White to Oliver M. Green, Esq.," October 5, 1926, LC; "N.A.A.C.P. to Fight Michigan Attack on Civil Rights War," press release October 8, 1926, NAACP Collection, LC.

68. "William Messinger Portrait and Biographical File," GRPL; "William Messinger," University of Michigan Yearbook, 1923, Law Class 23.

69. *Bolden v. Grand Rapids Operating Corporation*, vol. 239, Michigan Reports, June 1927, 323–24, 328; David Katzman, *Before the Ghetto: Black Detroit in the Nineteenth Century*, chap. 1.

70. William Messinger to NAACP Department, February 26, 1927; Walter White to William Messinger, February 28, 1927.

71. *NAACP*, Group I, Box G99, Grand Rapids 1927–1928, LC.

72. *Bolden v. Grand Rapids Operating Corporation*, 328, WMRA.

73. "Court Rules against Jim Crow Tactics: Reverses Decision in Theater Case," *Chicago Defender*, June 18, 1927; "NAACP Press Release," July 29, 1927, NAACP Collection, LC.

74. Oliver Green to Walter White, June 11, 1927, LC.

75. For comparison, see Reed, *Chicago NAACP.*

76. "Cab's Head Hasn't Swelled," *GRH*, July 24, 1933, 4; on Ramona Gardens, see Bennett, *Memories*, 22.

Chapter 5: "Southern Negroes Flock to Michigan"

1. "Southern Negroes Flock to Michigan," *GRP*, June 26, 1923, 22.

2. See Marks, "Social and Economic Life."

3. Kusmer, *Ghetto Takes Shape*, 172–73.

4. Thomas, *Life for Us*, chap. 2. Thomas has shown (regarding Detroit) that the availability of jobs in Henry Ford's automobile plants was a major impetus for the Southern Negro migration north. In Grand Rapids, the large furniture manufacturers (and the few new manufacturing plants related to the automobile industry) locked out Negro laborers from employment.

5. Katzman, *Before the Ghetto*; Spear, *Black Chicago*, chap. 3.

6. Sennett and Cobb, *Hidden Injuries*, 62: Sennett and Cobb use the idea of the "badge of ability" as the key to understanding class resentments. They write: "That ability is the badge of individual worth, that calculations of ability create an image of a few individuals standing out from the mass, that to be an individual by virtue of ability is to have the right to transcend social origin—these are the basic suppositions of a society that produces feelings of powerlessness and inadequacy in the lives of people . . . . To connect ideology and the people, we need to understand what happens to people when they wear badges of ability."

7. The literature on this subject has grown tremendously. Lasch-Quinn, *Black Neighbors*; Weisenfeld, "Harlem YWCA," 63–78; Salem, *Better Our World*; Scott, "Most Invisible," 3–22.

8. "Black History Collection," Collection #113, Box 3, Folder 38, GRPL.

9. "Failure to Report Shooting Affair Leads to a Probe," *GRP*, October 17, 1918, 1; "Find White Girl in Negro Resort," August 4, 1920, 3; "Police Raid Second 'House of Nations' Get Booze Supply," *GRH*, February 28, 1921, 3; "Negro Officer Arrests Eight of Own Race," *GRP*, October 30, 1922, 17; "Law Nabs 8 Disciples

of African Dominoes," *GRH*, December 3, 1922, 3; "Pastor, Crapshooter Character Witness," *GRH*, December 8, 1923, 12.

10. For the childcare concerns of African American women, see Jones, *Labor of Love*.

11. See Hine, "Black Migration."

12. Souvenir Program, 8;"Colored Folks Boast Baby Clinic," *GRH*, September 9, 1923.

13. Du Bois, *Social Betterment*, 102.

14. "New Bissell Activities Similar to Hull House Dedicated and Open," *GRP*, October 19, 1897; "Bissell House Short of Funds, Issues Public Appeal," *GRP*, September 29, 1902, 8; "Generous Contribution Prevents Closing of Bissell House," *GRP*, March 1, 1904, 2; "Women's Club Petition Board Aid to Secure Bissell House and Establish School for Wayward Girls," *GRP*, April 2, 1912, 3; "Bissell House Offered for Sale," *GRP*, April 25, 1912.

15. "Talk Much before Deciding to Act: Negroes Have a Bitter Meeting over Social Center Proposal," *GRP*, October 19, 1912, 14.

16. "Plan Social Center for Local Negroes: Zion Methodist Church Will Move to Commerce Avenue and Build Anew," *GRP*, March 20, 1915; "Plans to Erect YMCA for Local Negro Boys," *GRH*, March 22, 1915, 5.

17. "Will Ask Funds for Welfare of Negroes: Plans Also Include Rebuilding of St. Luke's African M.E. Zion Church," *GRP*, November 2, 1917, 22.

18. True Light Baptist Church 75th Anniversary Program.

19. Sarah Glover, interview with author, August 15, 1993.

20. "Will Ask for Funds," *GRP*.

21. "Fund Drive for New East End AME Church," *GRP*, May 24, 1919, 8; "Leading Citizens Plan Community Church for G.R. Negroes," *GRH*, April 25, 1920, religion section, 2; "AME Cornerstone," *GRP*, October 2, 1922, 2; "Dedicates Basement," *GRP*, March 24, 1923, 16; "Social Services," *GRP*, August 25, 1923, 5.

22. R. Maurice Moss, "A Survey of the Negro Population of Grand Rapids, Michigan, 1928," National Urban League Papers, LC, 35. Interestingly enough, Moss noted that the infant clinic Simms and Browning organized "served 90% of its clients from among white mothers in the neighborhood."

23. "St. James United AME," *GRP*, September 9, 1926, 2; "Church Solicitor Sought by Police," *GRP*, August 21, 1923, 2.

24. Beets, "Solve the Negro Problem," 613–14.

25. Burgess, "This I Believe," 334.

26. "The Negro Ministry," *GRP*, July 27, 1923, 6.

27. "Pop Bottle Broadcasts Kerosene Odor and Firebug Is Suspected of Blaze in True Light Church," *GRP*, May 4, 1927, 1; "Pop Bottle Gives No Clew [*sic*]; Blaze in Negro Church Still Mystery," *GRP*, May 5, 1927, 2.

28. Phillips, *Alabama North*, 128.

29. Moss, "A Survey," sec. II. In 1928, Moss reported that with more than five hundred members, True Light Baptist Church was the fastest-growing African American church in the city.

30. Gregg, *Sparks from the Anvil*; Sernett, *Promised Land*.

31. The treatment of proletarianization has been treated in the following:

Thomas, "Peasants to Proletarian"; Trotter, *Black Milwaukee*; Gottlileb, *Own Way*; Dickerson, *Black Steelworkers.*

32. "Strikers Threaten Trouble at Mines," June 12, 1917, *GRH*, 2.

33. "Protest Importation of Negroes as Strikebreakers," June 29, 1917, 8.

34. On the ambivalent role of unions among African Americans, see James Grossman, *Land of Hope,* chap. 8; Phillips, *Alabama North,* chap. 3; Thomas, *Life for Us.*

35. For more on East St. Louis, see Rudwick, *Race Riot;* "Church Solicitor Sought by Police," *GRP,* August 21, 1923, 2.

36. Beets, "Solve the Negro Problem," 613.

37. Ibid.

38. Moss, "A Survey," sec. 2, LC.

39. Ibid.

40. Ibid.

41. For comparable organizations, see Phillips, *Alabama North,* 123–24.

42. Harris, *Keeping the Faith.* This organization was more a social club than a collective bargaining agent. The ideological perspectives on unions shifted slowly as national labor organizer A. Philip Randolph won recognition for the Brotherhood of Sleeping Car Porters and Maids as a union in the 1930s.

43. "Vital Question of Racial Industrial," *GRH,* September 9, 1923, sec. 4, 2; "South and the Negro," *GRH,* September 14, 1923, 4; "Negroes Fear Cold Winter, Are Going Back to Southland," September 19, 1923, 16.

44. City of Grand Rapids, *City Commission,* May 7, 1923 to May 1, 1923, GRPL.

45. "Pop Bottle Broadcasts Kerosene Odor and Firebug Is Suspected of Blaze in True Light Church," *GRP,* May 4, 1927, 1; "Pop Bottle Gives No Clew [sic]; Blaze In Negro Church Still Mystery," *GRP,* May 5, 1927, 2; "3rd Negro Church Burns in Month," *GRH,* June 11, 1927, 2.

46. For the national reception of the Amos 'n' Andy show, see Melvin Ely, *The Adventures of Anos 'N' Andy: A Social History of an American Phenomenon.* (New York: Free Press, 1991).

47. "Popular Entertainers," *GRH,* March 9, 1930, 14.

48. Bagnall, "Land of Many Waters," 101–102, 123.

49. State of Michigan, "An Epitome of the Economic and Industrial Status of the Negro in Michigan," press release, April 21, 1927, Department of Labor and Industry, Bureau of Negro Welfare, Lansing, Michigan, SA.

50. Proceedings of Annual Conference, State Bureau of Negro Welfare at Detroit, Michigan, October 21, 1927, SA.

51. On the Family Service Association, see Lydens, *Story of Grand Rapids,* 573.

52. Charlotte C. Donnell to Eugene Kinckle Jones, August 2, 1926, National Urban League Papers, LC.

53. "Committee Report by Ethel B. Burgess, July 21, 197," National Urban League Papers, LC; "Bylaws Adopted by Inter-Racial Council," *GRP,* July 22, 1927, 2.

54. Ethel B. Burgess to Eugene Kinckle Jones, July 26, 1927, National Urban League Papers, LC.

55. Eugene Kinckle Jones to Mrs. Theodore Burgess July 29,1927, National Urban League Papers, LC.

56. Charles C. Stillman to Eugene Kinckle Jones August 24, 1927, National Urban League Papers, LC.

57. "Declares Negroes Need Social Work," *Grand Rapids Urban League*, September 23, 1927, 2; on Eugene Kinckle Jones's attempt to promote Negro Social Worker, see Armfield, "Eugene Kinckle Jones," and Moore, *Search for Equality*, chap. 3; Parris and Brooks, *Blacks in the City*, chap. 18; Weiss, *Urban League*, chap. 11.

58. "To Discuss Welfare of Colored Folk in City," *GRP*, September 30, 1927, 10.

59. Charles C. Stillman to Eugene Kinckle Jones, November 14, 1927, National Urban League Papers, LC.

60. The local debate in Grand Rapids follows the same line of thought as the one taking place between Du Bois and Walter White in 1934. See "Segregation—A Symposium," *The Crisis*, 41 (1934).

61. Ida W. Wilson to W. E. B. Du Bois, December 28, 1927, W. E. B. Du Bois Papers, University of Massachusetts, Reel 22.

62. W. E. B. Du Bois to Ida W. Wilson, December 30, 1927, W. E. B. Du Bois Papers, Reel 22.

63. Alice R. Yonkman to Eugene Kinckle Jones, December 20, 1927, National Urban League Papers, LC.

64. "Negro Part in U.S, Civilization Cited by Leader of Race," *GRH*, March 14, 1928, 3; "Holds Negro Aided Country's Growth," March 14, 1928, 18.

65. "R. Maurice Moss Preliminary Report to the Grand Rapids Inter Racial Council June 14, 1928," National Urban League Papers, LC.

66. Moss, "A Survey," Grand Rapids sections 3–4, National Urban League Papers, LC.

67. Ibid., 1–2.

68. Moss, "A Survey," Crime and Mortality section, 1.

69. Ibid, 2.

70. Ibid., 3.

71. Ibid., Crime and Mortality section, 1–3.

72. Moss, "American Cities," 12–15.

73. For an important comparative ethnic history, see Bodnar, *Lives of Their Own*.

74. Moss, "Survey," Conclusion, 1.

75. Ibid., 2.

76. "Need for Greater Social Work Among Negroes is Cited" *GRH*, January 22, 1929, 3.

77. Charles Stillman to Eugene Kinckle Jones, February 1, 1929, National Urban League Papers, LC.

78. Ibid.

79. "Negro Welfare Work," *Grand Rapids Spectator*, 17.

80. Ibid.

81. "A Gift the Negroes Do Not Want," *GRP*, May 17, 1930, 4.

82. Ibid.

83. "Tells of the Plan for Negro Center," *GRP*, May 21, 1930, 18.

84. "To Conduct Drive Here for Social Center," *GRP,* June 2, 1930, 20.

85. "Register Protest on Welfare Guild," *GRP,* June 10, 1930, 1; "Public Pulse: Reiterates Opposition of Colored Citizens of the Activities of the Negro Welfare Guild," *GRP,* July 25, 1930, 6.

86. Patterson, *America's Struggle,* chap. 2.

Chapter 6: The Making of the Brough Community Association

1. On Idlewild, see Wilson, *Rural Black;* Eugene Schoon, "Beautiful Idewild" CCH. On jazz, see "Jazz Blamed for Extraneous Evils, Musicians Claims" *GRH,* February 3, 1930, 3.

2. Harris, *Gospel Blues;* Dawley, *Struggles for Justice.*

3. The Grand Rapids NAACP Papers, LC.

4. For example, a check of the 1930 Polk Directories shows that dentist Emmett Bolden resided at his office. His address in 1927, when he was the successful plaintive in the case of *Bolden v. the Grand Rapids Operating Corporation,* showed him living a new section of the city on Philadelphia Street. The downturn in the economy forced him out of his home.

5. Mrs. Floyd H. Skinner, "File Clippings from *The Pittsburgh Courier,* September 1939–September 1941," GRPL.

6. "Permit Request from the Communist Party to the City Commission," April 28, 1930, CA; "Strike Demonstrate Flier," May 1, 1930; "Strike on May Day Flier," May 1, 1930, CA.

7. On communism, see Kelly, *Hammer and Hoe;* Mark Naison, *Communist in Harlem During the Depression* (Urbana: University of Illinois Press, 1983); Nell Irvine Painter, *The Narrative of Hosea Hudson: The Life and Times of a Black Radical* (New York: W. W. Norton, 1994).

8. Meier and Rudwick, *Black Detroit;* Thomas, *Life for Us,* chap. 2.

9. St. Philip's Episcopal Church, Fortieth Anniversary, 3; St. Philip's Episcopal Church, "The Canonical Register" (courtesy of St. Philip's Episcopal Church) shows twenty-seven names when the church was officially organized on December 1, 1912: Charles Stevenson, Ida Stevenson, Calvin Grayson, Wilhemina Grayson, Eva Day, Ida Woods, Bernice Wilson, Jennie Winburn, Robert Bowman, Miles Wood Sr., Sarah Hammond, Benjamin Hammond, Alice Green, Fay Elizabeth Gilbert, Leola Mabel Perkins, Linna Craig Corbin, Gertrude Corbin Browning, Daisey Lacey, Herbert Day, William Emmett Grant, Mamie P. Smith, Lena Saulter Gilbert, Edna Logan, Ethel Burgess, Theodore Burgess, Emeline Brown, George Lett.

10. Bishop John Burgess, telephone interview with the author, May 25, 2000.

11. St. Philip's Episcopal Church, Fortieth Anniversary, 4–5.

12. Ibid., 6; *St. Philip's Church New York Newsletter,* vol. 1, no. 6, February 20, 1938, on a biography of Jesse Anderson; "Episcopal Church, Diocese of Western Michigan Correspondence—Bishop, Parish, Mission," correspondence, Grand Rapids, St. Philip's Folder 1932 and 1936–38, St. Philip's Papers, BC.

13. *St. Philips Newsletter* 1, no.1 (June 1938): 3, Folder 1932, 1936–1939, BC.

14. Ibid.

15. Charles B. Hopper to Bishop Lewis Bliss Whittemore, February 23, 1944, St. Philip's Papers, Box 8, Folder 1944–1949, BHL.

16. On instrumentality see Sernett, *Promised Land*, 4. Sernett explores instrumentality only in terms of traditional African American denominations such as the Baptists. The case of Anderson in Grand Rapids sees this understanding of Christianity coming out of the Social Gospel and influencing the work of the educated Negro clergy.

17. Jesse Anderson to Henry Romyn, St. Philip's Papers, Folder 1939–1941. Romyn wrote: "I am exceedingly sorry that such a fault of race discrimination appeared evident to you. I have discussed this matter with the minstrel management, including members of your race, and have positive assurance that there was no pre-determined policy and the discrimination of which you accuse us was thoroughly unintentional. We also regret that you were embarrassed at being seated among your own people, or at being in attendance at an amusement enterprise of which you disapprove. We are grateful that you felt the cause was good, because dozen of Legionnaires of both white and colored races spent vast hours of time and considerable personal money to help advance the interests of the colored people of this community."

18. For a national point of view on Negroes and the Protestant establishment, see David Wells, "An Enduring Distance: Black Americans and the Protestant Establishment," in *In Between Times: The Travail of the Protestant Establishment in America*, William R. Hutchinson, ed. (New York: Cambridge University Press, 1989).

19. There were two representatives from the social services agencies: Jane Mulder, secretary of the Legal Aid Bureau, and Vesta Sturgis, executive secretary of the Grand Rapids Rehabilitation League. The municipality was represented by one police officer, Lt. Walter Coe. The committee members were lawyers Attorney Floyd Skinner and Donald Slawson of the firm Uhl, Bryant, and Snow; businesspeople Fred Yell (insurance agent), Raymond Bullock (a personnel director), and Howard Sluyter (the manger of the sales agency Wm. Iselin and Company); teacher and Grand Rapids Public Schools representative LeGrande Albee; Benedict McGinn, who represented the Employment Compensation Committee, a state agency; two homemakers, Ada Stearns (a widow), and Nelle Bell; and Raymond Bonini, whose occupation was not listed.

20. Weiss, *Urban League*, chap. 5.

21. Banner, *Negro Population*.

22. Banner, *Negro Population*, 11. Of the 319 families the survey team interviewed, 76 were natives of Michigan. In the next largest groups of families, 27 were natives of Indiana, followed by Alabama (20 families), then Georgia, Illinois, and Tennessee (19 families each). Interestingly, African American natives to the Great Lakes region represented the largest sector of the population in the city.

23. Gunnar Myrdal, *An American Dilemma: The Negro Problem and Modern Democracy* (New York: Harper Books, 1944). Before Gunnar Myrdal called the race problem an "American dilemma" in the late 1940s, blacks in the Great Lakes region faced this moral dilemma of racial exclusion in protestant dominated cities like Grand Rapids.

24. Morris, *Origins*.

25. Cohen, *New Deal*, 324. Cohen places heavy emphasis on the cultural unity the CIO attempted to create in the 1930s. Her work has to be put into a wider regional context than Chicago, however. White workers never shared this cultural unity that (perhaps) existed in Chicago.

26. Banner, *Negro Population*, 39–42.

27. Hazel Grant, interview with the author, January 1992. Grant was the first African American woman employed by city of Grand Rapids (as a secretary in 1930). This resulted from the advocacy of Floyd Skinner in the Progressive Voters League.

28. "Theola Ford's Wedding," *MSN*, April 26, 1920, 1.

29. Lewis Smith, interview with the author, July 20, 1998.

30. Banner, *Negro*, 128.

31. Ibid, 89–90.

32. For a read on black business, see Walker, *Black Business.*

33. Banner, *Negro Population*, 109.

34. Ibid., 115.

35. Bishop Lewis Bliss Whittemore to Maud Brough, March 20, 1942, Episcopal Church Diocese of Western Michigan, Box 8, Folder 1942–43.

36. Kelly Marsh to Bishop Lewis Bliss Whittemore, March 21, 1942, Episcopal Church Diocese of Western Michigan, Box 8, Folder 1942–43.

37. Bishop Lewis Bliss Whittemore to Helen Brough, March 10, 1942, Episcopal Church, Diocese of Western Michigan Box 8, Folder 1942–43.

38. Bishop Lewis Bliss Whittemore to St. Philip's, September 3, 1942, Episcopal Church, Diocese of Western Michigan Box 8, Folder 1942–43.

39. Bishop Lewis Bliss Whittemore to Rev. John Burgess, December 7, 1942, Episcopal Church, Diocese of Western Michigan Box 8, Folder 1942–43.

40. Bishop Lewis Bliss Whittemore to Maud Brough, December 17, 1942, Episcopal Church, Diocese of Western Michigan Box 8, Folder 1942–43.

41. Wendel Pasco to the Rt. Rev. Lewis Bliss Whittemore, December 22, 1942, Episcopal Church, Diocese of Western Michigan Box 8, Folder 1942–43; Bishop Lewis Bliss Whittemore to Wendell Pasco, December 31, 1942, Episcopal Church, Diocese of Western Michigan Box 8, Folder 1942–43.

42. Bishop Lewis Bliss Whittemore to Maud Brough, January 6, 1943, Episcopal Church, Diocese of Western Michigan, Box 8, Folder 1943–43.

43. See chapter 5; On Jones being a great promoter of Black Social Workers, see Armfield, "Eugene Kinckle Jones."

44. Lewis Bliss Whittemore, telegram to Maud Brough, January 11, 1943, Episcopal Church, Diocese of Western Michigan, Box 8, Folder 1943–43.

45. Maud Brough to Lewis Bliss Whittemore, January 12, 1943; Lewis Bliss Whittemore to Maud Brough, January 12, 1943, Episcopal Church, Diocese of Western Michigan, Box 8, Folder 1943–43; Maud Brough to Lewis Bliss Whittemore, January 13, 1943, Episcopal Church, Diocese of Western Michigan, Box 8, Folder 1943–43.

46. "Articles of Incorporation, The Brough Community Association, 1943,"Grand Rapids Urban League Papers," Box 1, Incorporation Folder, BC.

47. The Reverend Albert C. Keith to the Board of Directors of Brough Community Association, March 18, 1943, Episcopal Church, Diocese of Western Michigan, Box 8, Folder 1943–43.

48. First Annual Report of the Brough Community Association, 1943, Grand Rapids Urban League Papers, Annual Report Folder, BC.

49. Ibid., 7–8.

50. Bravid W. Harris to Lewis Bliss Whittemore, July 26, 1943, St. Philip's Papers, Folder 1943.

51. On the community tensions and the difficulty of this interracial funding, see Dickerson, *Militant Mediator*, 40–41.

52. Sennett and Cobb, *Hidden Injuries*, 22. Sennett and Cobb state (in referring to dignity) that "a poor man, therefore, has to want upward mobility in order to establish dignity in his own life, and dignity means, specifically, moving toward a position in which he deals with the world in some controlled, emotionally restrained way. People who have been educated, on the other hand, are supposed to already possess this capacity. They are supposed to have developed skills for taming the world without force or passion."

53. Wilkins, *Man's Life*, 48–49.

54. On Detroit in this period, see Capeci, *Wartime Detroit*.

Chapter 7: "Today's Negro and Tomorrow's World"

1. Floyd H. Skinner, press release to the editor of *Crisis Magazine*, April 1943, NAACP Papers, Group II, Box c 91, Folder 1940–1944, LC; "NAACP to Bring Pastor-Educator for Talk Tuesday," *GRP*, March 26, 1943; for more extensive biographical portraits of Adam Clayton Powell Jr., see Haygood *King of the Cats*, and Hamilton, *Adam Clayton Powell*.

2. On Daniel Lampkins, see chapter 4.

3. "Refection of an Editor" *GRH*, March 18, 1944, 2.

4. Floyd Skinner, unsigned memo and letter to Robert W. Bagnall, June 27, 1929, NAACP Papers, Group II, Box c 91, Folder 1927–1929, LC; "Ruffian Gets Term of Life," *GRP*, May 20, 1929.

5. Gerald Elliot, *Grand Rapids Renaissance on the Grand* (Tulsa: Continental Heritage Press, 1982), 112.

6. "Reflection of an Editor," *GRH*, March 8, 1944, 2; "First Negro Commission Candidate Sees Hope for the Nation," *GRP*, April 11, 1968, 39; "Obituary of Daniel Lampkins Boone," *GRP*, July 11, 1969, 2a; "Daniel Boone Lampkins' File," Black History Collection, Folder 9, GRPL.

7. "Branch News," *The Crisis*, 42 (January 1935): 27, 185.

8. "Resolution by Floyd H. Skinner, April 18, 1943," and "Report of Special Committee Investigating Brough Committee Center, June 20, 1943," NAACP Papers, Group II, Box c 91, Folder 1940–1944, LC.

9. "Report of Special Committee," NAACP Papers, Group II, Box c 91, Folder 1940–1944, LC; Carl Thomasson to Ella J. Baker, November 20, 1943, NAACP Papers, Group II, Box c 91, Folder 1940–1944, LC.

10. Tom Labelle, "The Man Who Could Talk to the Man," *GRP, Sunday Magazine*, November 1, 1970, 3.

11. Paul Phillips was born in 1914 in Omaha, Nebraska. In 1932, he received an athletic scholarship to Marquette University for track and field; he qualified for the 1936 Olympics, but he was a step behind his classmate and teammate at Marquette, Ralph Metcalf. Metcalf and Jesse Owens would go to the 1936 Olym-

pics and set records in front of Adolf Hitler. Instead of winning Olympics medals, Phillips completed his master's degree in social services at Fisk University and served in a variety of social agencies in Nashville, Tenn., and Milwaukee, Wis.

12. Phillips, "Intercultural Areas," 8. There was a sizable percentage of foreign-born whites. Among Afro-Southerners, the next largest group of migrants was from Tennessee. Also, see Clingman, "Human Relations Commission," 3. Clingman's study pointed out that by "1958, only 10% of the city's Negroes where native-born, whereas 75% had been born in one of the Southern states, [with] Mississippi alone contributing nearly 45% and Arkansas an additional 12%."

13. Ibid., 28–40; see also Stephen Tuuk, "The Transitions of Dutch-American and Black Population in Grand Rapids Housing," CCH.

14. Phillips, "Intercultural Areas," 49–50.

15. "Brief Account of our 25 years of Stewardship, 1971," Paul I. Phillips Papers, Collection 49, Box 1, Folder 15, Local History Collection, GRPL.

16. Dollard, *Caste and Class,* chapter 5.

17. See Harold Cruse, *Plural But Equal: A Critical Study of Blacks and Minorities and America's Plural Society* (New York: William Morrow, 1987).

18. McMillen, *Dark Journey,* 267–72.

19. Grossman, *Land of Hope,* 1.

20. Ibid., 2.

21. Scholars have begun exploring conceptions of time, work, and leisure during slavery. However, not enough scholarship has focused on the conception of work of former sharecroppers who moved to industrial employment, or on the regional aspects of work and time.

22. Bratt and Meehan, *Gathered at the River,* Appendix A (Directory of Congregations), 216–78; Phillips "Intercultural Areas", 17.

23. "Citizens Act to Save Negro from Mississippi Lynch Mob," *Michigan Herald Weekly,* October 20, 1946, 12, NAACP Papers, Box c.91, Folder 1945–1950, LC.

24. Fine, "'Jewel,'" 19–66; Fine's is quite helpful when it comes to the political machinations of the Fair Employment legislation. However, there is a serious omission on his part not taking up the role of the NAACP or the movement of Negroes in a number of political districts as having any influence on political representatives.

25. "Grand Rapids Branch N.A.A.C.P. Bulletin Vol.1 No.3 April 1945," NAACP Papers Box c.91, Folder1940–1945, LC.

26. Harms, "Bodies by Hayes," 51.

27. Floyd Skinner to Herbert Hill, November 2, 1951, LC; Hill to Skinner, November 20, 1951, LC.

28. On the history of Civil Rights and the UAW, see W. Michael Johnston, et al., *Lake Superior,* chap. 10. Johnston tells the regional history of the UAW. In this regard, UAW looks quite progressive. However, analyzing it from a regional perspective, the local looks quite conservative. Also see UAW Local 730, *Local 730 History* (Grand Rapids: UAW 730, 1988).

29. Correspondence between Floyd H. Skinner and Herbert Hill, November 2, 1951; November 20, 1951; December 5, 1951. Herbert Hill to Floyd H. Skinner, December 5, 1951, NAACP Papers Box c. 91, Folder 1950–1955.

30. See chapters 2 and 3.

31. Carl A. Thomasson to Lee Wilson Hutchins, August 22, 1945, NAACP Papers, Box c. 91, Folder1940–1945, LC.

32. One area that that needs more historical explanation is the recruitment of African American schoolteachers from the South. Cities like Grand Rapids and others throughout the Great Lakes region heavily recruited teachers from historically black colleges at the encouragement of African American leaders. Several of the issues that ought to be explored are the class conflict that this recruitment created in the communities, and the gender dimensions of this recruitment.

33. "The Autobiography of William Glenn," William Glenn Papers, Collection 49, Box 1, Folder 14, GRPL, 1.

34. Ibid.

35. Ibid., 2.

36. Ibid., 3.

37. William Glenn Papers, Collection, Box 1, Folder 17, GRPL.

38. See chapter 4.

39. "American Civil Liberties Union Western Michigan Chapter Presentation of 1971 Bill of Rights Award to William M. Glenn February 5, 1972," William Glenn Papers Collection 49, Box 1, Folder 14, GRPL.

40. "Autobiography of William Glenn," 4.

41. Ibid., 5.

42. Ibid.

43. "The Grand Rapids Branch N.A.A.C.P. Bulletin Vol. No.6 September 1945," NAACP Papers, Box 91, Folder 1945–1950, LC; on the International Workers Order, see Keeran "National Groups," 23–51.

44. Record, *Race and Radicalism;* Kelly, *Hammer and Hoe.*

45. "William Melbourne Glenn," Federal Bureau of Investigation File 100-306597, Headquarters, May 12, 1944, GRPL.

46. Ibid., memorandum, November 17, 1960.

47. "Activities in the Progressive Party," William Glenn Papers, Box 2, Folder 8 and 9.

48. *Civic Reminder,* vol. 1, no. 2 (March 1950), William Glenn Papers, Box 5.

49. William Glenn to Charles Velson, Secretary of the American Committee to Survey Labor Condition In Europe, August 31, 1951, William Glenn Papers, Box 1, Folder 15, GRPL.

50. "Glenn's Soviet Trip Checked," *GRH,* no date, 1952, William Glenn Papers, Box 5.

51. "Arbitrator Rules Glenn Back to Job," *GRH,* October 17, 1951, 1; "Layoff Delays Glenn Reinstatement," *GRH,* October 19, 1951.

52. "Testimony of William Glenn, Accompanied by His Counsel, Ernest Goodman," House Un-American Activities Committee, Communism in the Detroit Area, 1954, National Archives, Washington, D. C.; for testimony where Glenn is identified, see the "Testimony of Merton D. Sumner," Investigation of Communist Activities in the State of California, Part 3, Monday, April 12, 1954, 4623–4635; "Testimony of Berniece Baldwin," House Un-American Activities Committee, Communist Activities in the State of Michigan, 5297–5328, National Archives; "Testimony of Harold Mikkelsen," House Un-American Activities Committee, 5145–5201;"More in State Named as Reds," *Detroit Times,* February 28, 1952; "Accused Reds Talkative Enough Except When Asked About Member-

ship," *Detroit News*, March 13, 1952; "FBI Counterspy Finger at 30 Minor Red Officials at Detroit Hearing," *DFP*, May 5, 1954.

53. Bissell's maiden name was Rarden. She graduated from Greenville High School in 1930. *Greenville Daily*, obituary, March 3, 1975.

54. "Crusader in Rights Causes," *GRP*, obituary, March 3, 1975, 2-d.

55. *Sioux City Journal*, Sioux City, Iowa, June 26, 1943, 67; July 12, 1943, 1; April 22, 1949, sec. 2, 3; April 28, 1950, 8.

56. Hillary Bissell to Thurgood Marshall, undated 1949, NAACP Papers, Group II, Box 91, Folder 1945–1950, LC. Bissell was also elected state treasurer of the NAACP (see *GRP*, May 19, 1952, 2).

57. Ibid.

58. Hillary Bissel to Thurgood Marshall, January 15, 1950, NAACP Papers, Group II, Box 91, Folder 1945–1950, LC.

59. "Segregation of Students in Grand Rapids Protested," *Pittsburgh Courier* (Detroit Edition), June 16, 1951, 1.

60. "NAACP Membership Drive—Grand Rapids Hillary Bissell, Publicity Chairman," NAACP Papers, Group II, Box 91, Folder 1951, LC; Gloster B. Current, Director of Branches, to Mrs. Wadsworth Bissel, June 18, 1951, NAACP Papers, Group II, Box 91, LC.

61. Hillary Bissell to Gloster B. Current, June 15, 1951, NAACP Papers, Group II, Box 91, LC.

62. Hillary Bissell to Gloster B. Current, June 9, 1951, NAACP Papers, Group II, Box 91, LC.

63. Hillary Bissell to Roy Wilkins, NAACP Papers, Group II, Box 91, Folder 1952, LC.

64. Ibid.

65. Ibid.

66. Patricia Verdier to NAACP Office, May 29, 1952, NAACP Papers, Group II, Box 91, Folder 1952, LC.

67. Bissell to Gloster B. Current, June 9, 1951, NAACP Papers, Group II, Box 91, Folder 1952, LC.

68. Hillary Bissell to Gloster B. Current, June 10, 1952, NAACP Papers, Group II, Box 91, Folder 1952, LC. For more on Clark's psychological ideas, see Kluger, *Simple Justice.*

69. Wilkins, *Man's Life*, 18–20, 31–32. Also see Wilkins, *Standing Fast*, 86, 173–74.

70. Helen Claytor, record of oral interview, February 18, 1999, Black History Collection, GRPL.

71. Wilkins, *Man's Life*, chap. 3.

72. Clingman, *Human Relations Commission*, chap. 1.

73. Ibid.

74. For a nice overview of this period, see Polenberg, *One Nation*; also see Jackson, "Crabgrass Frontier."

75. For post–World War II Negro ghettoization, see Hirsch, *Second Ghetto*; Raymond Mohl, "Making the Second Ghetto in Metropolitan Miami, 1940–1960," in *The New African American Urban History*, Kenneth Goings and Raymond Mohl, eds. (Thousand Oaks, Calif.: Sage Publications, 1996).

Conclusion

1. Clingman, " Human Relations Commission," 2.

2. Plummer, "NAACP."

3. Rice, "Invasion-Succession."

4. Cato, "Racial Discrimination."

5. Hirsch, *Second Ghetto.* Hirsch distinguishes the second wave of the great migration from the first wave by calling it the second ghetto. While this is helpful in analyzing larger cities such as Chicago, with its distinct pre-Depression migration, the formulation does not fully hold true for cities the size of Grand Rapids. In fact, there is no first ghetto in Grand Rapids to speak of until the era in which Hirsch uses the term "second ghetto."

6. Meyer, "Evolution," 141–54; Meyer, "Residential Patterns," 151–67.

7. Kelley, " Riddle of the Zoot," 161–81; Cone, *Martin and Malcolm*; Perry, *Life of a Man.*

8. For the cultural shift in Black America, see VanDeburg, *New Day.*

9. For three different perspectives on the Grand Rapids race riot see George B. Kampius, "Riots of 1967"; Pertrusma, "Race Riots"; Travis Porter, "A Second Look at the 1967 Grand Rapids Race Riot: A Critique of the White Community's Explanation and Remedies," CCH.

10. Paul I. Philips Papers, Box 1, GRPL.

11. On the work of Cedric Ward and the Robeson Players, see the GRPL vertical file.

12. On Collins, see GRPL vertical file.

13. David K. Porter, "Grand Rapids' Historical Political Anomaly: The Election of Lyman S. Parks, Sr., as Mayor of Grand Rapids, MI in 1973," CCH.

BIBLIOGRAPHY

Notes on Sources

Locating the materials about African Americans in Grand Rapids was an adventure. Materials were gleaned from a number of archival collections and sources. The most notable collections were the Local History Collection of the Grand Rapids Public Library, the University of Michigan Bentley Historical Collection, Wayne State University Labor History Library, and the Library of Congress. Other smaller collections that provided important biographical information for individuals who appear in this history were local public libraries located in New York, Iowa, and Greenville, Michigan.

Since religion is a heavy theme of this book, smaller collections such as Kalamazoo College's archives of Baptist churches in western Michigan were essential to understanding the formation of key institutions that figure so prominently in this account. Finally, I would be remiss if I did not say that the Historical Collection of the Calvin College Library and the collection of senior papers written by Calvin College history majors were indispensable in tracking down sources for this book.

Manuscript Collections

THE GRAND RAPIDS PUBLIC LIBRARY LOCAL HISTORY COLLECTION, GRAND RAPIDS, MICHIGAN

Afro-American History Collection
Helen Claytor Papers
J. C. Craig Collection
Grand Rapids Study Collection
William and Virginia Glenn Papers
Paul I. Philips Papers
Richmond Family Papers
Robinson Photographic Collection

GRAND RAPIDS CITY ARCHIVES, GRAND RAPIDS, MICHIGAN

Proceedings of the Grand Rapids City Commission

MICHIGAN HISTORICAL COLLECTION, BENTLEY HISTORICAL
LIBRARY, ANN ARBOR

Helen Claytor Papers
Thomas Creswell Papers
The Diocese of Western Michigan, Episcopal Church in the U.S.A.
Fountain Street Church Papers
Grand Rapids Urban League Papers
Lyman Park Papers

LIBRARY OF CONGRESS, WASHINGTON, D.C.

Booker T. Washington Papers
National Association for the Advancement of Colored People Papers
National Urban League Papers

NATIONAL ARCHIVES, WASHINGTON, D.C.

Federal Employment Practice Commission
Freedman Bureau Papers
Testimony of the House Un-American Activities Committee

KALAMAZOO COLLEGE ARCHIVES, KALAMAZOO, MICHIGAN

The Grand Rapids Baptist Association
The Michigan Baptist Association

UNIVERSITY OF MASSACHUSETTS, AMHERST

W. E. B. Du Bois Papers (microfilm)

UNIVERSITY OF MINNESOTA, MINNEAPOLIS

Kantz Family Papers
YMCA Papers: Volunteers in World War I

THE STATE ARCHIVES OF MICHIGAN, LANSING

Bureau of Negro Welfare League
Department of Labor
Relief of Negroes

THE DETROIT PUBLIC LIBRARY, DETROIT, MICHIGAN

Burton Collection
Kimball Diary

CHICAGO HISTORICAL SOCIETY, CHICAGO, ILLINOIS

Claude Barnett Papers

WESTERN MICHIGAN UNIVERSITY REGIONAL ARCHIVES

Kent County Court Records

INTERVIEWS BY THE AUTHOR

Bishop John Burgess, June 15, 2000, Grand Rapids, Michigan
Helen Claytor, June 18, 1994, Grand Rapids, Michigan
Sarah Glover, July 10, 1999, Grand Rapids, Michigan
Melvin Gooselby, March 11, 1992, Grand Rapids, Michigan
Hazel Grant, June 12, 1993, Grand Rapids, Michigan
Pierson Smith, Grand Rapids, Michigan

NEWSPAPERS AND MAGAZINES

The Banner (Magazine of the Christian Reformed Church of North America),
    Grand Rapids, Michigan
Chicago Defender, Chicago, Illinois
The Crisis, New York, New York
Detroit Free Press, Detroit, Michigan
Detroit Plaindealer, Detroit, Michigan
Detroit Tribune, Detroit, Michigan
Grand Rapids Eagle, Grand Rapids, Michigan
Grand Rapids Evening Leader, Grand Rapids, Michigan
Grand Rapids Herald, Grand Rapids, Michigan
Grand Rapids Magazine, Grand Rapids, Michigan
Grand Rapids Post, Grand Rapids, Michigan
Grand Rapids Spectator, Grand Rapids, Michigan
Grand Rapids Times, Grand Rapids, Michigan
Michigan State News, Grand Rapids, Michigan
Pittsburgh Courier, Pittsburgh, Pennsylvania

Primary Articles, Books, and Published Reports

Allen, Richard. *The Life Experience and Gospel Labors of the Rt. Rev. Richard
    Allen.* Philadelphia: Martin and Boston, 1833.
Bagnall, Robert W. "Recruiting in the Mid-West." *The Crisis* 18 (July 1919): 3.
———. "Michigan: The Land of Many Waters." *The Messenger*, 8 (1926): 101–
    23.
Baker, Ray Stannard. *Following the Color Line: American Negro Citizenship in
    the Progressive Era.* New York: Harper and Row, 1964.
Banner, Warren M. *The Negro Population of Grand Rapids, MI: 1940.* New York:
    National Urban League, 1940.
Baxter, Albert. *History of the City of Grand Rapids, Michigan.* New York and
    Grand Rapids: Munsell and Company, 1891.
Beets, Henry. "The Dutch People and the Negro." *The Banner* 51 (January 10,
    1916).
———. "How to Solve the Negro Problem." *The Banner* 54 (October 2, 1919).

———. "Negro Education Injustice." *The Banner* 47 (November 14, 1912).

———."The Negro in the South." *The Banner* 53 (April 11, 1918).

———. "The Tuskegee Institute For Negroes." *The Banner* 53 (January 31, 1918).

Bolden (Mildred) v. Bolden (Emmett), Circuit Court of Kent County, Case No. 26115, June 12, 1924, Kent County Clerk's Office, Hall of Justice, Grand Rapids, Mich.

Booker v. Grand Rapids Medical College. Michigan Reports: Cases Decided in the Supreme Court of Michigan. Grand Rapids Court Records, 156.

Bragg, George F. *History of the Afro-American Group of the Episcopal Church.* Baltimore: Church Advocate Press, 1922.

Brawley, Benjamin G. *The History of Morehouse College.* College Park, Md.: McGrath Publishing Co., 1970. First published 1917 by Morehouse College.

Burgess, John M. "This I Believe." In *Many Shades of Black,* edited by Stanley L. Wormely and Lewis H. Fenderson. New York: William Morrow and Company, 1969.

Chapman, Charles. *History of Kent County Michigan.* Chicago: Chapman and Company, 1881.

Community African Methodist Episcopal Church, Grand Rapids, Michigan. *Souvenir Program: 82nd Anniversary, June 4, 1956.* Ann Arbor: Michigan Historical Collection, Bentley Historical Library, University of Michigan.

Du Bois, W. E. B. *The Souls of Black Folk.* 1904. Reprint, New York: Penguin Press, 1989.

———. *Efforts for Social Betterment among Negro Americans.* 1909. Reprinted in *The Atlanta University Publications.* New York: Arno Press and The New York Times, 1968.

Edmond, Mary, comp. *We Honor Them: African American Women's Clubs and Organizational Endeavors in Grand Rapids.* Grand Rapids, Mich.: Alpha Kappa Alpha Sorority, Theta Chi Omega Chapter, 1997.

Everett, Franklin. *Memorials of the Grand River Valley.* Chicago: The Chicago Legal News Company, 1878.

Goss, Dwight. *History of Grand Rapids and Its Industries.* Vol. 2. Chicago: C. F. Cooper and Company, 1906.

Grand Rapids, City of. *Proceedings of the City Commission, City of Grand Rapids, Michigan.*

Grand Rapids Spectator."Negro Welfare Work." No. 10 (May 17, 1930), 19.

Jones, Eugene Kinckle. "Negro in Community Life." In *Proceedings of the National Conference of Social Work: 56th Annual Session, San Francisco, Calif., 1929,* 388. Chicago: University of Chicago Press, 1929.

Kinsey, W. H. Kinsey, and F. A. Baldwin, eds. *Park Congregational Church: The Story of One Hundred Years 1836–1936.* Grand Rapids, Mich.: Park [First] Congregational Church, 1936.

McKee, James. *Negro Leadership in Grand Rapids.* East Lansing: Institute for Community Development, Continuing Education Service, Michigan State University, May 1962.

McLaughlin, Robert William. *The Negro Problem: A Sermon.* Manuscript, February 28, 1904, Local History Collection, GRPL.

"*Meisner v. Detroit Belle Isle and Windsor Ferry Company.*" *Northwestern Reporter* 118 (1909).

Michigan, State of. Department of Labor and Industry, Bureau of Negro Welfare Lansing, Michigan (State of Michigan, State Archives).

——. *Proceedings of Annual Conference, State Bureau of Negro Welfare at Detroit, Michigan, October 21, 1927.* State of Michigan Archives, Lansing.

——. *Public Acts, 1885, No. 130.* Lansing, Michigan.

——. *Public Acts, 1919, No. 375.* Lansing, Michigan.

Moss, R. Maurice. "American Cities—Grand Rapids." *Opportunity,* January 1929, 12–15.

Owens, A. A., and Harvey C. Jackson. "Report on Negroes in The State of Michigan." In *State of Michigan Sixteenth Annual Report of the Bureaus of Labor and Industrial Statistics, under Direction of Joseph L. Cox, Commissioner of Labor.* Lansing: Robert Smith Printing Company, 1899.

Park Congregational Church. *Memorial of the Rev. James Ballard, 1805–1881.* Grand Rapids: C. M. Loomis Book and Job Printer, 1881.

Philips, Paul I. "The Negro In Grand Rapids." Unpublished manuscript, Grand Rapids Urban League Papers, Grand Rapids Local History Collection, Grand Rapids Public Library.

——. "A Study of Ten Inter-Cultural Areas in Grand Rapids, Michigan." Unpublished manuscript, Grand Rapids Public Library, Grand Rapids, Mich., November 13, 1947.

Plummer, W. W. "What the NAACP Means To Me," *Faces in Places* 2, no. 1 (January 1958): 2.

St. Luke African Methodist Episcopal Zion Church, Grand Rapids, Michigan. *125th Anniversary Souvenir Journal Historical Sketches,* October 9, 1988. Grand Rapids: Local History Collection, Grand Rapids Public Library.

St. Philip's Episcopal Church, Grand Rapids, Michigan. *Fortieth Anniversary, 1911–1951.* Ann Arbor: Michigan Historical Collection, Bentley Historical Library, University of Michigan.

True Light Baptist Church. *75th Anniversary Program: August 24, 1997.* Grand Rapids: Local History Collection, Grand Rapids Public Library.

United States House of Representatives Committee On Un-American Activities. Washington, D.C.: National Archives.

University of Michigan. *University of Michigan Yearbook, 1923.* Ann Arbor: University of Michigan.

University of Michigan. *University of Michigan Yearbook, 1924.* Ann Arbor: University of Michigan.

University of Michigan. *University of Michigan Yearbook, 1926.* Ann Arbor: University of Michigan.

Warren, Frances H. *Michigan Manual of Freedman's Progress.* Lansing: The State of Michigan, 1915.

White, Walter. *A Man Called White.* New York: Viking Press, 1948.

Wilkins, Roger. *A Man's Life: An Autobiography.* New York: Simon and Schuster, 1985.

Wilkins, Roy. *Standing Fast: The Autobiography of Roy Wilkins.* New York: Viking Press, 1982.

Works Project Administration. *Inventory of the Church Archives of Michigan: African Methodist Episcopal Church Michigan Conference.* Detroit: The Michigan Historical Records Survey Project, 1940.

Secondary Books and Articles

Anderson, Benedict. *Imagined Communities: Reflection on the Origin and Spread of Nationalism.* Revised edition. New York: Verso, 1991.

Baltzell, E. Digby. *The Protestant Establishment: Aristocracy and Caste in America.* New York: Random House, 1964.

———. *The Protestant Establishment Revisited.* New Brunswick, N.J.: Transaction Publishers, 1991.

Barron, Hal S. "Staying Down on the Farm: Social Processes of Settled Rural Life in the Nineteenth-Century North." In *The Countryside in the Age of Capitalist Transformation: Essays in the Social History of Rural America,* edited by Steve Hahn and Jonathan Prude. Chapel Hill: University of North Carolina Press, 1985.

Bennett, William L., *Memories of East Grand Rapids, 1834–1982.* East Grand Rapids: City of East Grand Rapids, 1982.

Berlin, Ira. *Slaves without Masters: The Free Negro in the Antebellum South.* New York: Pantheon Books, 1975.

Berreman, Gerald. "The Concept of Caste." In the *International Encyclopedia of the Social Sciences,* edited by David L. Sills, 333–34. New York: Macmillan, 1968.

Blackwell, James E., and Morris Janowitz, eds. *The Black Sociologist: Historical and Contemporary Perspectives.* Chicago: University of Chicago Press, 1974.

Blumin, Stuart. *The Emergence of the Middle Class: Social Experience in the American City, 1760–1900.* New York: Cambridge University Press, 1989.

Bodnar, John. *Lives of Their Own: Blacks, Italians, and Poles in Pittsburgh, 1900–1960.* Urbana: University of Illinois Press, 1982.

Borchert, James. *Alley Life in Washington: Family, Community, Religion, and Folklife in the City, 1850–1970.* Urbana: University of Illinois Press, 1980.

Boxill, Bernard. "Self Respect and Protest." *Philosophy and Public Affairs* 6:1 (1976): 58–69.

Bratt, James. *Dutch Calvinism in Modern America: A History of a Conservative Subculture.* Grand Rapids, Mich.: W. B. Eerdmans, 1984.

Bratt, James D., and Christopher Meehan. *Gathered at the River: Grand Rapids, Michigan, and Its People of Faith.* Grand Rapids, Mich.: Grand Rapids Area Council for the Humanities and W. B. Eerdmans, 1993.

Campbell, James T. *Songs of Zion: The African Methodist Church in the United States and South Africa.* New York: Oxford University Press, 1995.

Campbell, Susan. "'Black Bolsheviks' and Recognition of African-America's Right to Self-Determination by the Communist Party USA." *Science and Society* 58, no. 4 (Winter 1994–95): 440–70.

Capeci, Dominic. *Race Relations in Wartime Detroit: The Sojourner Truth Housing Controversy of 1942.* Philadelphia: Temple University Press, 1984.

Carron, Christian. *Grand Rapids Furniture: The Story of America's Furniture City.* Edited by Karen McCarthy. Grand Rapids, Mich.: Public Museum of Grand Rapids, 1998.

Cashin, Joan E. "Black Families in the Old Northwest." *Journal of the Early Republic* 15, no. 3 (1995): 449–75.

Cohen, Lizabeth. *Making a New Deal: Industrial Workers in Chicago, 1919–1939.* New York: Cambridge University Press, 1990.

Cohen, William. *At Freedom's Edge: Black Mobility and the Southern White Quest for Racial Control 1861–1915.* Baton Rouge: Louisiana State University Press, 1991.

Cone, James H. *Martin and Malcolm in America: A Dream or a Nightmare.* Maryknoll, N.Y.: Orbis Books, 1991.

Cox, Anna-Lisa. "A Pocket of Freedom: Blacks in Covert, Michigan, in the Nineteenth Century." *Michigan Historical Review* 21, no. 1 (Spring 1995): 1–18.

Cox, Oliver C. *Caste, Class and Race: A Study in Social Dynamics.* Garden City, N.Y.: Doubleday, 1948.

Curry, Leonard. *The Free Black in Urban America, 1800–1850.* Chicago: University of Chicago Press, 1981.

Dalfiume, Richard M. "The 'Forgotten Years' of the Negro Revolution." *Journal of American History* 55, no. 1 (June 1968): 90–106.

Dawley, Alan. *Struggle for Justice: Social Responsibility and the Liberal State.* Cambridge, Mass.: Harvard University Press, 1991.

DeVries, James E. *Race and Kinship in a Midwestern Town: The Black Experience in Monroe, Michigan, 1900–1915.* Urbana: University of Illinois Press, 1984.

Dickerson, Dennis. *Militant Mediator: Whitney M. Young Jr.* Lexington: University of Kentucky Press, 1998.

———. *Out of the Crucible: Black Steelworkers in Western Pennsylvania, 1875–1980.* New York: State University of New York Press, 1986.

Dollard, John. *Caste and Class in a Southern Town.* New York: Anchor Books, 1937.

Dormon, James H. "Shaping the Popular Image of Post Reconstruction American Blacks: 'The Coon Song' Phenomenon of the Gilded Age." *American Quarterly* 40 (December 1988): 450–71.

Douglas, Mary. *Purity and Danger: An Analysis of Concepts of Pollution and Taboo.* New York: Praeger Publishers, 1966.

Drake, St. Clair. "The Tuskegee Connection: Booker T. Washington and Robert E. Park." *Society* 20, no. 4 (May/June 1983): 82–92.

Du Bois, W. E. B. *Black Reconstruction in America 1860–1880.* New York: Atheneum, 1973.

Dunbar, Willis F., and William G. Shade. "The Black Man Gains the Vote: The Centennial of 'Impartial Suffrage' in Michigan." *Michigan History* 56, no. 1 (Spring 1972): 42–57.

Elsthain, Jean Bethke. *Democracy on Trial.* New York: Basic Books, 1995.

Fabre, Geneviéve. "African-American Commerative Celebrations in the Nineteenth-century." In *History and Memory in African American Culture,* Geneviéve Fabre and Robert O'Meally, eds. New York: Oxford University Press, 1994.

Fennimore, Jean Joy L. "Austin Blair: Civil War Governor, 1861–1862." *Michigan History* 49 (September 1965): 344–69.

Fine, Sidney. *Expanding the Frontiers of Civil Rights: Michigan, 1948–1968.* Detroit: Wayne State University Press, 2000."

———. 'A Jewel in the Crown of All of Us': Michigan Enacts a Fair Employment

Practices Act, 1941–1958." *Michigan Historical Review* 22, no. 1 (Spring 1996): 18–66.

———. *Violence in the Model City: The Cavanaugh Administration, Race Relations, and the Detroit Riot of 1967.* Ann Arbor: University of Michigan Press, 1989.

Foner, Eric. *Free Soil, Free Labor, Free Men: The Ideology of the Republican Party before the Civil War.* New York: Oxford University Press, 1970.

———. *Reconstruction: America's Unfinished Revolution 1863–1877.* New York: Harper and Row, 1989.

Formisano, Ronald P. "The Edge of Caste: Colored Suffrage in Michigan, 1827–1861." *Michigan History* 56 (Spring 1972): 19–40.

———. *Boston against Busing: Race, Class, and Ethnicity in 1960s and 1970s.* Chapel Hill: University of North Carolina Press, 1991.

Franklin, John Hope. "'Birth of a Nation': Propaganda as History." *Massachusetts Review* 20, no. 3 (Autumn 1979): 417–34.

Fredrickson, George. *The Black Image in the White Mind: The Debate on Afro-American Character and Destiny, 1817–1914.* New York: Harper and Row, 1971.

———. *White Supremacy: A Comparative Study in American and South African History.* New York: Oxford University Press, 1981.

Freedmen's Progress Commission. *Michigan Manual of Freedman's Progress.* Compiled by Francis H. Warren. Detroit: Freedmen's Progress Commission, 1915.

Gaines, Kevin K. *Uplifting the Race: Black Leadership, Politics, and Culture in the Twentieth Century.* Chapel Hill: University of North Carolina Press, 1996.

Gamble, Vanessa Northington. *Making a Place for Ourselves: The Black Hospital Movement, 1920–1945.* New York: Oxford University Press, 1995.

Gates, Henry Louis Jr. "The Trope of a New Negro and the Reconstruction of the Image of the Black." *Representations* 24 (1988): 129–55.

Gay, Peter. *The Bourgeois Experience: Victoria to Freud.* New York: Oxford University Press, 1984.

Gerould, Winifred Gregory. *American Newspapers, 1821–1936: A Union List of Files Available in the United States and Canada.* New York: Kraus Reprint Corporation, 1967.

Giddens, Anthony. *Capitalism and Modern Social Theory: An Analysis of the Writings of Marx, Durkheim, and Max Weber.* New York: Cambridge University Press, 1971.

Giddings, Paula. *When and Where I Enter: The Impact of Black Women on Race and Sex in America.* New York: Bantam Books, 1984.

Gilroy, Paul. "One Nation under a Groove: The Politics of 'Race' and Racism in Britain." In *Anatomy of Racism,* edited by David Theo Golberg, 263–82. Minneapolis: University of Minnesota Press, 1990.

Goggins, Jacqueline A. *Carter G. Woodson: A Life in Black History.* Baton Rouge: Louisiana State University Press, 1993.

Goings, Kenneth. *The NAACP Comes of Age: The Defeat of Judge John J. Parker.* Bloomington: Indiana University Press, 1990.

Goings, Kenneth, and Raymond Mohl, eds. *The New African American Urban History*. Thousands Oaks, Calif.: Sage Publications, 1996.

Gordon, John M. "Michigan Journal, 1836." Edited by Douglas H. Gordon and George S. May. *Michigan History* 43 (December 1959): 433–79.

Gottlileb, Peter. *Making Their Own Way: Southern Blacks' Migration to Pittsburgh, 1916–1930*. Urbana: University of Illinois Press, 1987.

Gray, Susan E. *The Yankee West: Community Life on the Michigan Frontier*. Chapel Hill: University of North Carolina Press, 1996.

Greenfeld, Liah. *Nationalism: Five Roads to Modernity*. Cambridge, Mass.: Harvard University Press, 1992.

Greenwood, Janette Thomas. *The Bittersweet Legacy: The Black and White "Better Classes" in Charlotte, 1850–1910*. Chapel Hill: University of North Carolina Press, 1994.

Gregg, Robert. *Sparks from the Anvil of Oppression: Philadelphia's African Methodists and Southern Migrants, 1890–1940*. Philadelphia: Temple University Press, 1993.

Grossman, James R. *Land of Hope: Chicago, Black Southerners and the Great Migration*. Chicago: University of Chicago Press, 1989.

Hale, Grace Elizabeth. *Making Whiteness: The Culture of Segregation in the South, 1890–1940*. New York: Pantheon Books, 1995.

Halpern, Martin. "The Politics of Auto Union Factionalism: The Michigan CIO in the Cold War Era." *Michigan Historical Review* 13 (Fall 1987): 51–73.

Hamilton, Charles. *Adam Clayton Powell, Jr.: The Political Biography of An American Dilemma*. New York: Atheneum, 1991.

Harlan, Louis. *Booker T. Washington: The Making of a Black Leader, 1856–1901*. New York: Oxford University Press, 1972.

———. *Booker T. Washington: The Wizard of Tuskegee, 1901–1915*. New York: Oxford University Press, 1983.

Harms, Richard H. "Bodies by Hayes." *Grand Rapids Magazine*, April 1995, 51.

———. "Comstock's Row." *Grand Rapids Magazine*, August 1995.

———. "Jess Elster: Grand Rapids' Mr. Baseball." *Michigan History Magazine*, January/February 1993.

Harris, Michael W. *The Rise of Gospel Blues: The Music of Thomas Andrew Dorsey in the Urban Church*. New York: Oxford University, 1992.

Harris, William H. *Keeping the Faith: A. Philip Randolph, Milton P. Webster, and the Brotherhood of Sleeping Car Porters, 1925–1937*. Urbana: University of Illinois Press, 1977.

Hatch, Nathan O. *The Democratization of American Christianity*. New Haven, Conn.: Yale University Press, 1989.

Haygood, Will. *King of the Cats: The Life and Times of Adam Clayton, Jr.* New York: Houghton Mifflin Company, 1993.

Hellwig, David J. "Strangers in Their Own Land: Patterns of Black Nativism, 1830–1930." *American Studies* 23, no.1 (1982): 85–98.

Higginbotham, Evelyn Brooks. *Righteous Discontent: The Women's Movement in the Black Baptist Church, 1880–1920*. Cambridge, Mass.: Harvard University Press, 1993.

Hill, Christopher *The English Bible and the Seventeenth-Century Revolution.* New York: Penguin Books, 1993.

Himmelfarb, Gertrude. *Poverty and Compassion: The Moral Imagination of the Late Victorians.* New York: Knopf, 1991.

Hine, Darlene Clark. "Black Migration to the Urban Midwest: The Gender Dimension, 1915–1945." In *The Great Migration in Historical Perspective: New Dimensions of Race, Class, and Gender,* edited by Joe William Trotter Jr., 127–46. Bloomington: Indiana University Press, 1991.

———. *Black Women in White: Racial Conflict and Cooperation in the Nursing Profession, 1890–1950.* Bloomington: Indiana University Press, 1989.

———. *Black Women in the Middle West: The Michigan Experience.* Ann Arbor: Michigan Historical Society, 1990.

———. *The State of Afro-American History: Past, Present and Future.* Baton Rouge: Louisiana State University Press, 1986.

Hirsch, Arnold R. *Making the Second Ghetto: Race and Housing in Chicago, 1940–1960.* 2nd ed. Chicago: University of Chicago Press, 1983.

Hobbes, Thomas. *The Leviathan.* Edited by Nelle Fuller. Reprint, Chicago: Encyclopedia Britannica, Inc., 1952.

Hobsbawm, Eric. *The Age of Capital, 1848–1875.* London: Abacus, 1995.

Holt, Thomas. *Black Over White: Negro Political Leadership in South Carolina during Reconstruction.* Urbana: University of Illinois Press, 1977.

Horsman, Reginald. *Race and Manifest Destiny: The Origins of American Racial Anglo-Saxonism.* Cambridge, Mass.: Harvard University Press, 1981.

Horton, James Oliver. *Free People of Color: Inside the African-American Community.* Washington, D.C.: Smithsonian Institution Press, 1993.

Horton, James Oliver, and Lois E. Horton. *In Hope of Liberty: Community and Protest among Northern Free Blacks, 1700–1860.* New York: Oxford University Press, 1997.

Huggins, Nathan Irvin. *Harlem Renaissance.* New York: Oxford University Press, 1971.

Jackson, Kenneth T. "Crabgrass Frontier: 150 Years of Suburban Growth in America." In *The Urban Experience: Themes in American History,* edited by Raymond A. Mohl and James F. Richardson, 196–221. Belmont, Calif.: Wadsworth Publishing Company, 1973.

Jaynes, Gerald David. *Branches without Roots: Genesis of the Black Working Class in the American South, 1862–1882.* New York: Oxford University Press, 1986.

Jelks, Randal M. *"Bolden v. Keith's Theatre." Grand River Valley History* 11 (1993): 10–15.

———. "The Character and Work of a Spiritual Watchman Described: The Preaching of Lemuel Haynes and the Quest for Personal Freedom." *Fides et Historia: Journal of the Conference on Faith and History* 26, no. 1 (1994): 126–33.

———. "'Making Opportunity': The Struggle against Jim Crow in Grand Rapids, Michigan, 1890–1927." *Michigan Historical Review* 19, no. 2 (Fall 1993): 23–48.

Johnston, W. Michael. *From Lake Superior to Indiana: The Story of UAW Region 1–D.* Grand Rapids, Michigan: UAW 1–D, 1988.

Jones, Jacqueline. *American Work: Four Centuries of Black and White Labor.* New York: W. W. Norton and Company, 1998.

———. *Labor of Love, Labor of Sorrow: Black Women, Work and the Family, From Slavery to the Present.* New York: Basic Books, 1985.

Katzman, David M. *Before the Ghetto: Black Detroit in the Nineteenth Century.* Urbana: University of Illinois Press, 1973.

———. "Black Slavery in Michigan." *Midcontinent American Studies Journal* (Fall 1970): 56–66.

Kelley, Robin D. G. *Hammer and Hoe: Alabama Communists during the Great Depression.* Chapel Hill: University of North Carolina Press, 1990.

———. "The Riddle of the Zoot: Malcolm Little and Black Cultural Politics during World War II." Chapter 7 in *Race Rebels: Culture, Politics, and the Black Working Class.* New York: Free Press, 1994.

———. "'We Are Not What We Seem': Rethinking Black Working Class Opposition in the Jim Crow South." *Journal of American History* 80, no. 1 (June 1993): 75–112.

Keeran, Roger. "National Groups and the Popular Front: The Case of the International Workers Order." *Journal of American Ethnic History* 14, no. 3 (Spring 1995): 23–51.

Kellogg, Charles Flint. *NAACP: A History of the National Association for the Advancement of Colored People.* Vol. 1, 1909–1920. Baltimore, Md.: Johns Hopkins University Press, 1967.

Kluger, Richard, *Simple Justice: The History of* Brown v. Board of Education *and Black America's Struggle for Equality.* New York: Knopf, 1977.

Kusmer, Kenneth L. *A Ghetto Takes Shape: Black Cleveland, 1870–1930.* Urbana: University of Illinois Press, 1976.

Lal, Barbara Ballis. "Black and Blue in Chicago: Robert E. Park's Perspective on Race Relations in Urban America, 1914–1944." *British Journal of Sociology* 38, no. 4 (December 1987): 546–66.

Lasch-Quinn, Elisabeth. *Black Neighbors: Race and the Limits of Reform in the American Settlement House Movement, 1890–1945.* Chapel Hill: University of North Carolina Press, 1993.

Lemons, J. Stanley. "Black Stereotypes as Reflected in Popular Culture, 1880–1920." *American Quarterly* 29 (Spring 1977): 102–16.

Levine, Lawrence. *Black Culture and Black Consciousness: Afro-American Folk Thought from Slavery to Freedom.* New York: Oxford University Press, 1976.

Littlejohn, Edward J., and Donald L. Hobson. *Black Lawyers, Law Practice, and Bar Association, 1844 to 1970: A Michigan History.* Detroit: The Wolverine Bar Association, 1972.

Litwack, Leon F. *North of Slavery: The Free Negro in the Free States, 1790–1860.* Chicago: University of Chicago Press, 1961.

Logan, Rayford W. *The Betrayal of the Negro: From Rutherford B. Hayes to Woodrow Wilson.* New York: Collier Books, 1965.

Lott, Eric. *Love and Theft: Blackface Minstrelsy and The American Working Class.* New York: Oxford University Press, 1995.

Lowell, Michigan, city of. *100 Years of History, 1831–1931.* Lowell, Michigan: 1931. Grand Rapids Public Library.

Luker, Ralph E. *The Social Gospel in Black and White: American Racial Reform, 1885–1912.* Chapel Hill: University of North Carolina, 1991.

Lydens, Z. Z. *The Story of Grand Rapids.* Grand Rapids, Mich.: Kregels Publishing, 1966.

MacPherson, James M. *The Abolitionist Legacy: From Reconstruction to the NAACP.* Princeton, N.J.: Princeton University Press, 1975.

Maffly-Kipp, Laurie F. "Mapping the World, Mapping the Race: The Negro Race History, 1874–1915." *Church History* 64 (December 1995): 610–26.

Mandle, Jay R. *Not Slave, Not Free: The African American Economic Experience since the Civil War.* Durham, N.C.: Duke University Press, 1992.

Marks, Carole. "Social and Economic Life of Southern Blacks." In *Black Exodus: The Great Migration from the American South,* edited by Alferdteen Harrison, 36–50. Jackson: University Press of Mississippi, 1991.

Martin, Waldo E., Jr. *The Mind of Frederick Douglass.* Chapel Hill: University of North Carolina Press, 1984.

Marx, Karl. "The German Ideology." In *The Marx-Engels Reader,* edited by Robert C. Tucker. 2nd ed. New York: W. W. Norton, 1978.

Mays, Benjamin Elijah, and Joseph William Nicholson. *The Negro's Church.* New York: Arno Press and The New York Times, 1969.

———. *The Negro's God: As Reflected in His Literature.* New York: Atheneum, 1968.

McCain, Rea, Aris A. Mallas Jr., and Magaret K. Hedden. *Forty Years in Politics: The Story of Ben Pelham.* Detroit: Wayne State University Press, 1957.

McFeely, William S. *Frederick Douglass.* New York: Simon and Schuster, 1991.

McKivigan, John R., and Jason H. Silverman. "Monarchial Liberty and Republican Slavery: West Indies Emancipation Celebration in Upstate New York and Canada West." *Afro-American in New York Life and History* (January 1986): 7–18.

McLaughlin, Tom L. "Grass Roots Attitudes toward Black Rights in Twelve Nonslaveholding States, 1846–1846." *Mid-America* 56 (1974): 175–81.

McMillen, Neil R. *Dark Journey: Black Mississippian in the Age of Jim Crow.* Urbana: University of Illinois Press, 1989.

McNeil, Genna Rae. *Groundwork: Charles Hamilton Houston and the Struggle for Civil Rights.* Philadelphia: University of Pennsylvania Press, 1983.

Meier, August. *Negro Thought In America 1880–1915.* Ann Arbor: University of Michigan Press, 1963.

Meier, August, and Elliot Rudwick. *Black Detroit and the Rise of the U.A.W.* New York: Oxford University Press, 1979.

Meyer, Douglas K. "Changing Negro Residential Patterns in Michigan's Capital, 1915–1970." *Michigan History* 56, no. 2 (1972): 151–67.

———. "Evolution of a Permanent Negro Community in Lansing." *Michigan History* 55, no. 2 (1971): 141–54.

Michigan Department of State. *Pathway to Michigan's Black Heritage.* Lansing: Michigan Department of State, 1988.

Moore, Jesse Thomas, Jr. *A Search for Equality: The Urban League, 1910–1960.* University Park: The Pennsylvania State University Press, 1981

Morris, Aldon. *The Origins of the Civil Rights Movement: Black Communities Organizing for Change.* New York: Free Press and Collier Macmillan, 1984.

Moses, Wilson Jeremiah. *The Golden Age of Black Nationalism, 1850–1925.* New York: Oxford University Press, 1978.

———. *Wings of Ethiopia: Studies in African American Life and Letters.* Ames: Iowa State University Press, 1990.

Murphy, Marjorie. "Prairie Politics: Black Life in the Midwest, 1890–1940." *Reviews in American History* 13 (June 1985): 251–56.

Murray, Pauli, ed. *States' Laws on Race and Color.* Cincinnati: Women's Division of Christian Services, Board of Mission and Church Extension, Methodist Church, 1951.

Nash, Gary. *Forging Freedom: The Formation of Philadelphia's Black Community 1720–1840.* Cambridge, Mass.: Harvard University Press, 1988

Neverdon-Morton, Cynthia. *Afro-American Women in the South and the Advancement of the Race, 1895–1925.* Knoxville: University of Tennessee, 1989

Norton, Wesley. "The Methodist Church in Michigan and the Politics of Slavery: 1850–1860." *Michigan History* 48 (September 1964): 193–213.

Ogbu, John. *Minority Education and Caste: The American System in Cross-Cultural Perspective.* New York: Academic Press, 1978.

Olson, Gordon. *The Grand Rapids Sampler.* Grand Rapids, Mich.: The Grand Rapids Historical Commission, 1992.

Osofsky, Gilbert. "The Enduring Ghetto." *Journal of American History* 55 (September 1968): 243–55.

Parris, Guichard, and Lester Brooks. *Blacks in the City: A History of the National Urban League.* Boston: Little, Brown and Company, 1971.

Patterson, James. *America's Struggle against Poverty, 1900–1985.* Cambridge, Mass.: Harvard University Press, 1986.

Patterson, Orlando. *Slavery and Social Death.* Cambridge, Mass.: Harvard University Press, 1983.

———. *Freedom in the Making of Western Culture.* New York: Basic Books, 1991.

Perry, Bruce. *Malcolm: The Life of a Man Who Changed Black America.* Barrytown, N.Y.: Station Hill, 1991.

Pettigrew, Thomas F. "Actual Gains and Psychological Losses: The Negro American Protest." *Journal of Negro Education* 32 (Fall 1963): 493–506.

Phillips, Kimberly. *Alabama North: African-American Migrants, Community and Working-Class Activism in Cleveland, 1915–1945.* Urbana: University of Illinois Press, 1999.

Piersen, William D. *Black Yankees: The Development of an Afro-American Subculture in Eighteenth-Century New England.* Amherst: University of Massachusetts Press, 1988.

Pieterse, Jan Nederveen. *White on Black: Images of Africa and Blacks in Western Popular Culture.* New Haven, Conn.: Yale University Press, 1992.

Polenberg, Richard. *One Nation Divisible: Class, Race, and Ethnicity in the United States Since 1938.* New York: Viking Penguin, 1980.

Porter, Kenneth W. "Negroes and the Fur Trade." *Minnesota History* 15 (December 1934): 421–33.

Quist, John W. "'The Great Majority of Our Subscribers Are Farmers': The Michigan Abolitionist Constituency of the 1840s." *Journal of the Early Republic* 14, no. 3 (1994): 325–58.

Rancière, Jacques. *The Nights of Labor: The Worker's Dream in Nineteenth-Century France.* Translated by John Drury. Philadelphia: Temple University Press, 1989.

Record, Wilson. *Race and Radicalism: The NAACP and the Communist Party in Conflict.* Ithaca, N.Y.: Cornell University Press, 1964.

Reed, Christopher R. *The Chicago NAACP and the Rise of Black Professional Leadership, 1910–1966.* Bloomington: Indiana University Press, 1997.

Richardson, Heather Cox. *The Death of Reconstruction: Race, Labor and Politics in the Post–Civil War North, 1865–1901.* Cambridge, Mass.: Harvard University Press, 2002.

Roark, James L. "American Black Leaders: The Response to Colonialism and the Cold War, 1943-1953." *African Historical Studies* 4, no. 2 (1971): 253–70.

Roediger, David R. *The Wages of Whiteness: Race and the Making of the American Working Class.* New York: Verso, 1991.

Rudwick, Elliot M. *Race Riot at East St. Louis, July 2, 1917.* Cleveland and New York: World Publishing Company, 1966.

Salem, Dorothy. *To Better Our World: Black Women in Organized Reform, 1890–1920.* Brooklyn, N.Y.: Carlson Publishing, 1990.

Scott, Anne Firor. "Most Invisible of All: Black Women's Voluntary Associations," *Journal of Southern History* 56, no. 1 (February 1990): 3–22.

Scott, Daryl Michael. *Contempt and Pity: Social Policy and the Image of the Damaged Black Psyche, 1880–1896.* Chapel Hill: University of North Carolina Press, 1997.

Sennett, Richard, and Jonathan Cobb. *The Hidden Injuries of Class.* New York: W. W. Norton and Company, 1993.

Sernett, Milton C. *Bound for the Promised Land: African American Religion and the Great Migration.* Durham, N.C.: Duke University Press, 1997.

Sitkoff, Harvard. *A New Deal for Blacks: The Emergence of Civil Rights as a National Issue; The Depression Decade.* New York: Oxford University Press, 1978.

Smith, Michael O. "Raising a Black Regiment in Michigan: Adversity and Triumph." *Michigan Historical Review* 16, no. 2 (1990): 22–41.

Southern, David W. *The Malignant Heritage: Yankee Progressives and the Negro Question, 1901–1914.* Chicago: Loyola University Press, 1968.

Spear, Allen H. *Black Chicago: The Making of a Negro Ghetto, 1890–1920.* Chicago: University of Chicago Press, 1967.

Stokes, Curtis. "Tocqueville and the Problem of Racial Inequality." *Journal of Negro History* 75, nos. 1–2 (1990): 1–15.

Strum, Carol W. "School Segregation in Michigan." *Michigan History* 38 (March 1954): 1–23.

Stuckey, Sterling. *Slave Culture: Nationalist Theory and the Foundations of Black America.* New York: Oxford University Press, 1987.

Thomas, Richard W. "The Historical Roots of Contemporary Urban Black Self-Help in the United States." In *Contemporary Urban America: Problems, Issues and Alternatives,* edited by Marvel Lang, 253–91. Lanham, Md.: University Press of America, 1991.

———. *Life for Us Is What We Make It: Building Black Community in Detroit, 1915–1945.* Bloomington: Indiana University Press, 1992.

Thompson, E. P. *The Making of the English Working Class.* New York: Vintage Books, 1966.

Thurman, Howard. *Jesus and the Disinherited.* Nashville: Abingdon-Cokesbury, 1949.

Tocqueville, Alexis de. *Democracy in America.* Reprint. New York: Harper and Row: 1966.

Toll, Robert C. *Blacking Up: The Minstrel Show in Nineteenth-Century America.* New York: Oxford University Press, 1974

Trotter, Joe W. "African Americans in the City: The Industrial Era, 1900–1950." In *The New African American Urban History,* edited by Kenneth W. Goings and Raymond A. Mohl. Thousand Oaks, Calif.: Sage Publications, 1996.

———. *Black Milwaukee: The Making of Industrial Proletariat, 1915–1945.* Urbana: University of Illinois Press, 1985.

Turner, Victor. *Dramas, Fields, and Metaphors: Symbolic Action in Human Society.* Ithaca, N.Y.: Cornell University Press, 1974.

———. *The Ritual Process: Structure and Anti-Structure.* Chicago: Aldine Publishing co., 1969.

Tuttle, William M. *Chicago in the Red Summer of 1919.* New York: Atheneum Press, 1970.

Van Deburg, William L. *New Day in Babylon: The Black Power Movement and American Culture, 1965–1975.* Chicago: University of Chicago Press, 1992.

———. *Slavery and Race in American Popular Culture.* Madison: University of Wisconsin, 1984.

VanVulpen, James. *A Faith Journey: In Celebration of One Hundred Fifty Years, First (Park) Congregational Church, United Church of Christ.* Grand Rapids: First Park United Church of Christ, 1985.

Voegli, V. Jacques. *Free but Not Equal: The Midwest and the Negro during the Civil War.* Chicago: University of Chicago Press, 1967.

Walker, Juliet E. K. *The History of Black Business in America: Capitalism, Race, Entrepreneurship.* New York: Prentice Hall International, 1998.

Walker, Lewis, and Benjamin Wilson. *Black Eden: The Idlewild Community.* Lansing: Michigan State University Press, 2002.

Walters, Raymond. *The New Negro on Campus: Black College Rebellions of the 1920s.* Princeton, N.J.: Princeton University Press, 1975.

Weisenfeld, Judith. "The Harlem YWCA and the Secular City, 1904–1945," *Journal of Women's History* 3 (Fall 1994): 62–78.

Weiss, Nancy. *Farewell to the Party of Lincoln: Black Politics in the Age of FDR.* Princeton, N.J.: Princeton University Press, 1983.

———. "From Black Separatism to Interracial Cooperation: The Origins of Organized Efforts for Racial Advancement, 1890–1920." In *Twentieth-Century America: Recent Interpretations,* edited by Barton J. Bernstein and Allan Matusow. 2nd ed. New York: Harcourt Brace Jovanovich, 1972.

———. *The National Urban League, 1910–1940.* New York: Oxford University Press, 1974.

West, Dorothy. *The Wedding.* New York: Doubleday, 1995.

White, Deborah Gray. *Arn't I a Woman: Female Slaves in the Plantation South.* New York: W. W. Norton Company, 1985.

White, Shane. "'It Was a Proud Day': African Americans, Festivals, and Parades in the North, 1741–1834." *Journal of American History* 18, no. 1 (June 1994): 13–50.

Williams, Lillian S. *Strangers in the Land of Paradise: The Creation of An American Community, Buffalo, New York 19110–1940.* Bloomington: Indiana University Press, 1999.

Wills, David W. "Womanhood and Domesticity in the A.M.E. Tradition: The Influence of Daniel Payne. " In *Black Apostles at Home and Abroad: Afro-Americans and the Christian Mission from the Revolution to Reconstruction,* edited by David W. Wills and Richard Newman, 133–46. Boston: G. K. Hall and Company, 1982.

Wilmore, Gayraud. *Black Religion and Black Radicalism: An Interpretation of the Religious History of Afro-American People.* 2nd ed. Maryknoll, N.Y.: Orbis Press, 1983.

Wilson, Benjamin C. *The Rural Black Heritage Between Chicago and Detroit, 1850–1929: A Photograph Album and Random Thoughts.* Kalamazoo, Mich.: New Issues Press, Western Michigan University, 1985.

Wood, Peter. *Black Majority: Negroes in Colonial South Carolina from 1670 through the Stono Rebellion.* New York: W. W. Norton, 1974.

Woodward, C. Vann. *Reunion and Reaction.* New York: Doubleday Anchor, 1956.

———. *The Strange Career of Jim Crow.* New York: Oxford University Press, 1957.

Wright, George C. *Life Behind a Veil: Blacks in Louisville Kentucky, 1865–1930.* Baton Rouge; Louisiana State University Press, 1985.

Yzenbaard, John H. "The Crosswhite Case," *Michigan History* 53, no. 2 (1969): 131–43.

Zilversmith, Arthur. *The First Emancipation: The Abolition of Slavery in the North.* Chicago: University of Chicago Press, 1967.

Zunz, Olivier. *The Changing Face of Inequality: Urbanization, Industrial Development and Immigrants in Detroit 1880–1920.* Chicago: University of Chicago Press, 1982.

Dissertations, Theses, and Unpublished Papers

Armfield, Felix. "Eugene Kinckle Jones and Black Social Workers." Ph.D. diss., Michigan State University, 1998.

Browne, S. Henri. "The Negro in Grand Rapids." Manuscript, Grand Rapids Public Library, April 6, 1913.

Cato, Kevin. "Racial Discrimination in Northern Cities: The Land Tract Sale in Grand Rapids to Four Afro-Americans and the Reaction to the Sale." Calvin College History Seminar, Grand Rapids, Mich., Spring 1995.

Clingman, Lewis B. "The History of the Grand Rapids Human Relations Commission." Ph.D. diss., Michigan State University, 1976.

Elder, Mary Ruth. "Rowing, Not Drifting: The Grand Rapids Study Club, 1904–1964." Calvin College History Seminar, Grand Rapids, Mich., Fall 1994.

Kamper, Dennis. "The Christian Reformed Church and the Negro: The Attitude of the *Banner*." Calvin College History Seminar, Grand Rapids, Mich., Spring 1970.

Kampius, George B. "The Racial Riots of 1967: A Comparison of Reactions." Calvin College History Seminar, Grand Rapids, Mich., Fall 1978.

Kleiman, Jeffrey D. "The Great Strike: Religion, Labor and Reform in Grand Rapids, Michigan, 1890–1916." Ph.D. diss., Michigan State University, 1985.

Konow, Gary George. "The Establishment of Theatrical Activity in a Remote Settlement: Grand Rapids, Michigan, 1827–1862." Ph.D. diss., University of Michigan, 1985.

Manion, Joel. "The Negro Question and Slavery: Michigan Soldiers and Northern Thought." Calvin College History Seminar, Grand Rapids, Mich., Spring 1993.

Mesaros, Elaine J. "The American Negro and the Christian Reformed Church." Calvin College History Seminar, Grand Rapids, Mich., 1964.

Morgan, Ben. "A Local Perspective of Black Suffrage and Civil Rights during the Reconstruction Period." Calvin College History Seminar, Grand Rapids, Mich., Spring 1993.

Mulhern, Henry. "The Twenty-Fifth Anniversary of the Fountain Street Baptist Church April 1st 1894, and an Account of the Origin, Growth, and Present State of Each Baptist Church in Grand Rapids, Mich." Manuscript, Kalamazoo College Archives, Kalamazoo, Michigan.

Pertrusma, Ed. "The Race Riots and Disturbances in Grand Rapids (1967–68)." Calvin College History Seminar, Grand Rapids, Mich., Fall 1979.

Rice, Rodger Reid. "An Analysis of Invasion-Succession and Areal Differentiation as Process Operative in the Development of Ecological Variation within a Negro Community." Master's thesis, Michigan State University, 1962.

Sawyer, Marcia Renee. "Surviving Freedom: African American Farm Households in Cass County, Michigan, 1832–1880." Ph.D. diss., Michigan State University, 1990.

Thomas, Richard W. "From Peasants to Proletarian: The Formation and Organization of the Black Industrial Working Class in Detroit, 1915–1945." Ph.D. diss., University of Michigan, 1976.

Vanderstel, David Gordon. "The Dutch of Grand Rapids, Michigan: A Study of Social Mobility in a Midwestern Urban Community, 1850–1970." Master's thesis, Kent State University, 1978.

———."The Dutch of Grand Rapids, Michigan, 1848–1900; Immigrant neighborhood and Community Development in a Nineteenth-Century City." Ph.D. diss., Kent State University, 1983.

Wilson, Benjamin C. "Michigan's Antebellum Black Haven: Cass County, 1835–1870." Ph.D. diss., Michigan State University, 1974.

INDEX

Progressive Voter's League, 123
The Protestant Ethic and the Spirit of Capitalism (Weber), xiii
Protestant religious ethos and the black middle class, xii–xiii, xv; and cultural nationalism, 22; and democratic tradition, 33; Depression-era class issues, 108, 182n23; and idea of historical progress, 26–27; and nineteenth-century civil society, 22, 26–27, 33; post-Reconstruction and early twentieth-century politics, 61–62; and "respectability," xiii–xiv; and self-respect, xiv

railroad employees, 10, 87, 108–9
Ramona Gardens, 77–78
Rancière, Jacques, xvi
Ray, Basil, 68
Record, Wilson, 136
Redd, Robert, 111
Republican Party: and abolitionist legacy, 51–52; and Hardy's election as county supervisor, 16–17; and Lampkins, 68; late nineteenth-century civil society and patronage politics, 27–29; and suffrage rights, 14–15
respectability and the black middle class, xiii–xvi; and honor, 158n17; and late nineteenth-century black churches, 33; post–World War II politics of respectability, 150–55; tensions over social welfare and Northern migration, 80–81
Rice, Rodger, 151
Richard Allen Home for Colored Girls, 81–83
Richmond, Rebecca, 6
Ridge, C. C., 107
Robbins, John W., 28
Robert Gould Shaw House, 115
Roberts, David, 8, 12
Robeson, Paul, 153
Robeson Singers, 153
Romyn, Henry, 106, 182n17
Roosevelt, Franklin, 73, 121
Russian War Relief Committee, 136

Saints of Christ Church, 83
"Sambo and Abie" (radio show), 89
Schermer, George, 146
Scott, John, 4
Sennett, Richard, 177n6, 184n52
Shields, Edward, Sr., 115
Shillady, John R., 69
Simms, Edward P., 115–16
Simms, Grace Craig, 82
Sims, Grace, 25
Skinner, Floyd, 72, 98, 111, 132, 151; and the BCA, 124; and Bolden case, 122, 174n41; and post–World War II NAACP leadership, 122–25, 141; and Pratt case, 122–23
Smith, George M., 68, 69, 98, 123, 889
Smith, Hezekiah, 5
Smith, Lewis, 109
Smith, William Alden, 50–53
Social Service Council of Grand Rapids, 104–5
social welfare and twentieth-century Northern migration, 79–101, 108; calls for a social welfare agency, 89–93; and employment opportunities, 80, 86–88, 93–94, 177n4; and the Interracial Council, 90, 92, 93, 98–99; and labor tensions, 86–88; local Negro Welfare Guild, 98–100; local Urban League and debate between integrationists and self-segregation, 91–92; Moss's NUL survey (1928), 84, 87–88, 93–96, 97–98, 108; new churches and tensions, 83–86; and population growth, 80, 89, 93–94; racial tensions and white responses to new migrants, 88–90; respectability and proper social outlets, 80, 83, 177n6; tensions over social welfare programs, 80–81, 97–98; and urban respectability, 80–81; women leaders and community centers, 81–83; the YMCA and YWCA, 97–98, 100
Sojourner Truth Housing Project, 119
South Division School, 41–42
Southern Normal and Industrial Institute (Brewton, Alabama), 49, 61

RANDAL MAURICE JELKS is an associate professor of history and the director of African and African Diaspora studies at Calvin College, Grand Rapids, Michigan.

The University of Illinois Press
is a founding member of the
Association of American University Presses.

University of Illinois Press
1325 South Oak Street
Champaign, IL 61820-6903
www.press.uillinois.edu